TEENAGE MUTANT NINJA
TURTLES
VOL. 7 · CITY FALL, PART 2

Story by Kevin Eastman, Bobby Curnow, and Tom Waltz · Script by Tom Waltz

Art by Mateus Santolouco   Layouts by Kevin Eastman (Issue #25)

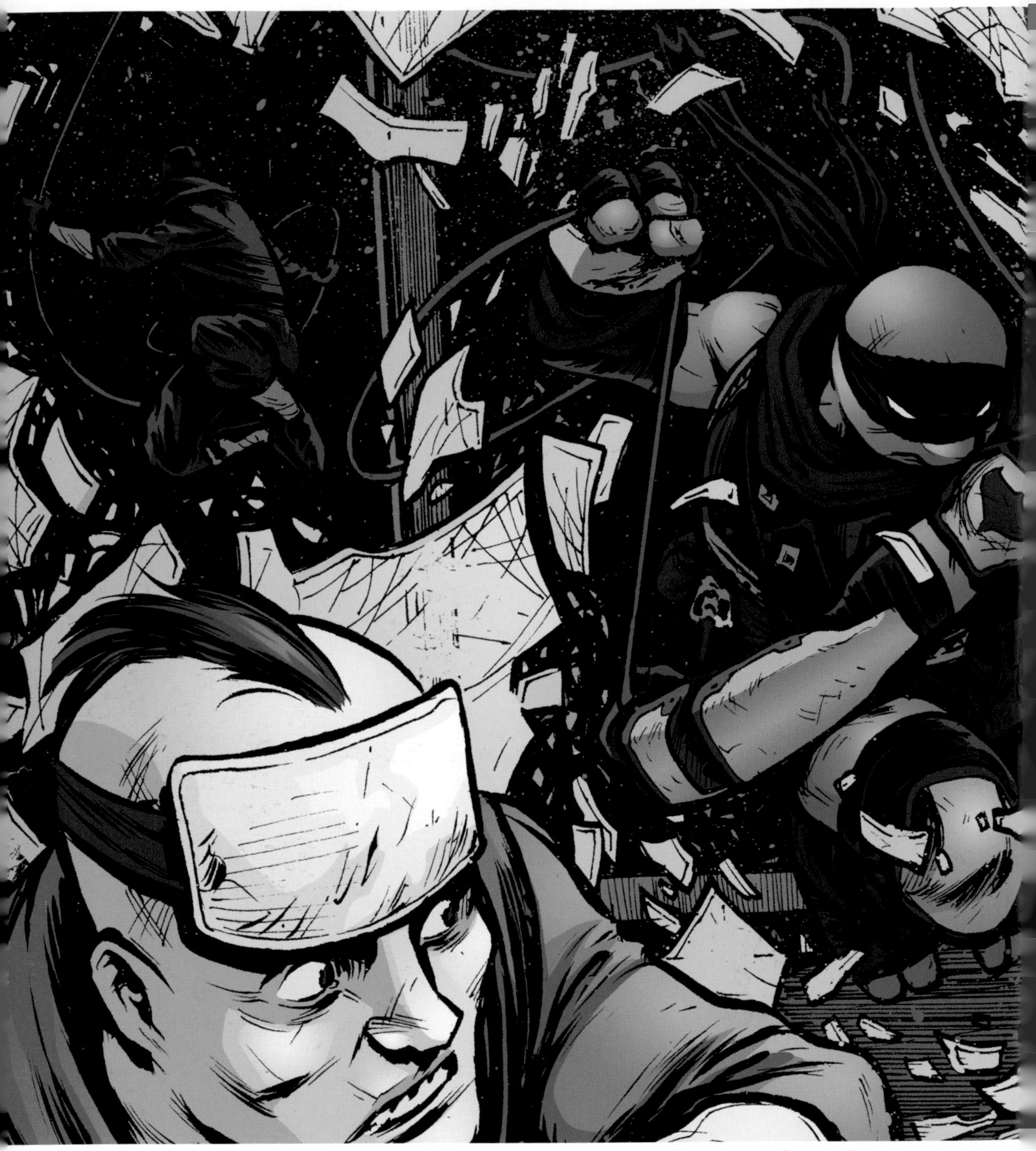

Special thanks to Joan Hilty, Linda Lee, and Kat van Dam for their invaluable assistance.

IDW founded by Ted Adams, Alex Garner, Kris Oprisko, and Robbie Robbins

ISBN: 978-1-61377-876-0

17 16 15 14   2 3 4 5

IDW

Ted Adams, CEO & Publisher
Greg Goldstein, President & COO
Robbie Robbins, EVP/Sr. Graphic Artist
Chris Ryall, Chief Creative Officer/Editor-in-Chief
Matthew Ruzicka, CPA, Chief Financial Officer
Alan Payne, VP of Sales
Dirk Wood, VP of Marketing
Lorelei Bunjes, VP of Digital Services

Originally published as TEENAGE MUTANT NINJA TURTLES issues #25–28.

Additional Art by Charles Paul Wilson III (Issue #26, pp. 1-2) • Colors by Ronda Pattison

Additional Colors by Ian Herring (Issue #28) • Letters by Shawn Lee and Tom B. Long

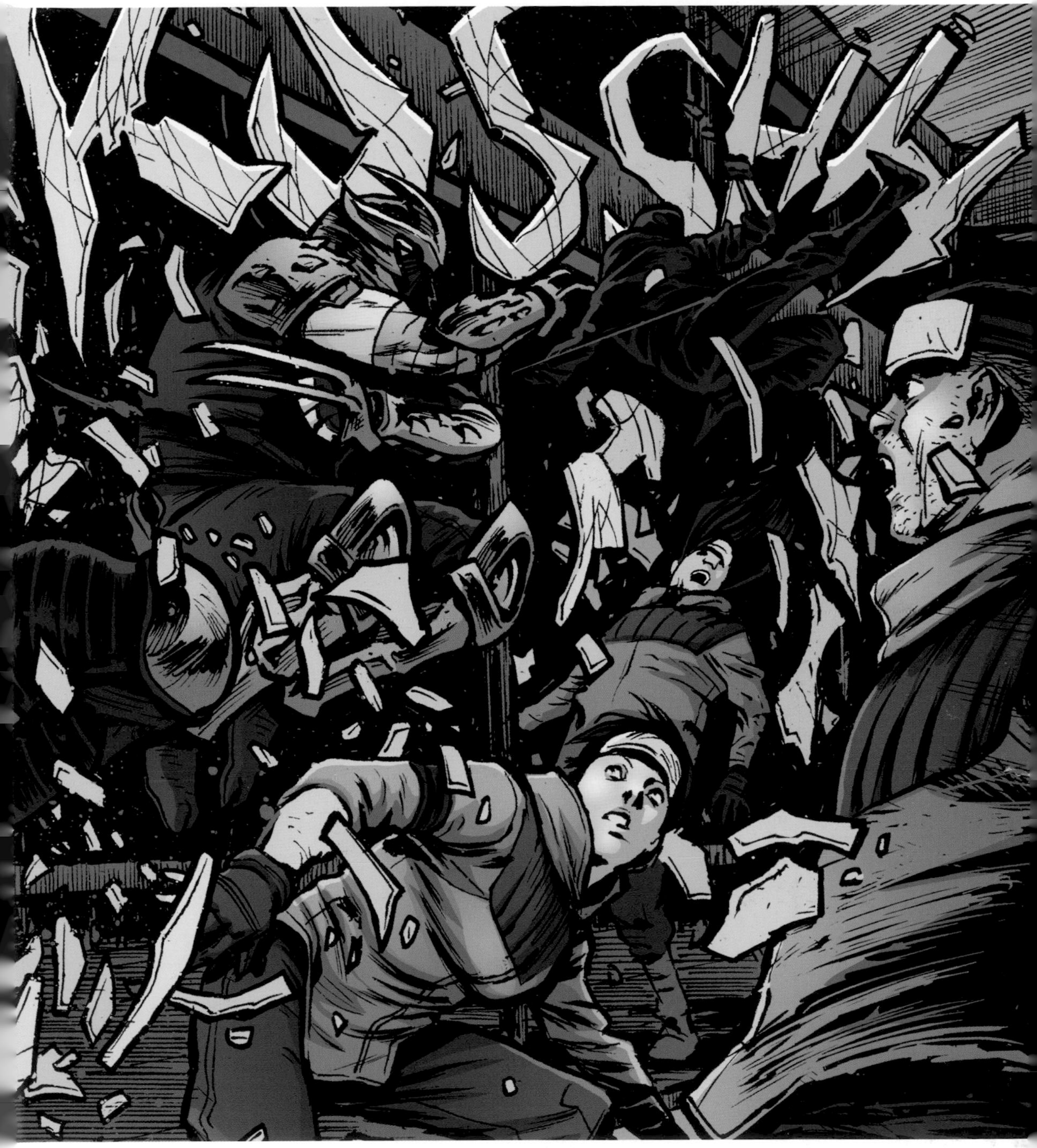

Series Edits by Bobby Curnow

Collection Edits by Justin Eisinger & Alonzo Simon

Collection Design by Tom B. Long • Cover by Mateus Santolouco

Based on characters created by Peter Laird and Kevin Eastman

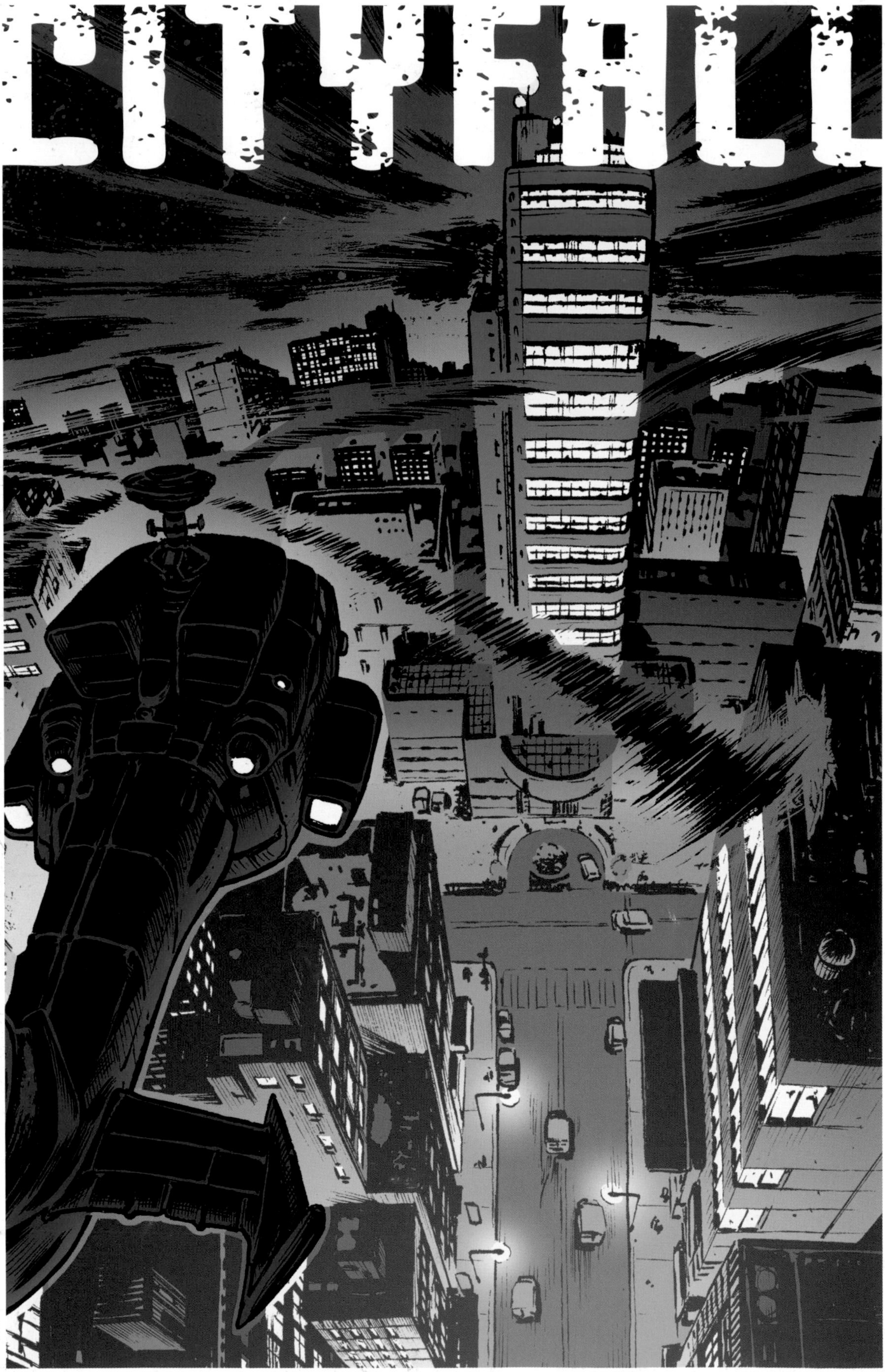

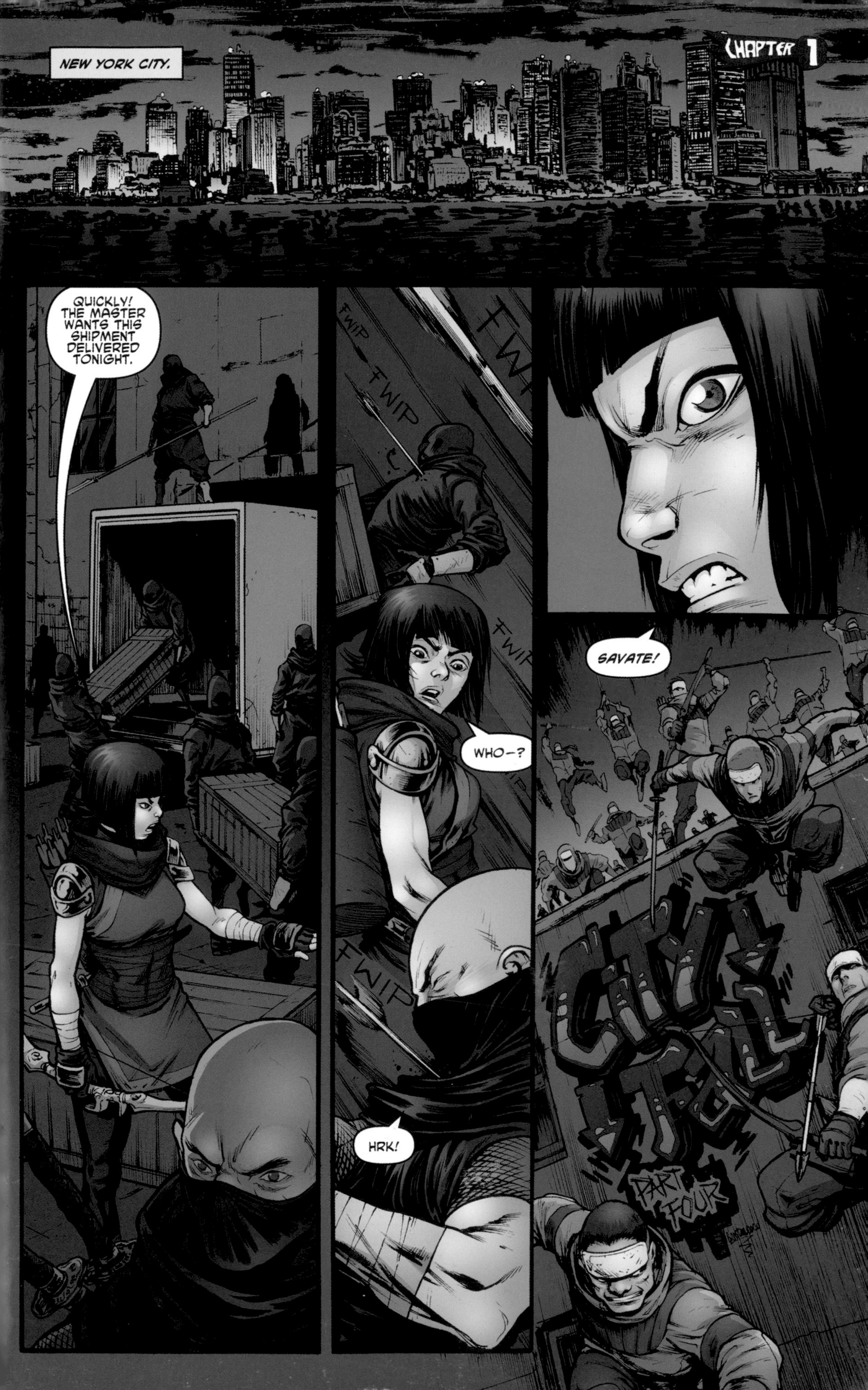
NEW YORK CITY.
CHAPTER 1
QUICKLY! THE MASTER WANTS THIS SHIPMENT DELIVERED TONIGHT.
FWIP
FWIP
FWIP
WHO-?
FWIP
HRK!
SAVATE!
CITY FALL
PART FOUR

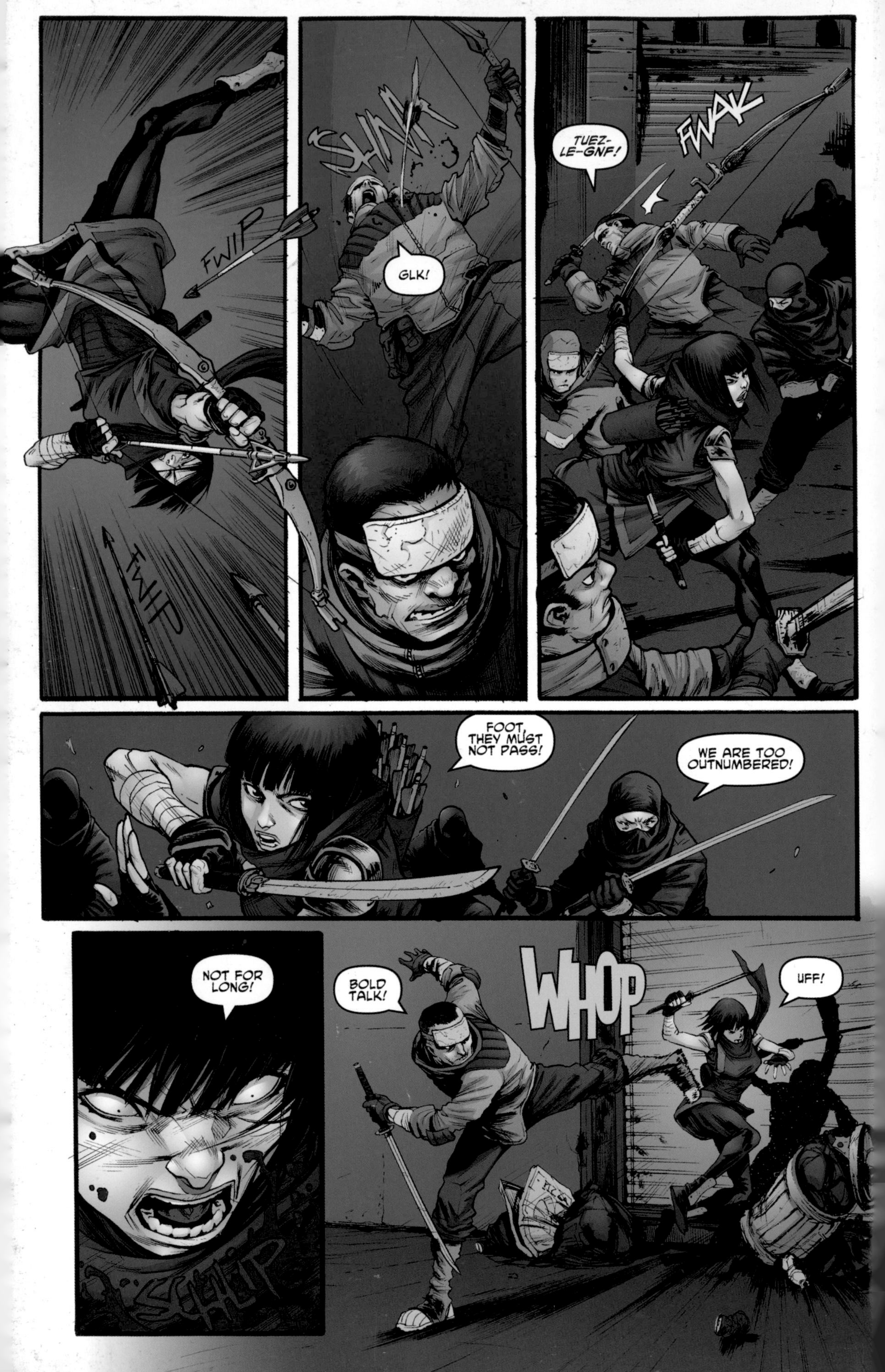
FWIP
FWIP
GLK!
TUEZ-LE-GNF!
FWAK
FOOT, THEY MUST NOT PASS!
WE ARE TOO OUTNUMBERED!
NOT FOR LONG!
BOLD TALK!
WHOP
UFF!

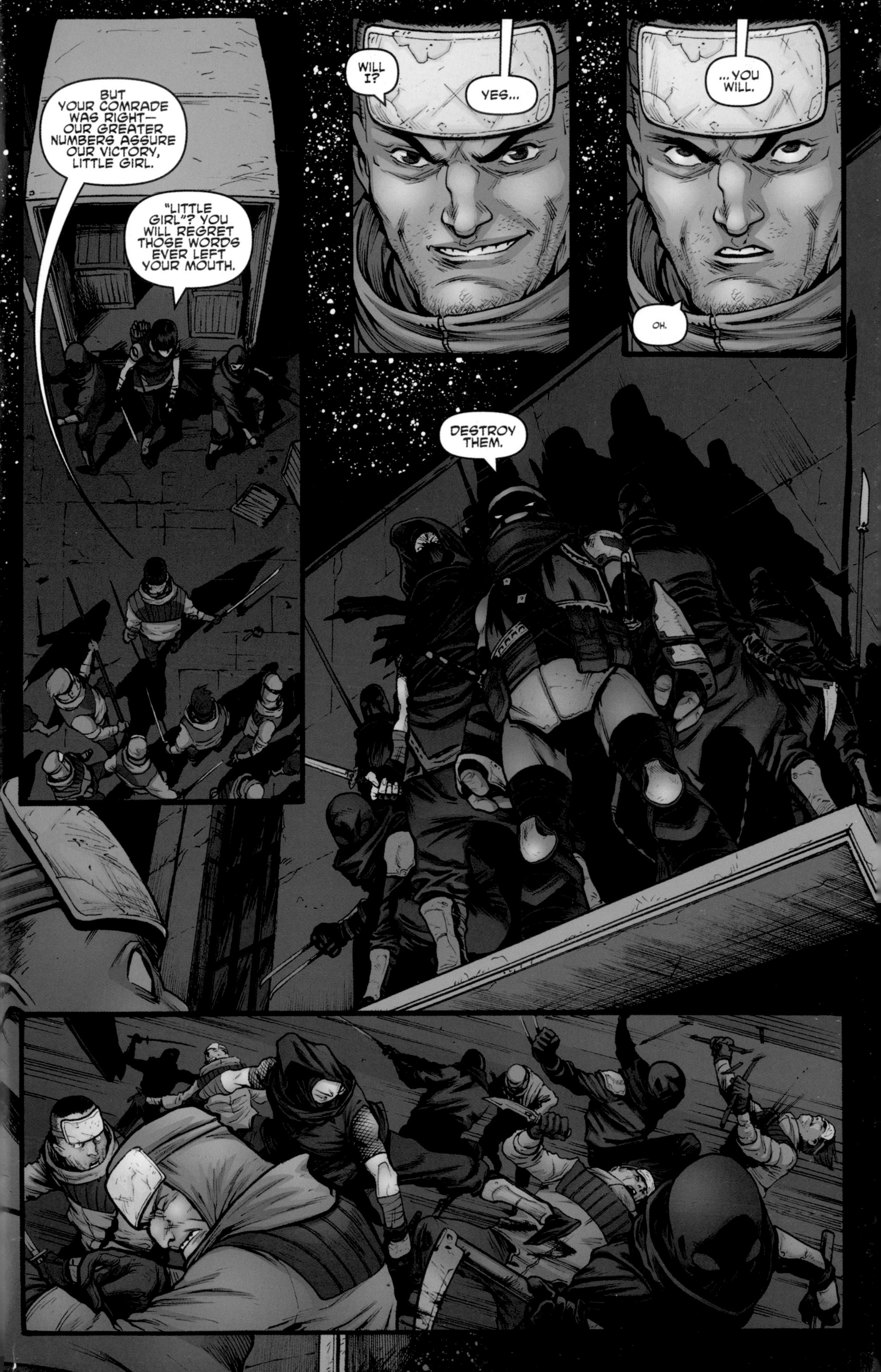
BUT YOUR COMRADE WAS RIGHT— OUR GREATER NUMBERS ASSURE OUR VICTORY, LITTLE GIRL.
"LITTLE GIRL"? YOU WILL REGRET THOSE WORDS EVER LEFT YOUR MOUTH.
WILL I?
YES...
...YOU WILL.
OH.
DESTROY THEM.

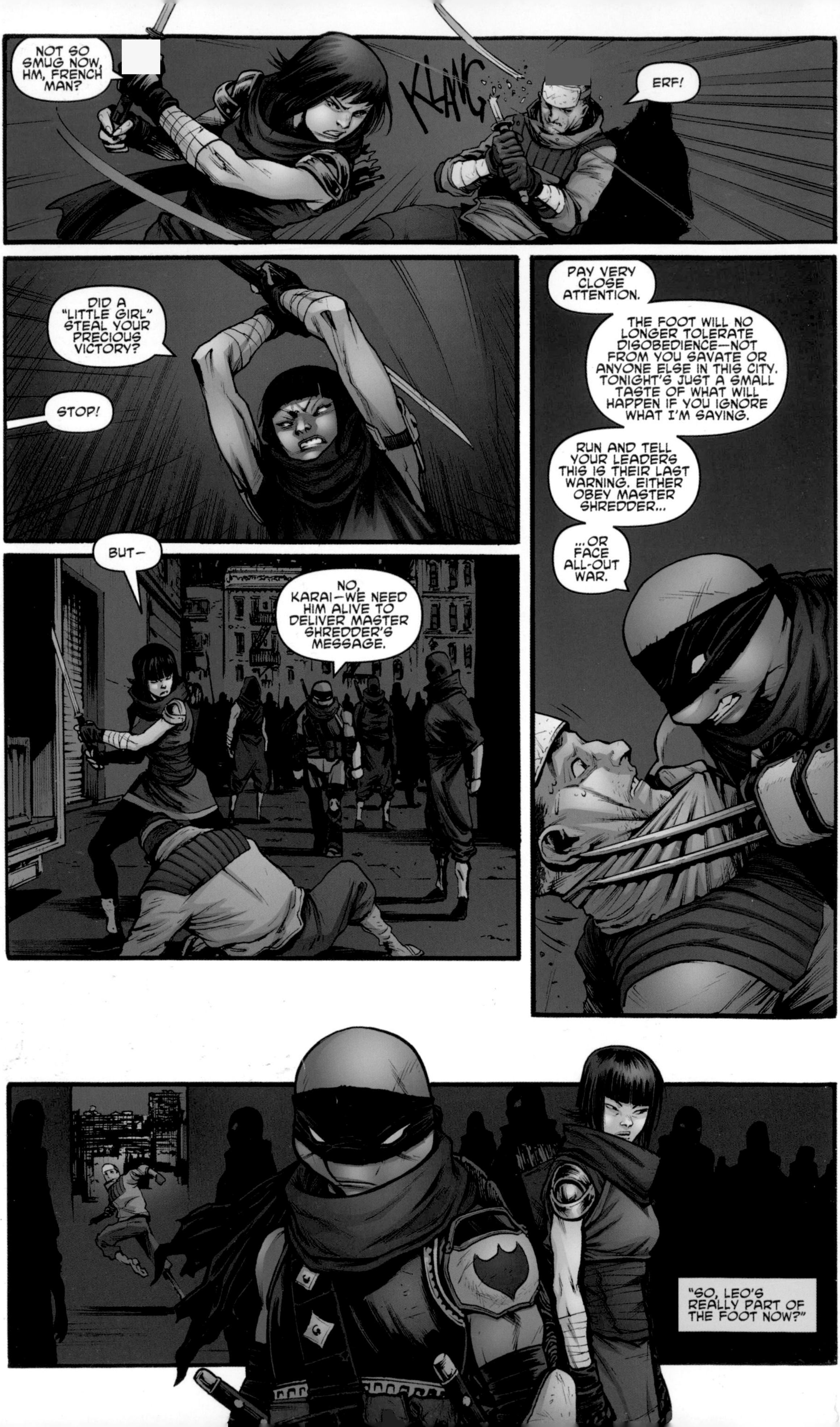
NOT SO SMUG NOW, HM, FRENCH MAN?
KLANG
ERF!
DID A "LITTLE GIRL" STEAL YOUR PRECIOUS VICTORY?
STOP!
BUT—
NO, KARAI—WE NEED HIM ALIVE TO DELIVER MASTER SHREDDER'S MESSAGE.
PAY VERY CLOSE ATTENTION.
THE FOOT WILL NO LONGER TOLERATE DISOBEDIENCE—NOT FROM YOU SAVATE OR ANYONE ELSE IN THIS CITY. TONIGHT'S JUST A SMALL TASTE OF WHAT WILL HAPPEN IF YOU IGNORE WHAT I'M SAYING.
RUN AND TELL YOUR LEADERS THIS IS THEIR LAST WARNING. EITHER OBEY MASTER SHREDDER...
...OR FACE ALL-OUT WAR.
"SO, LEO'S REALLY PART OF THE FOOT NOW?"

"MAN, THAT... THAT'S A HARD ONE TO SWALLOW, DONNIE."

EMERGENCY

IT'S BEEN ALMOST TWO WEEKS SINCE WE SAW HIM LAST. THINGS HAVEN'T BEEN SO GOOD AROUND HERE.

YEAH, APRIL TOLD ME RAPH TOOK IT PRETTY HARD.

WE *ALL* HAVE. BUT YOU KNOW RAPH—HE DOESN'T ALWAYS DEAL WITH STRESS IN... *CONSTRUCTIVE* WAYS. HE'S OFF ON HIS OWN DOING GOD KNOWS WHAT RIGHT NOW.

AND IT'S NOT JUST HIM—MASTER SPLINTER'S GONE, TOO, TAKING CARE OF SOME KIND OF "URGENT MATTER" WITH OLD HOB AND SLASH.

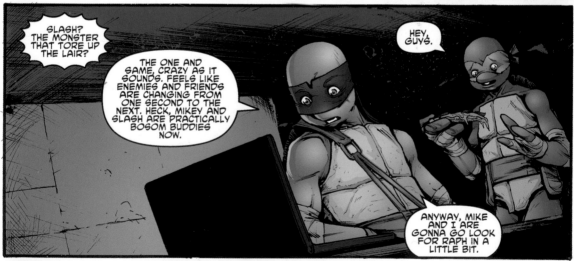

SLASH? THE MONSTER THAT TORE UP THE LAIR?

THE ONE AND SAME, CRAZY AS IT SOUNDS. FEELS LIKE ENEMIES AND FRIENDS ARE CHANGING FROM ONE SECOND TO THE NEXT. HECK, MIKEY AND SLASH ARE PRACTICALLY BOSOM BUDDIES NOW.

HEY, GUYS.

ANYWAY, MIKE AND I ARE GONNA GO LOOK FOR RAPH IN A LITTLE BIT.

ANYTHING'S BETTER THAN SITTING AROUND HERE DOING NOTHING, YOU KNOW?

I HEAR YA. I'M GONNA GO NUTSO IF I GOTTA STAY IN THIS STUPID BED MUCH LONGER.

OKAY, WE BETTER RUN. REALLY GOOD TALKING TO YOU, CASEY. HOPEFULLY WE'LL HAVE BETTER NEWS FOR YOU NEXT TIME.

YEAH—HANG IN THERE, GUYS.

SEE YA.

9

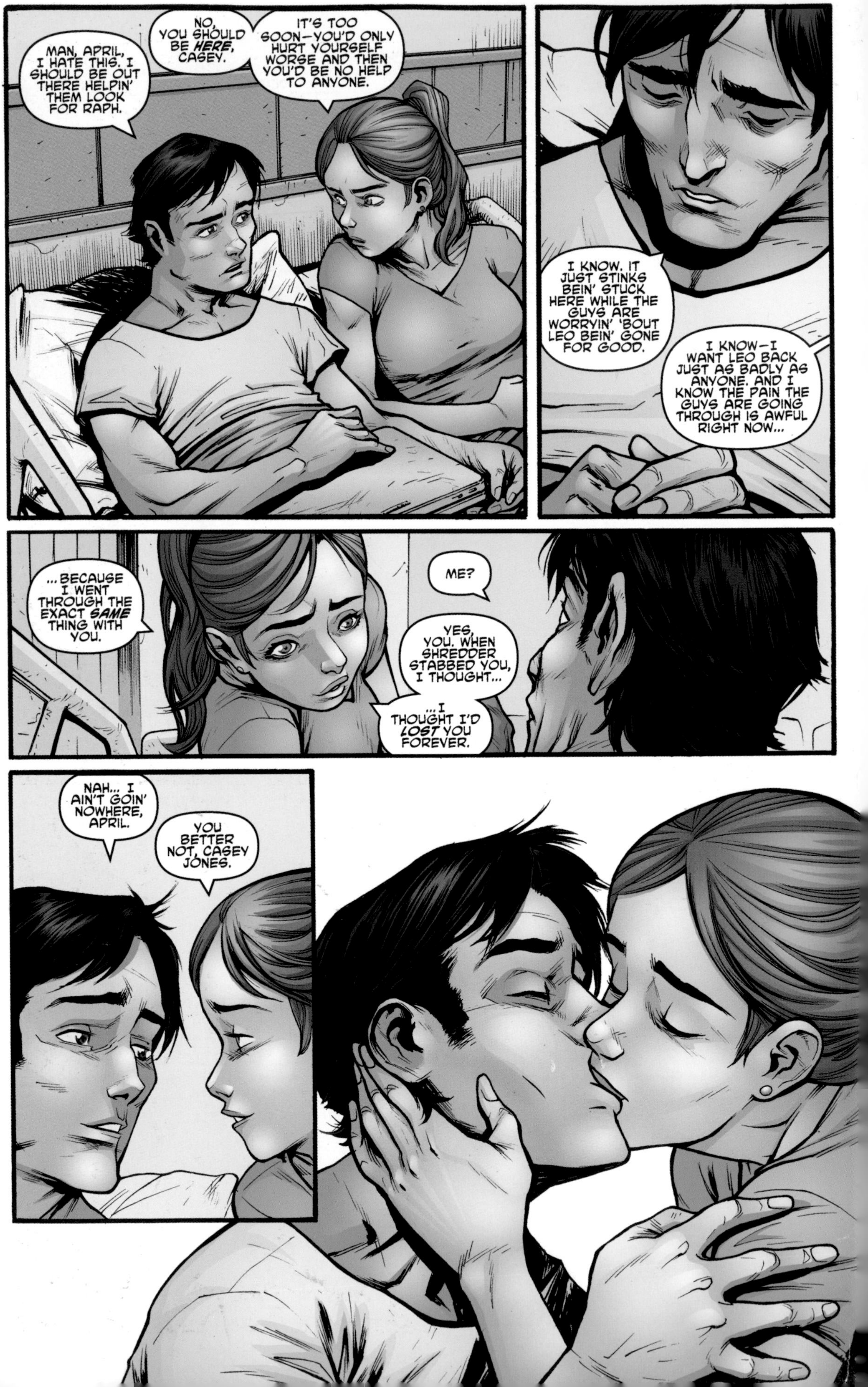

MAN, APRIL, I HATE THIS. I SHOULD BE OUT THERE HELPIN' THEM LOOK FOR RAPH.
NO, YOU SHOULD BE HERE, CASEY.
IT'S TOO SOON—YOU'D ONLY HURT YOURSELF WORSE AND THEN YOU'D BE NO HELP TO ANYONE.
I KNOW. IT JUST STINKS BEIN' STUCK HERE WHILE THE GUYS ARE WORRYIN' 'BOUT LEO BEIN' GONE FOR GOOD.
I KNOW—I WANT LEO BACK JUST AS BADLY AS ANYONE. AND I KNOW THE PAIN THE GUYS ARE GOING THROUGH IS AWFUL RIGHT NOW...
...BECAUSE I WENT THROUGH THE EXACT SAME THING WITH YOU.
ME?
YES, YOU. WHEN SHREDDER STABBED YOU, I THOUGHT...
...I THOUGHT I'D LOST YOU FOREVER.
NAH... I AIN'T GOIN' NOWHERE, APRIL.
YOU BETTER NOT, CASEY JONES.

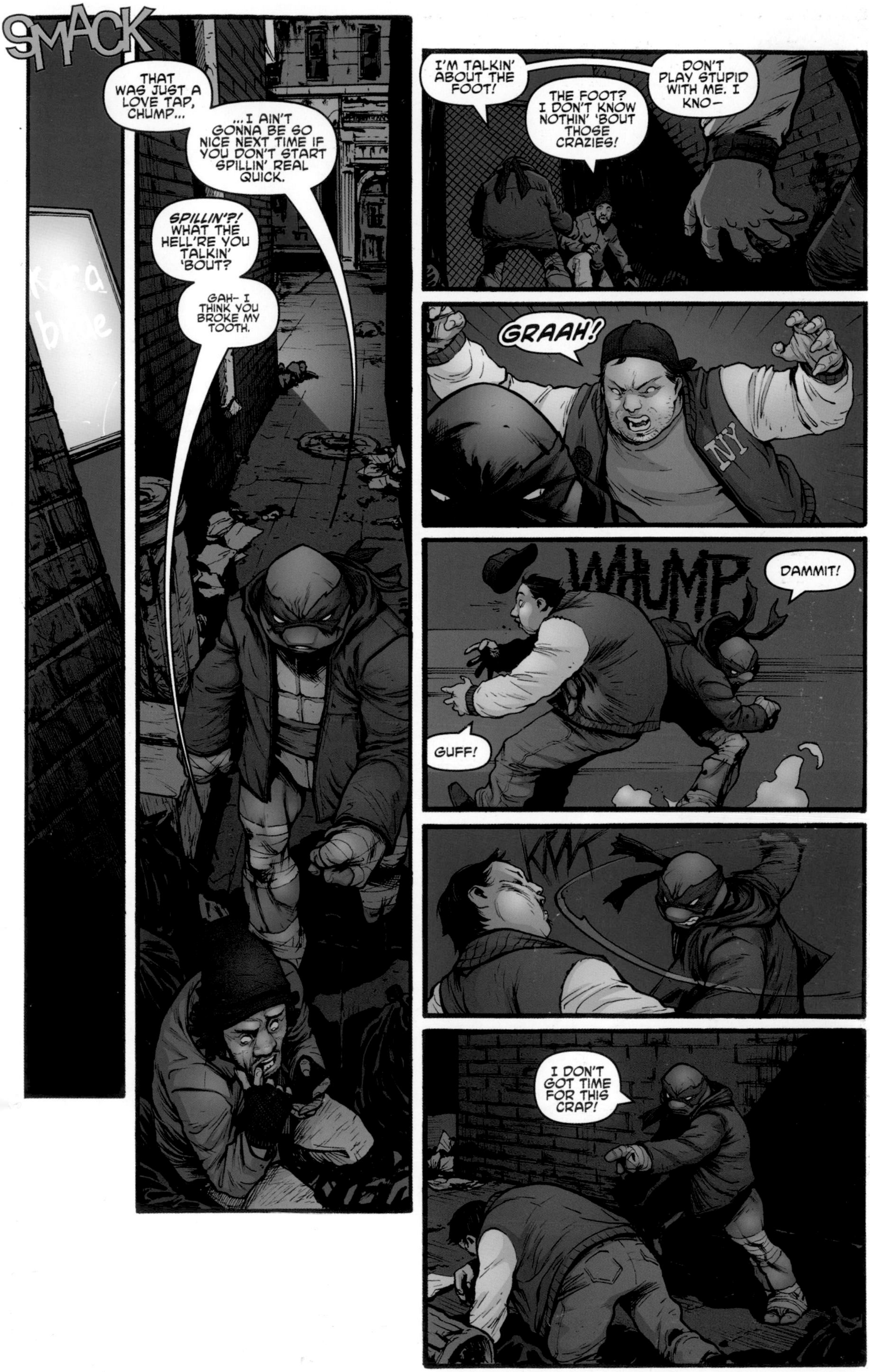
SMACK
THAT WAS JUST A LOVE TAP, CHUMP...
...I AIN'T GONNA BE SO NICE NEXT TIME IF YOU DON'T START SPILLIN' REAL QUICK.
SPILLIN'?! WHAT THE HELL'RE YOU TALKIN' 'BOUT?
GAH- I THINK YOU BROKE MY TOOTH.
I'M TALKIN' ABOUT THE FOOT!
THE FOOT? I DON'T KNOW NOTHIN' 'BOUT THOSE CRAZIES!
DON'T PLAY STUPID WITH ME. I KNO—
GRAAH!
NY
WHUMP
DAMMIT!
GUFF!
I DON'T GOT TIME FOR THIS CRAP!

MUTANT FREAK!

FWK

DIDN'T I JUST WARN YOU 'BOUT BEIN' STUPID?

I... GRK... YEAH, YOU... HLRK... DID. SORRY...

SAVE YOUR APOLOGIES AND LISTEN UP.

I REMEMBER YOU AND DUMBO OVER THERE FROM THAT BRIEFCASE THING WITH THE FOOT AND SAVATE.*

YOU WERE KNEE DEEP IN THAT MESS AND SOMETHIN' TELLS ME YOU'RE MIXED UP IN THE CRAP GOIN' ON 'ROUND THE CITY RIGHT NOW, TOO.

N-NO... URF... MAN, YOU'RE WRONG... HUK... WE AIN'T—

*See TMNT Annual #1 – B.C.

SHUT UP. I AIN'T DONE.

THE FOOT NEARLY WAXED MY BEST FRIEND AND STOLE MY BROTHER. I'M GONNA GET HIM BACK, BUT I GOTTA FIND WHERE THOSE JACKASSES ARE KEEPIN' HIM FIRST. SO, LIKE I SAID, TIME FOR YOU TO START SPILLIN' WHAT YOU KNOW OR I START SPILLIN' MORE BLOOD.

GOT ME?

MM-HM.

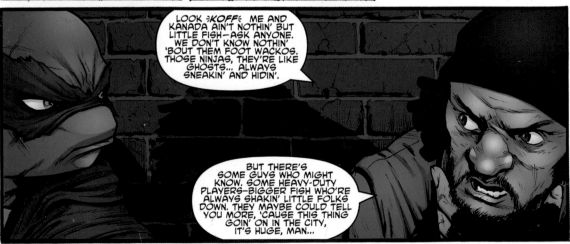

LOOK =KOFF= ME AND KANADA AIN'T NOTHIN' BUT LITTLE FISH—ASK ANYONE. WE DON'T KNOW NOTHIN' 'BOUT THEM FOOT WACKOS. THOSE NINJAS, THEY'RE LIKE GHOSTS... ALWAYS SNEAKIN' AND HIDIN'.

BUT THERE'S SOME GUYS WHO MIGHT KNOW. SOME HEAVY-DUTY PLAYERS—BIGGER FISH WHO'RE ALWAYS SHAKIN' LITTLE FOLKS DOWN. THEY MAYBE COULD TELL YOU MORE, 'CAUSE THIS THING GOIN' ON IN THE CITY, IT'S HUGE, MAN...

"...GOES ALL THE WAY TO THE TOP."

KRAK

RAAH!

HE WAS THE LAST, BOSS. WE'VE WON.

OF COURSE.

IT AIN'T NO SOCIAL CALL, THAT'S FOR SURE.

VICTOR!

MARCELLO? WHAT BRINGS YOU INTO THE TRENCHES, MON AMI?

THE FAMILIES ARE GETTIN' A LITTLE EDGY. THEY CALLED A MEETIN' TO DISCUSS THINGS AND SENT ME TO PICK YOU UP.

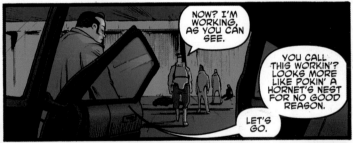

NOW? I'M WORKING, AS YOU CAN SEE.

YOU CALL THIS WORKIN'? LOOKS MORE LIKE POKIN' A HORNET'S NEST FOR NO GOOD REASON.

LET'S GO.

"THANK YOU FOR JOINING US ON SUCH SHORT NOTICE, VICTOR..."

...WE WOULD NOT HAVE CALLED YOU HERE IN SUCH AN ABRUPT FASHION IF IT WEREN'T A MATTER OF *DIRE* CONCERN.

DIRE CONCERN, ANTONIO?

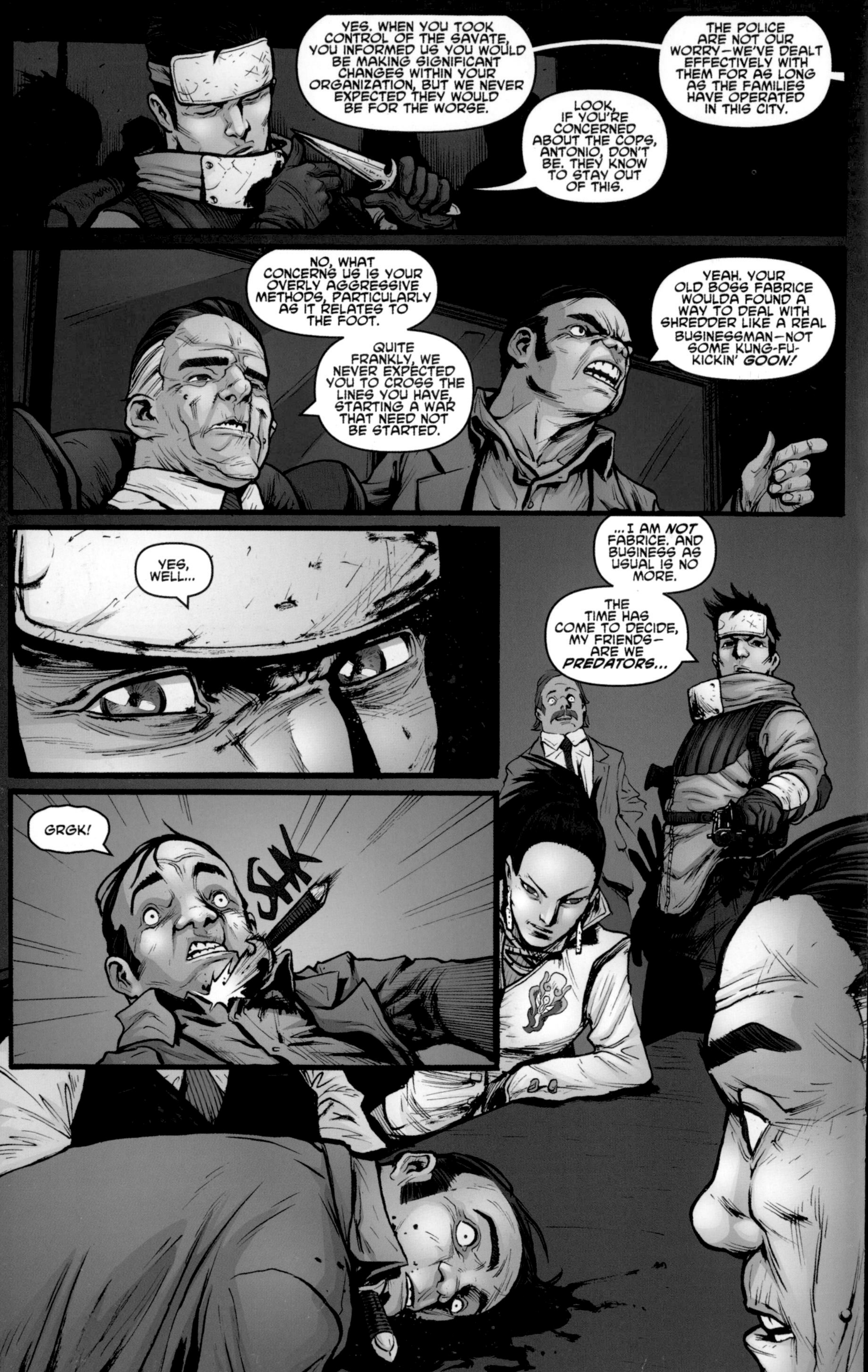
YES. WHEN YOU TOOK CONTROL OF THE SAVATE, YOU INFORMED US YOU WOULD BE MAKING SIGNIFICANT CHANGES WITHIN YOUR ORGANIZATION, BUT WE NEVER EXPECTED THEY WOULD BE FOR THE WORSE.
THE POLICE ARE NOT OUR WORRY—WE'VE DEALT EFFECTIVELY WITH THEM FOR AS LONG AS THE FAMILIES HAVE OPERATED IN THIS CITY.
LOOK, IF YOU'RE CONCERNED ABOUT THE COPS, ANTONIO, DON'T BE. THEY KNOW TO STAY OUT OF THIS.
NO, WHAT CONCERNS US IS YOUR OVERLY AGGRESSIVE METHODS, PARTICULARLY AS IT RELATES TO THE FOOT.
QUITE FRANKLY, WE NEVER EXPECTED YOU TO CROSS THE LINES YOU HAVE, STARTING A WAR THAT NEED NOT BE STARTED.
YEAH. YOUR OLD BOSS FABRICE WOULDA FOUND A WAY TO DEAL WITH SHREDDER LIKE A REAL BUSINESSMAN—NOT SOME KUNG-FU-KICKIN' *GOON!*
YES, WELL...
...I AM *NOT* FABRICE. AND BUSINESS AS USUAL IS NO MORE.
THE TIME HAS COME TO DECIDE, MY FRIENDS—ARE WE *PREDATORS...*
GRGK!
SHK

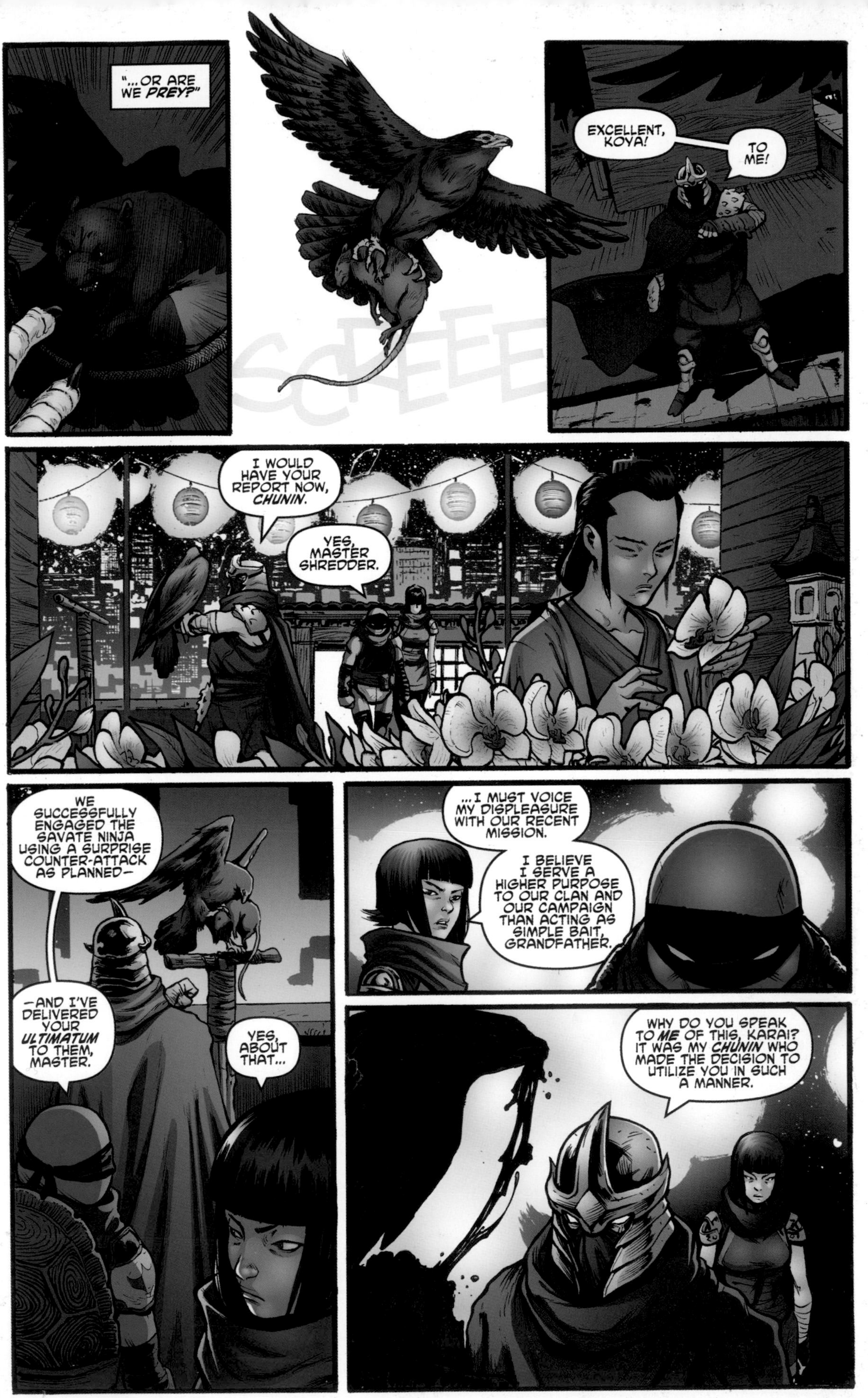
"...OR ARE WE PREY?"
SCREEE
EXCELLENT, KOYA!
TO ME!
I WOULD HAVE YOUR REPORT NOW, CHUNIN.
YES, MASTER SHREDDER.
WE SUCCESSFULLY ENGAGED THE SAVATE NINJA USING A SURPRISE COUNTER-ATTACK AS PLANNED—
—AND I'VE DELIVERED YOUR ULTIMATUM TO THEM, MASTER.
YES, ABOUT THAT...
...I MUST VOICE MY DISPLEASURE WITH OUR RECENT MISSION.
I BELIEVE I SERVE A HIGHER PURPOSE TO OUR CLAN AND OUR CAMPAIGN THAN ACTING AS SIMPLE BAIT, GRANDFATHER.
WHY DO YOU SPEAK TO ME OF THIS, KARAI? IT WAS MY CHUNIN WHO MADE THE DECISION TO UTILIZE YOU IN SUCH A MANNER.

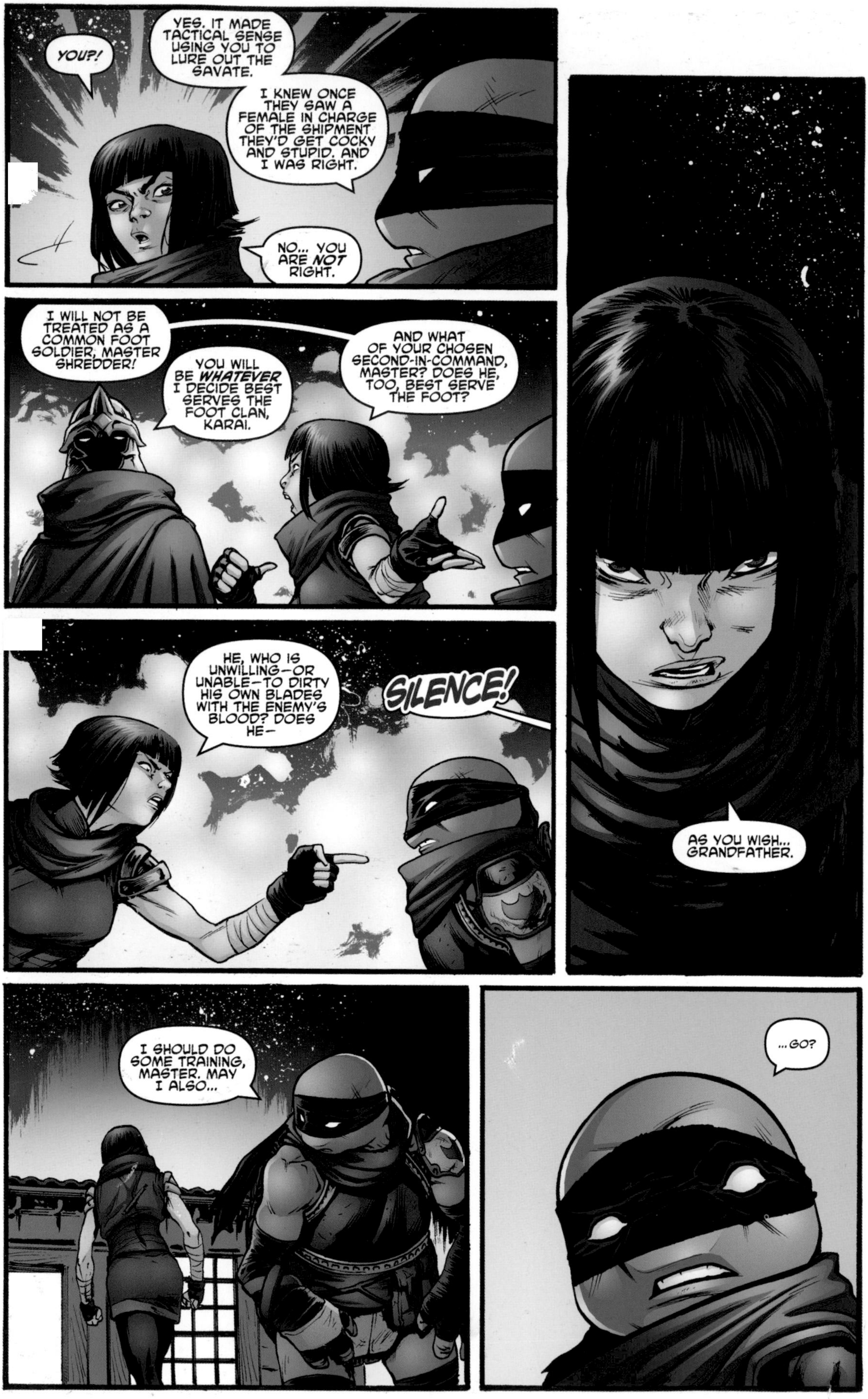
YOU?!
YES. IT MADE TACTICAL SENSE USING YOU TO LURE OUT THE SAVATE.
I KNEW ONCE THEY SAW A FEMALE IN CHARGE OF THE SHIPMENT THEY'D GET COCKY AND STUPID. AND I WAS RIGHT.
NO... YOU ARE NOT RIGHT.
I WILL NOT BE TREATED AS A COMMON FOOT SOLDIER, MASTER SHREDDER!
YOU WILL BE WHATEVER I DECIDE BEST SERVES THE FOOT CLAN, KARAI.
AND WHAT OF YOUR CHOSEN SECOND-IN-COMMAND, MASTER? DOES HE, TOO, BEST SERVE THE FOOT?
HE, WHO IS UNWILLING—OR UNABLE—TO DIRTY HIS OWN BLADES WITH THE ENEMY'S BLOOD? DOES HE—
SILENCE!
AS YOU WISH... GRANDFATHER.
I SHOULD DO SOME TRAINING, MASTER. MAY I ALSO...
...GO?

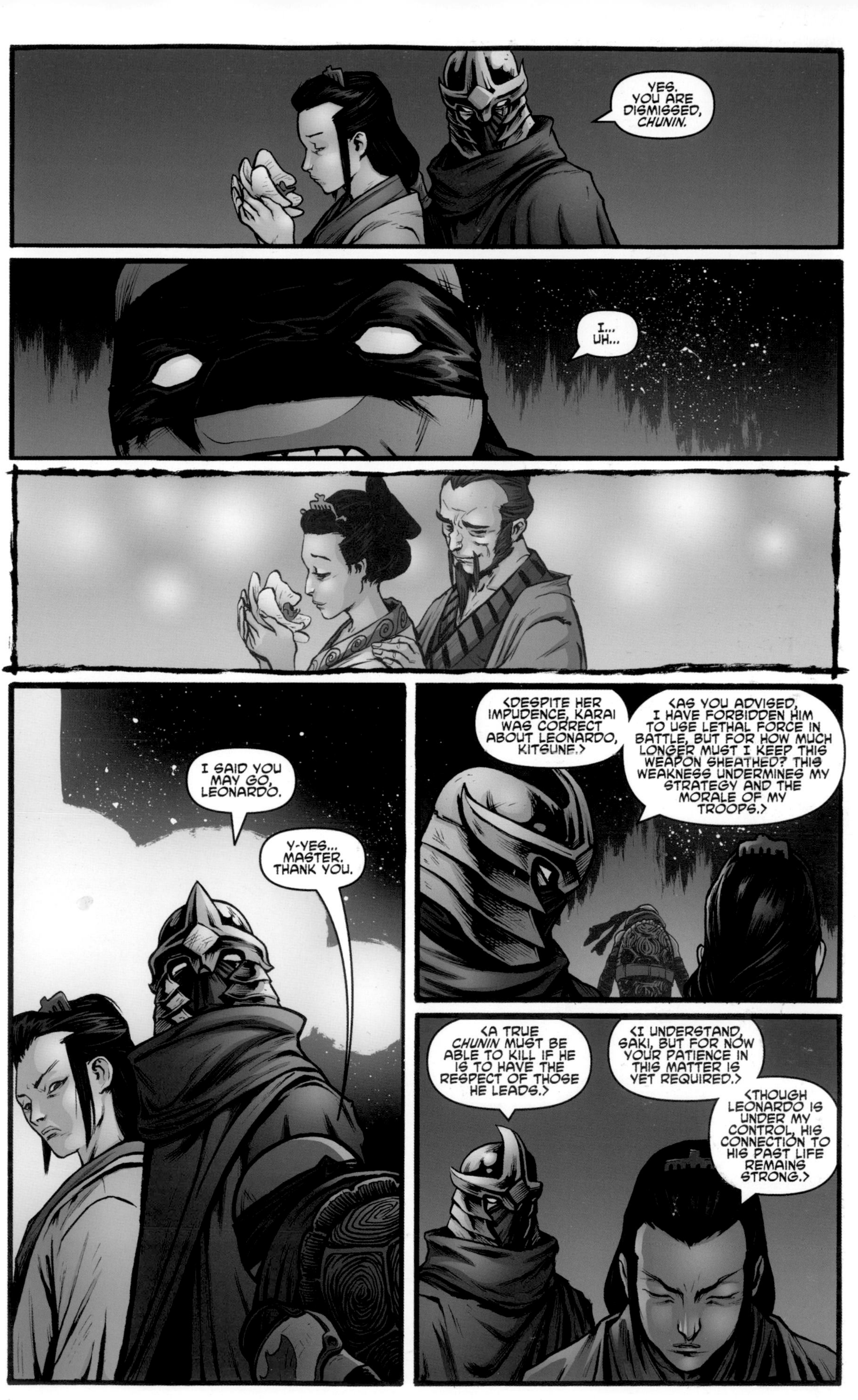
YES. YOU ARE DISMISSED, *CHUNIN.*
I... UH...
I SAID YOU MAY GO, LEONARDO.
Y-YES... MASTER. THANK YOU.
<DESPITE HER IMPUDENCE, KARAI WAS CORRECT ABOUT LEONARDO, KITSUNE.>
<AS YOU ADVISED, I HAVE FORBIDDEN HIM TO USE LETHAL FORCE IN BATTLE, BUT FOR HOW MUCH LONGER MUST I KEEP THIS WEAPON SHEATHED? THIS WEAKNESS UNDERMINES MY STRATEGY AND THE MORALE OF MY TROOPS.>
<A TRUE *CHUNIN* MUST BE ABLE TO KILL IF HE IS TO HAVE THE RESPECT OF THOSE HE LEADS.>
<I UNDERSTAND, SAKI, BUT FOR NOW YOUR PATIENCE IN THIS MATTER IS YET REQUIRED.>
<THOUGH LEONARDO IS UNDER MY CONTROL, HIS CONNECTION TO HIS PAST LIFE REMAINS STRONG.>

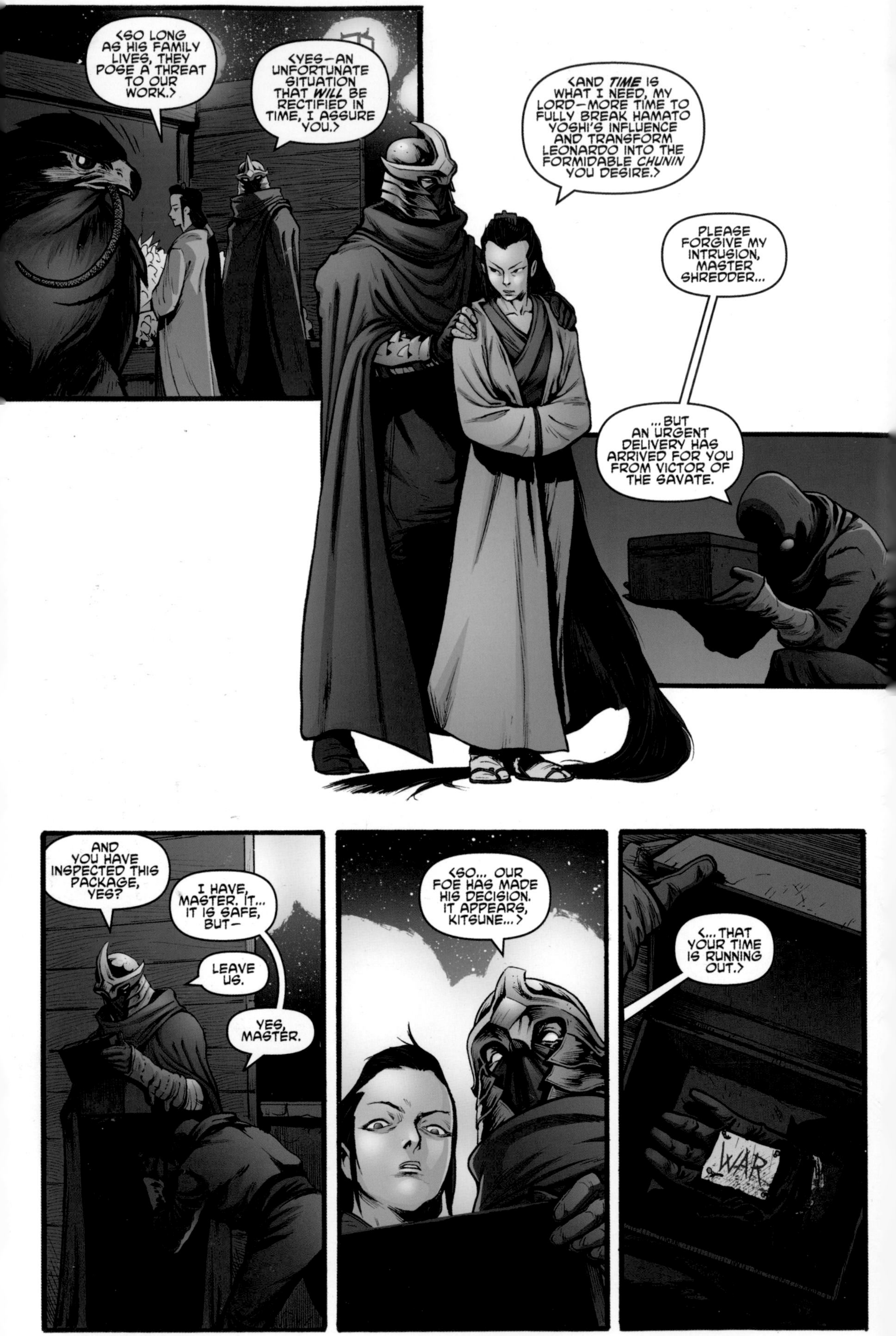

<SO LONG AS HIS FAMILY LIVES, THEY POSE A THREAT TO OUR WORK.>
<YES—AN UNFORTUNATE SITUATION THAT *WILL* BE RECTIFIED IN TIME, I ASSURE YOU.>
<AND *TIME* IS WHAT I NEED, MY LORD—MORE TIME TO FULLY BREAK HAMATO YOSHI'S INFLUENCE AND TRANSFORM LEONARDO INTO THE FORMIDABLE *CHUNIN* YOU DESIRE.>
PLEASE FORGIVE MY INTRUSION, MASTER SHREDDER...
...BUT AN URGENT DELIVERY HAS ARRIVED FOR YOU FROM VICTOR OF THE SAVATE.
AND YOU HAVE INSPECTED THIS PACKAGE, YES?
I HAVE, MASTER. IT... IT IS SAFE, BUT—
LEAVE US.
YES, MASTER.
<SO... OUR FOE HAS MADE HIS DECISION. IT APPEARS, KITSUNE...>
<...THAT YOUR TIME IS RUNNING OUT.>
WAR

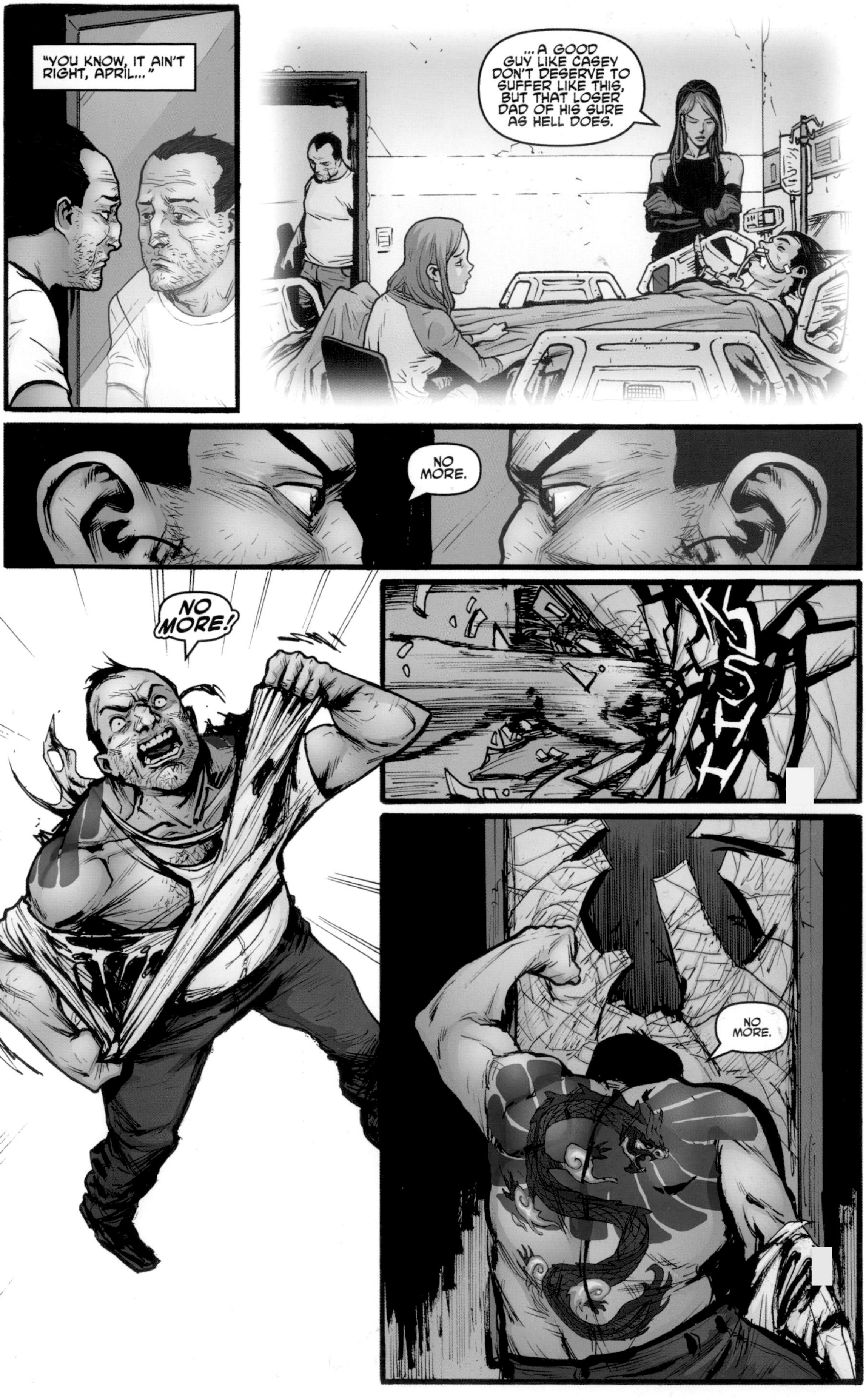
"YOU KNOW, IT AIN'T RIGHT, APRIL..."
...A GOOD GUY LIKE CASEY DON'T DESERVE TO SUFFER LIKE THIS, BUT THAT LOSER DAD OF HIS SURE AS HELL DOES.
NO MORE.
NO MORE!
KSSHH
NO MORE.

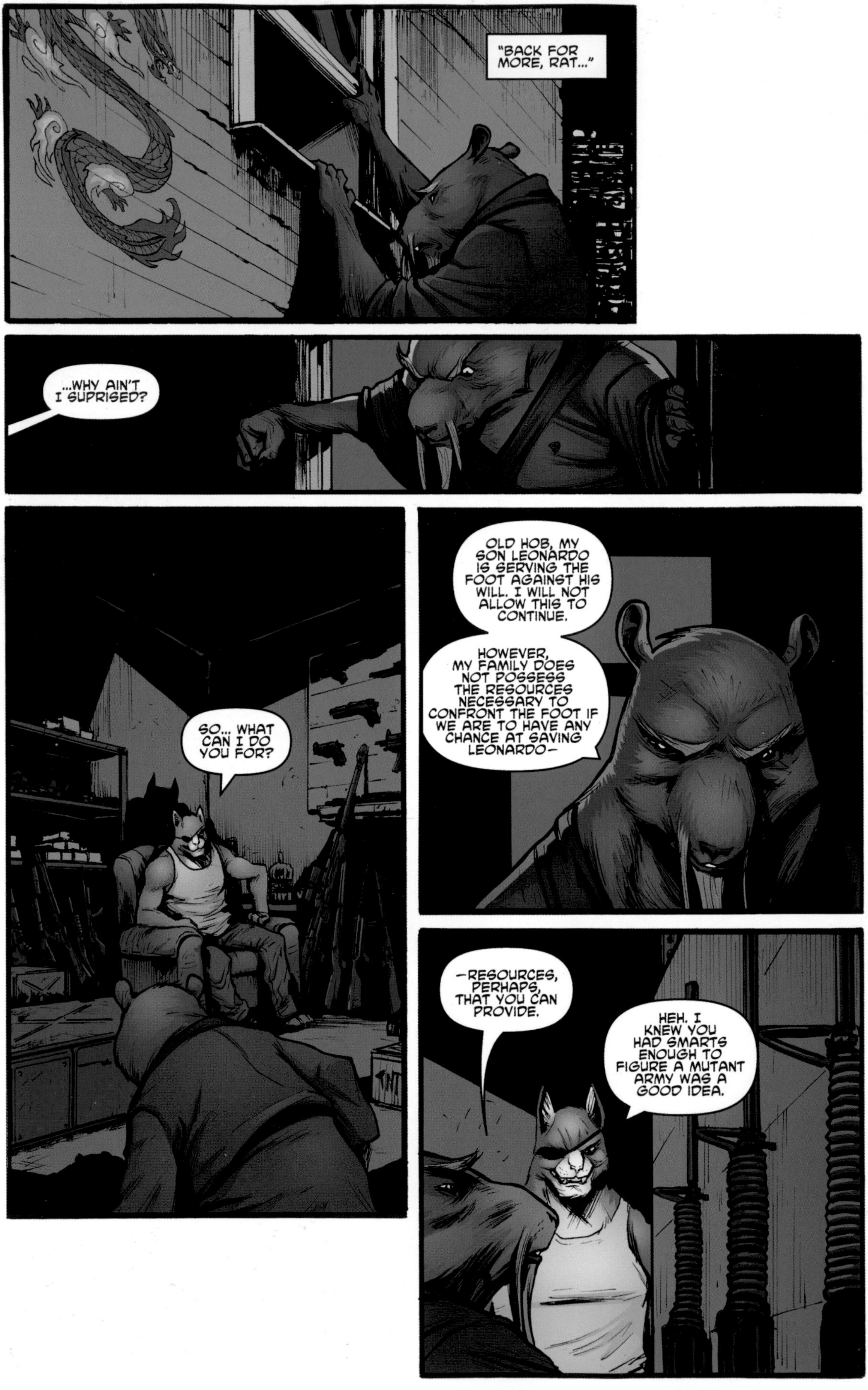
"BACK FOR MORE, RAT..."
...WHY AIN'T I SUPRISED?
SO... WHAT CAN I DO YOU FOR?
OLD HOB, MY SON LEONARDO IS SERVING THE FOOT AGAINST HIS WILL. I WILL NOT ALLOW THIS TO CONTINUE.
HOWEVER, MY FAMILY DOES NOT POSSESS THE RESOURCES NECESSARY TO CONFRONT THE FOOT IF WE ARE TO HAVE ANY CHANCE AT SAVING LEONARDO—
—RESOURCES, PERHAPS, THAT YOU CAN PROVIDE.
HEH. I KNEW YOU HAD SMARTS ENOUGH TO FIGURE A MUTANT ARMY WAS A GOOD IDEA.

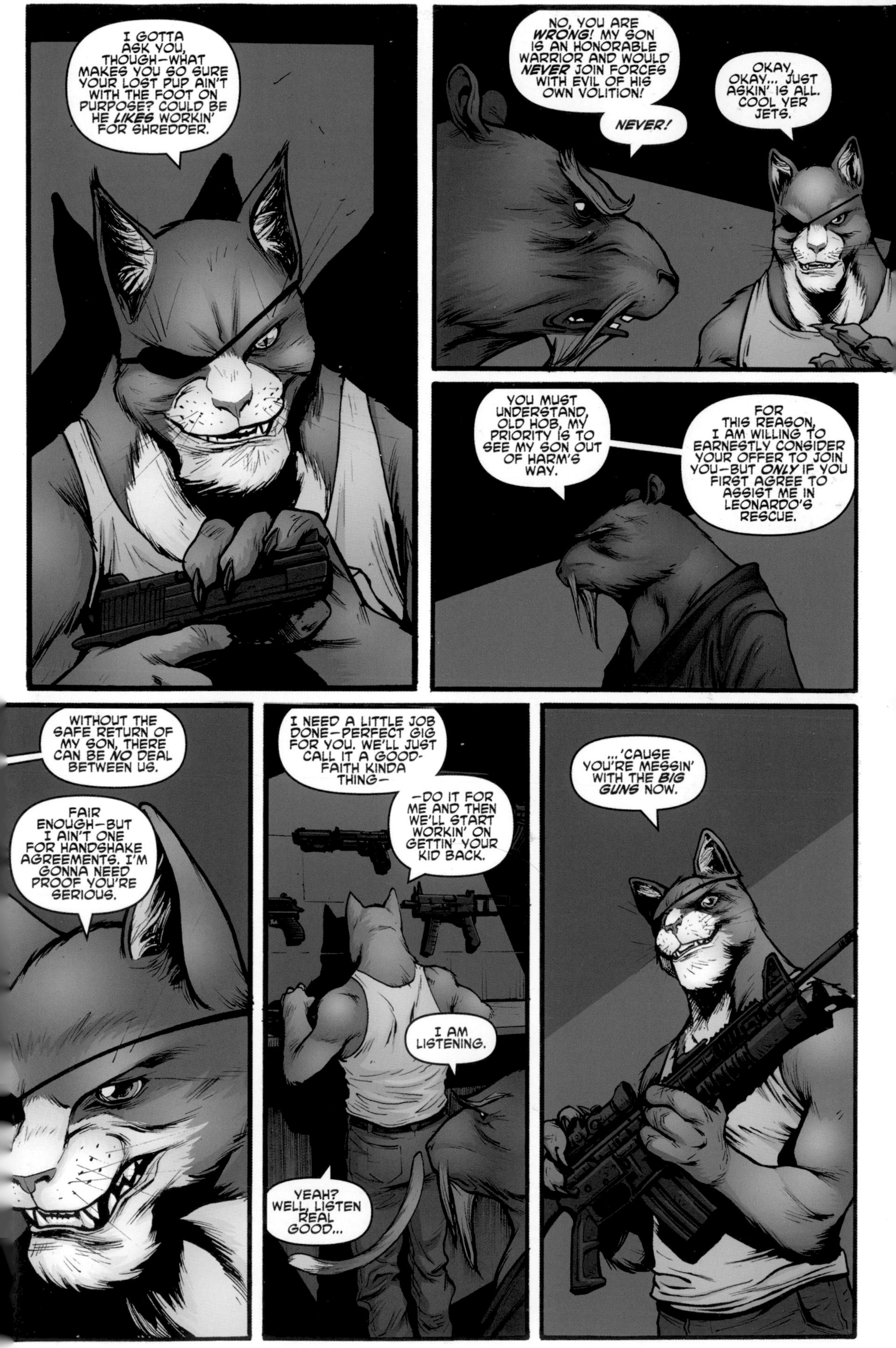
I GOTTA ASK YOU, THOUGH—WHAT MAKES YOU SO SURE YOUR LOST PUP AIN'T WITH THE FOOT ON PURPOSE? COULD BE HE LIKES WORKIN' FOR SHREDDER.
NO, YOU ARE WRONG! MY SON IS AN HONORABLE WARRIOR AND WOULD NEVER JOIN FORCES WITH EVIL OF HIS OWN VOLITION!
NEVER!
OKAY, OKAY... JUST ASKIN' IS ALL. COOL YER JETS.
YOU MUST UNDERSTAND, OLD HOB, MY PRIORITY IS TO SEE MY SON OUT OF HARM'S WAY.
FOR THIS REASON, I AM WILLING TO EARNESTLY CONSIDER YOUR OFFER TO JOIN YOU—BUT ONLY IF YOU FIRST AGREE TO ASSIST ME IN LEONARDO'S RESCUE.
WITHOUT THE SAFE RETURN OF MY SON, THERE CAN BE NO DEAL BETWEEN US.
FAIR ENOUGH—BUT I AIN'T ONE FOR HANDSHAKE AGREEMENTS. I'M GONNA NEED PROOF YOU'RE SERIOUS.
I NEED A LITTLE JOB DONE—PERFECT GIG FOR YOU. WE'LL JUST CALL IT A GOOD-FAITH KINDA THING—
—DO IT FOR ME AND THEN WE'LL START WORKIN' ON GETTIN' YOUR KID BACK.
I AM LISTENING.
YEAH? WELL, LISTEN REAL GOOD...
...'CAUSE YOU'RE MESSIN' WITH THE BIG GUNS NOW.

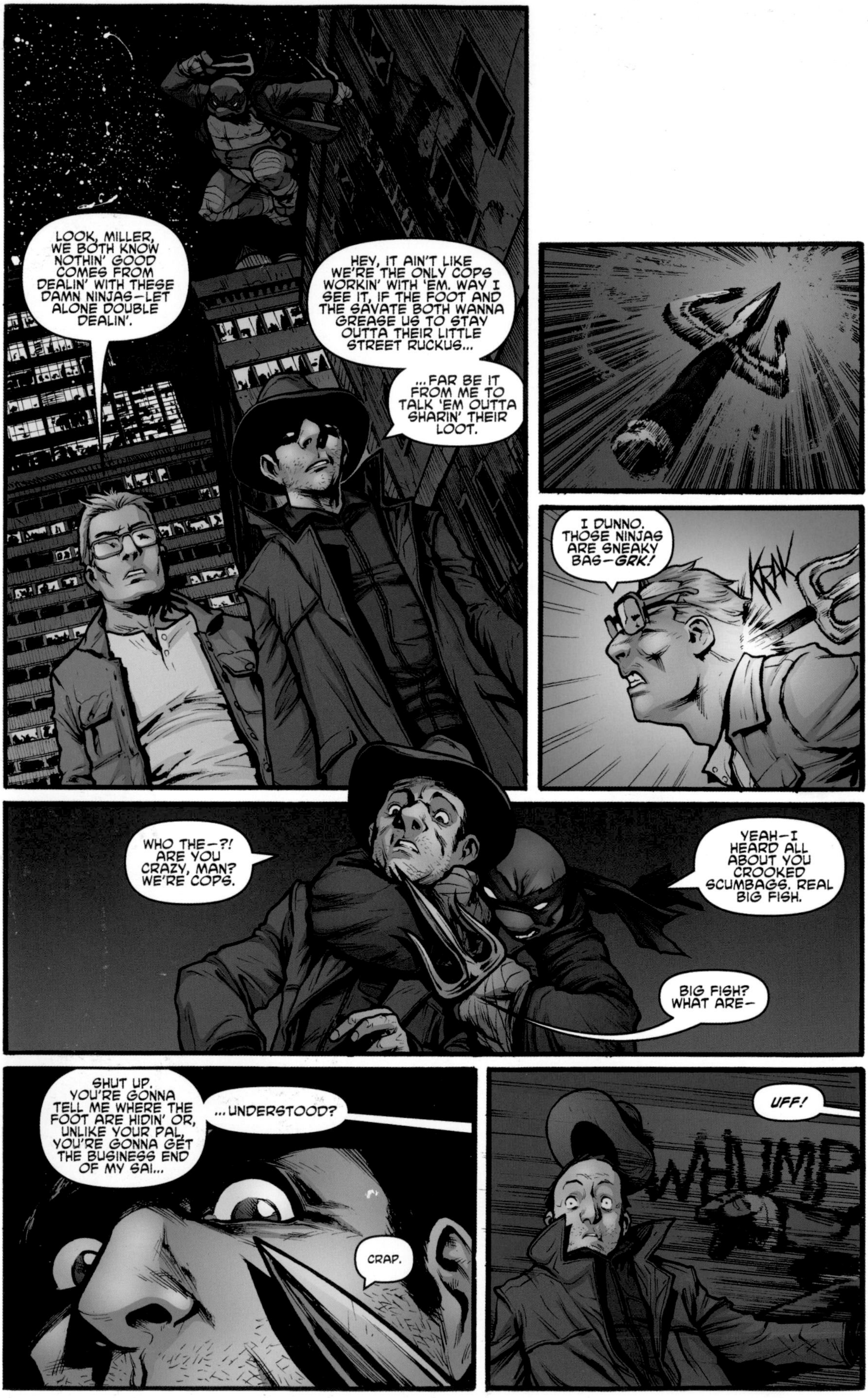
LOOK, MILLER, WE BOTH KNOW NOTHIN' GOOD COMES FROM DEALIN' WITH THESE DAMN NINJAS—LET ALONE DOUBLE DEALIN'.
HEY, IT AIN'T LIKE WE'RE THE ONLY COPS WORKIN' WITH 'EM. WAY I SEE IT, IF THE FOOT AND THE SAVATE BOTH WANNA GREASE US TO STAY OUTTA THEIR LITTLE STREET RUCKUS...
...FAR BE IT FROM ME TO TALK 'EM OUTTA SHARIN' THEIR LOOT.
I DUNNO. THOSE NINJAS ARE SNEAKY BAS—GRK!
KRAK
WHO THE—?! ARE YOU CRAZY, MAN? WE'RE COPS.
YEAH—I HEARD ALL ABOUT YOU CROOKED SCUMBAGS. REAL BIG FISH.
BIG FISH? WHAT ARE—
SHUT UP. YOU'RE GONNA TELL ME WHERE THE FOOT ARE HIDIN' OR, UNLIKE YOUR PAL, YOU'RE GONNA GET THE BUSINESS END OF MY SAI...
...UNDERSTOOD?
CRAP.
UFF!
WHUMP

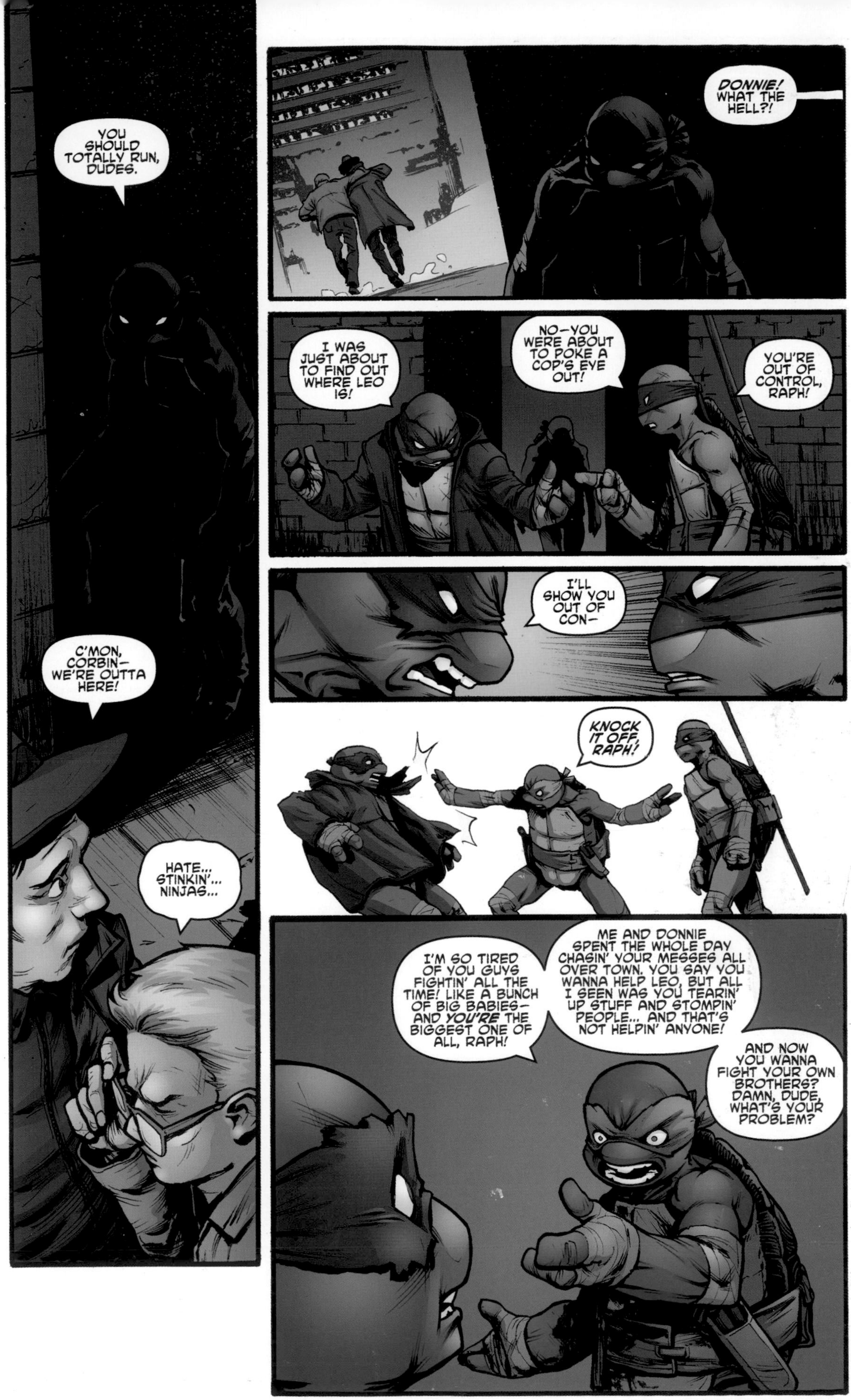
YOU SHOULD TOTALLY RUN, DUDES.
C'MON, CORBIN— WE'RE OUTTA HERE!
HATE... STINKIN'... NINJAS...
DONNIE! WHAT THE HELL?!
I WAS JUST ABOUT TO FIND OUT WHERE LEO IS!
NO—YOU WERE ABOUT TO POKE A COP'S EYE OUT!
YOU'RE OUT OF CONTROL, RAPH!
I'LL SHOW YOU OUT OF CON—
KNOCK IT OFF, RAPH!
I'M SO TIRED OF YOU GUYS FIGHTIN' ALL THE TIME! LIKE A BUNCH OF BIG BABIES— AND YOU'RE THE BIGGEST ONE OF ALL, RAPH!
ME AND DONNIE SPENT THE WHOLE DAY CHASIN' YOUR MESSES ALL OVER TOWN. YOU SAY YOU WANNA HELP LEO, BUT ALL I SEEN WAS YOU TEARIN' UP STUFF AND STOMPIN' PEOPLE... AND THAT'S NOT HELPIN' ANYONE!
AND NOW YOU WANNA FIGHT YOUR OWN BROTHERS? DAMN, DUDE, WHAT'S YOUR PROBLEM?

GAH, I KNOW IT'S STUPID. IT'S JUST... IT'S ALL MY FAULT. IF I DIDN'T LET CASEY GET TAKEN BY THE FOOT, IF I DIDN'T LOSE IT WHEN SHREDDER HURT 'IM... LEO WOULDN'T BE GONE LIKE THIS.

I DON'T KNOW WHAT'S MAKIN' LEO DO THIS CRAZY STUFF. I JUST KNOW IT'S ALL ON ME, AND I GOTTA DO SOMETHIN' TO FIX IT.

WE ALL FINALLY FOUND EACH OTHER AND NOW, 'CAUSE OF MY STUPID TEMPER, WE'RE BROKEN AGAIN.

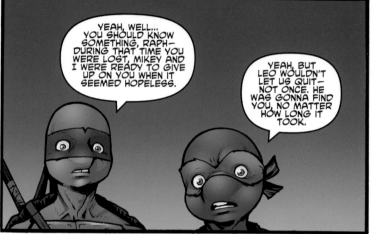

YEAH, WELL... YOU SHOULD KNOW SOMETHING, RAPH— DURING THAT TIME YOU WERE LOST, MIKEY AND I WERE READY TO GIVE UP ON YOU WHEN IT SEEMED HOPELESS.

YEAH, BUT LEO WOULDN'T LET US QUIT— NOT ONCE. HE WAS GONNA FIND YOU, NO MATTER HOW LONG IT TOOK.

HE WAS ALWAYS OUR LEADER—NO MATTER HOW MUCH I USED TO FIGHT HIM ABOUT IT.

AND LEO'D BE THE FIRST ONE TO TELL YOU THIS ISN'T YOUR FAULT, RAPH. BAD THINGS HAPPEN SOMETIMES—THAT'S JUST LIFE.

YOU CAN'T CONTROL IT, SO YOU GOTTA QUIT BEATING YOURSELF UP, MAN... NOT TO MENTION EVERY LOWLIFE THUG AND CROOKED COP IN THE CITY.

IT'S TIME FOR US TO BE THE TEAM LEO MADE US INTO.

WORKING TOGETHER IS THE ONLY WAY WE'RE GONNA GET THROUGH THIS. THE ONLY WAY WE'RE GONNA SAVE HIM.

I...

...YEAH, YOU'RE RIGHT, DON. THANKS.

AWESOME! SO WHERE DO WE START, TEAM?

WELL, WHAT WOULD LEO SAY?

HEH— THAT'S EASY. HE'D SAY...

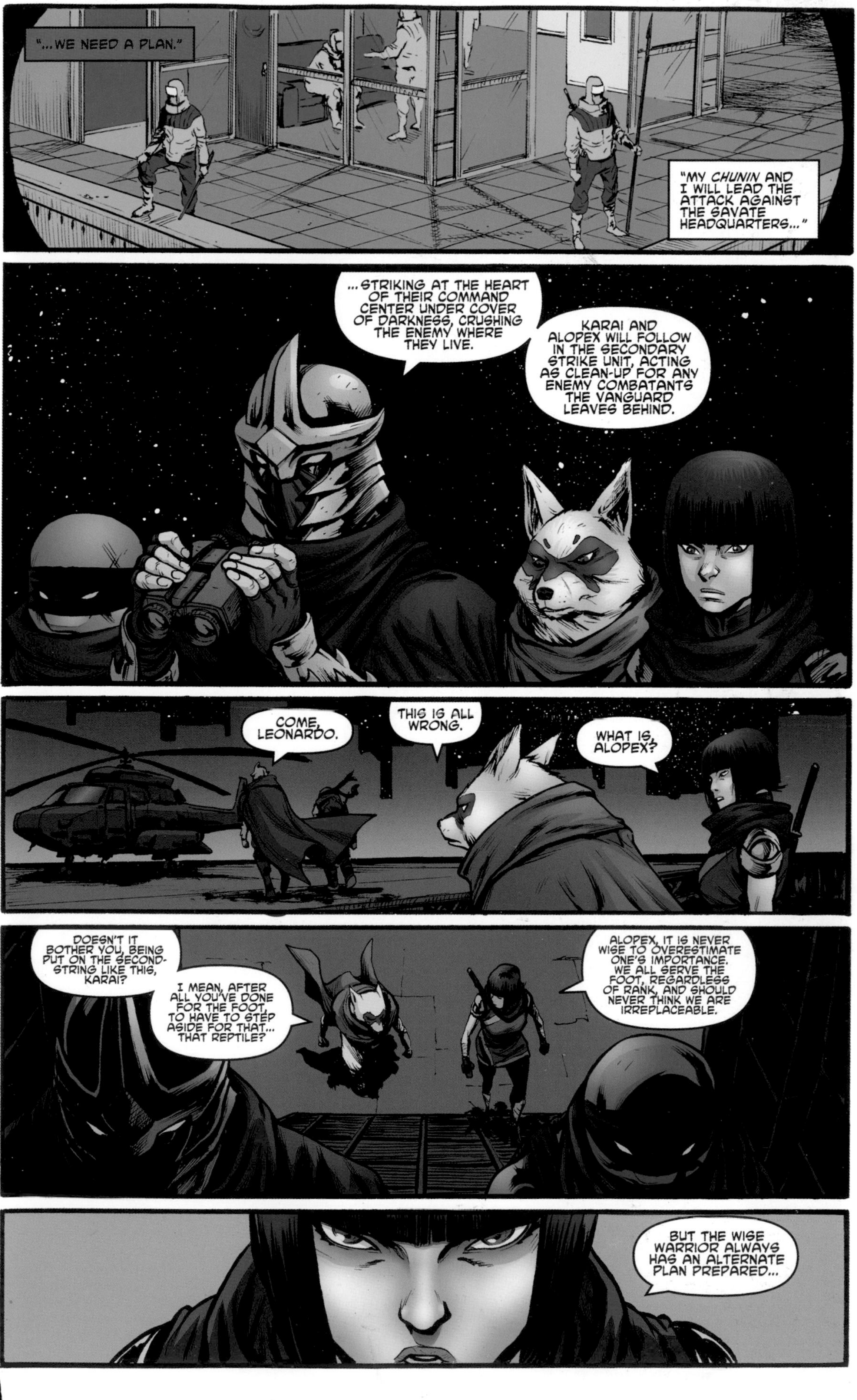
"...WE NEED A PLAN."
"MY CHUNIN AND I WILL LEAD THE ATTACK AGAINST THE SAVATE HEADQUARTERS..."
...STRIKING AT THE HEART OF THEIR COMMAND CENTER UNDER COVER OF DARKNESS, CRUSHING THE ENEMY WHERE THEY LIVE.
KARAI AND ALOPEX WILL FOLLOW IN THE SECONDARY STRIKE UNIT, ACTING AS CLEAN-UP FOR ANY ENEMY COMBATANTS THE VANGUARD LEAVES BEHIND.
COME, LEONARDO.
THIS IS ALL WRONG.
WHAT IS, ALOPEX?
DOESN'T IT BOTHER YOU, BEING PUT ON THE SECOND-STRING LIKE THIS, KARAI?
I MEAN, AFTER ALL YOU'VE DONE FOR THE FOOT, TO HAVE TO STEP ASIDE FOR THAT... THAT REPTILE?
ALOPEX, IT IS NEVER WISE TO OVERESTIMATE ONE'S IMPORTANCE. WE ALL SERVE THE FOOT, REGARDLESS OF RANK, AND SHOULD NEVER THINK WE ARE IRREPLACEABLE.
BUT THE WISE WARRIOR ALWAYS HAS AN ALTERNATE PLAN PREPARED...

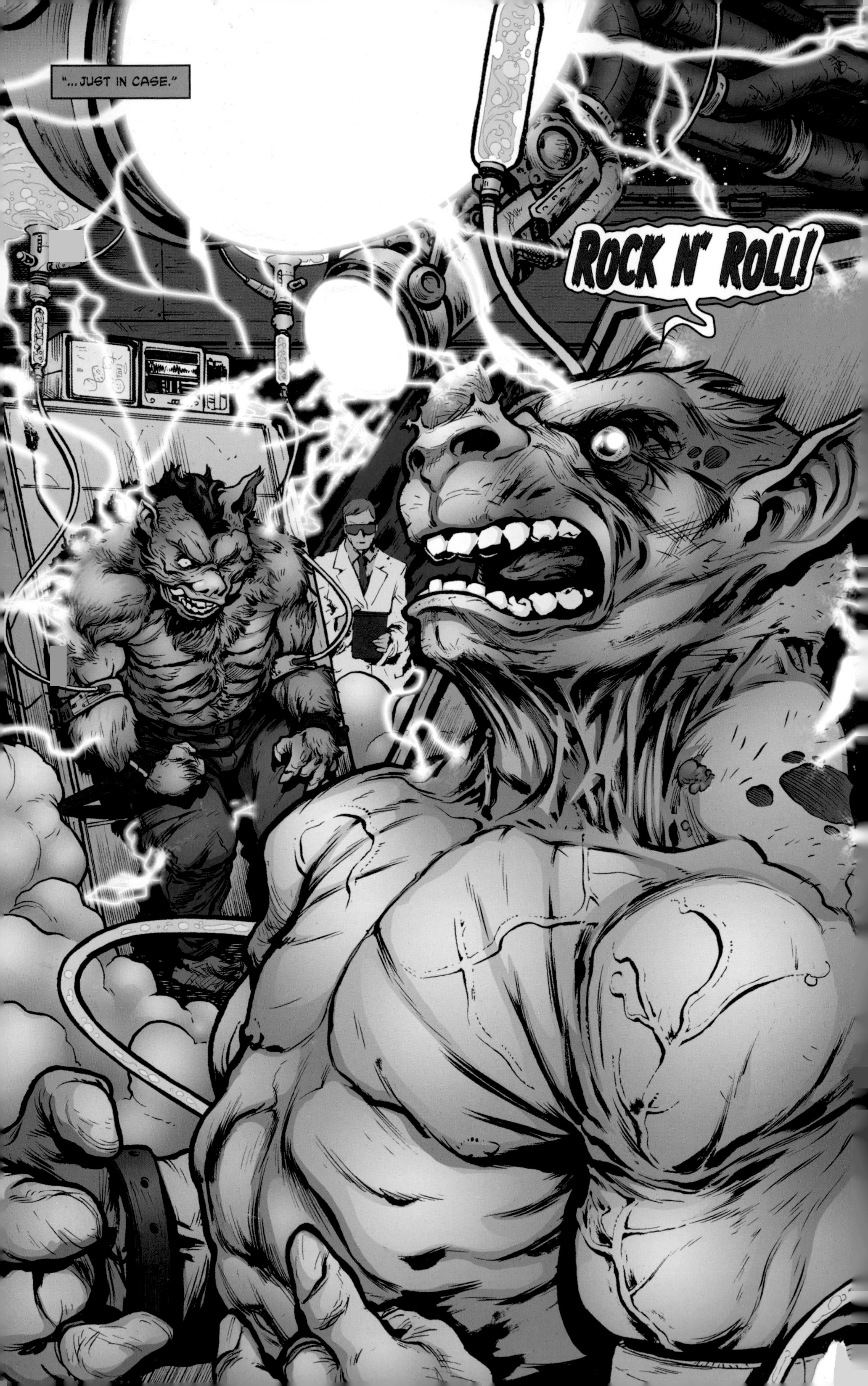
"...JUST IN CASE."
ROCK N' ROLL!

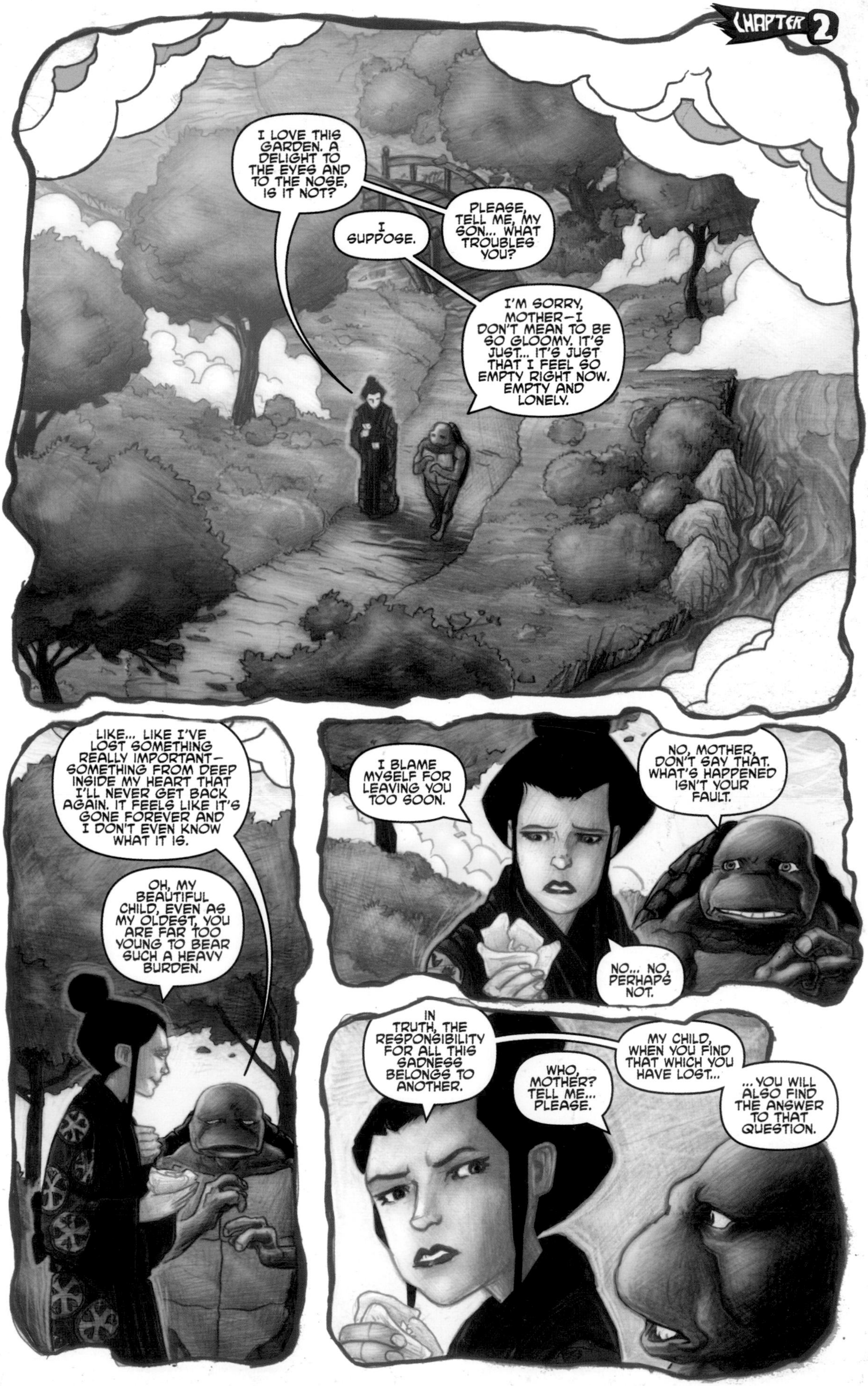
CHAPTER 2
I LOVE THIS GARDEN. A DELIGHT TO THE EYES AND TO THE NOSE, IS IT NOT?
I SUPPOSE.
PLEASE, TELL ME, MY SON... WHAT TROUBLES YOU?
I'M SORRY, MOTHER—I DON'T MEAN TO BE SO GLOOMY. IT'S JUST... IT'S JUST THAT I FEEL SO EMPTY RIGHT NOW. EMPTY AND LONELY.
LIKE... LIKE I'VE LOST SOMETHING REALLY IMPORTANT—SOMETHING FROM DEEP INSIDE MY HEART THAT I'LL NEVER GET BACK AGAIN. IT FEELS LIKE IT'S GONE FOREVER AND I DON'T EVEN KNOW WHAT IT IS.
OH, MY BEAUTIFUL CHILD, EVEN AS MY OLDEST, YOU ARE FAR TOO YOUNG TO BEAR SUCH A HEAVY BURDEN.
I BLAME MYSELF FOR LEAVING YOU TOO SOON.
NO, MOTHER, DON'T SAY THAT. WHAT'S HAPPENED ISN'T YOUR FAULT.
NO... NO, PERHAPS NOT.
IN TRUTH, THE RESPONSIBILITY FOR ALL THIS SADNESS BELONGS TO ANOTHER.
WHO, MOTHER? TELL ME... PLEASE.
MY CHILD, WHEN YOU FIND THAT WHICH YOU HAVE LOST...
...YOU WILL ALSO FIND THE ANSWER TO THAT QUESTION.

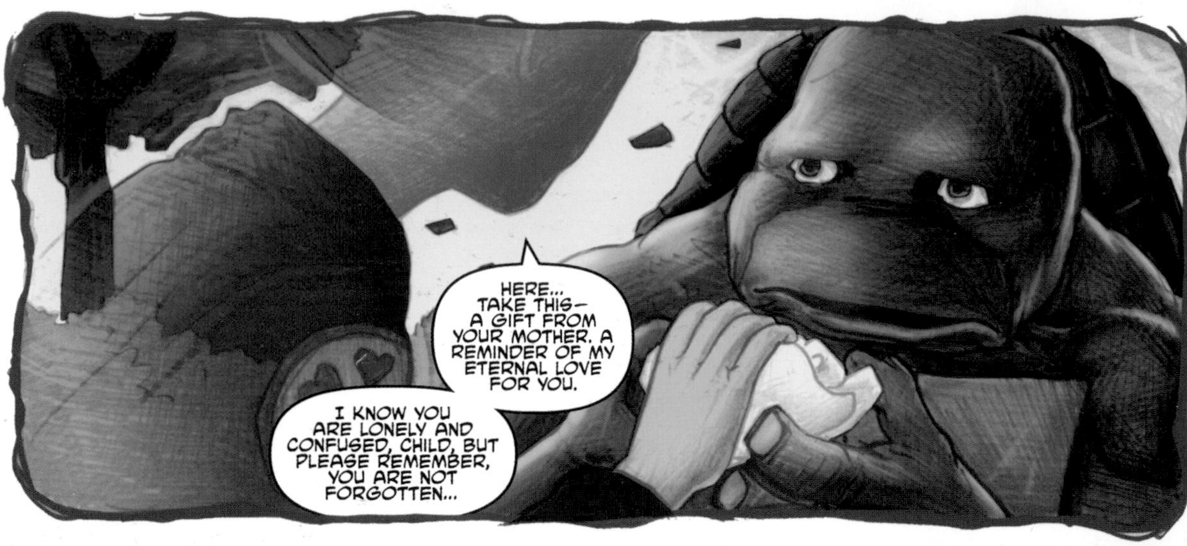
HERE... TAKE THIS— A GIFT FROM YOUR MOTHER. A REMINDER OF MY ETERNAL LOVE FOR YOU.
I KNOW YOU ARE LONELY AND CONFUSED, CHILD, BUT PLEASE REMEMBER, YOU ARE NOT FORGOTTEN...

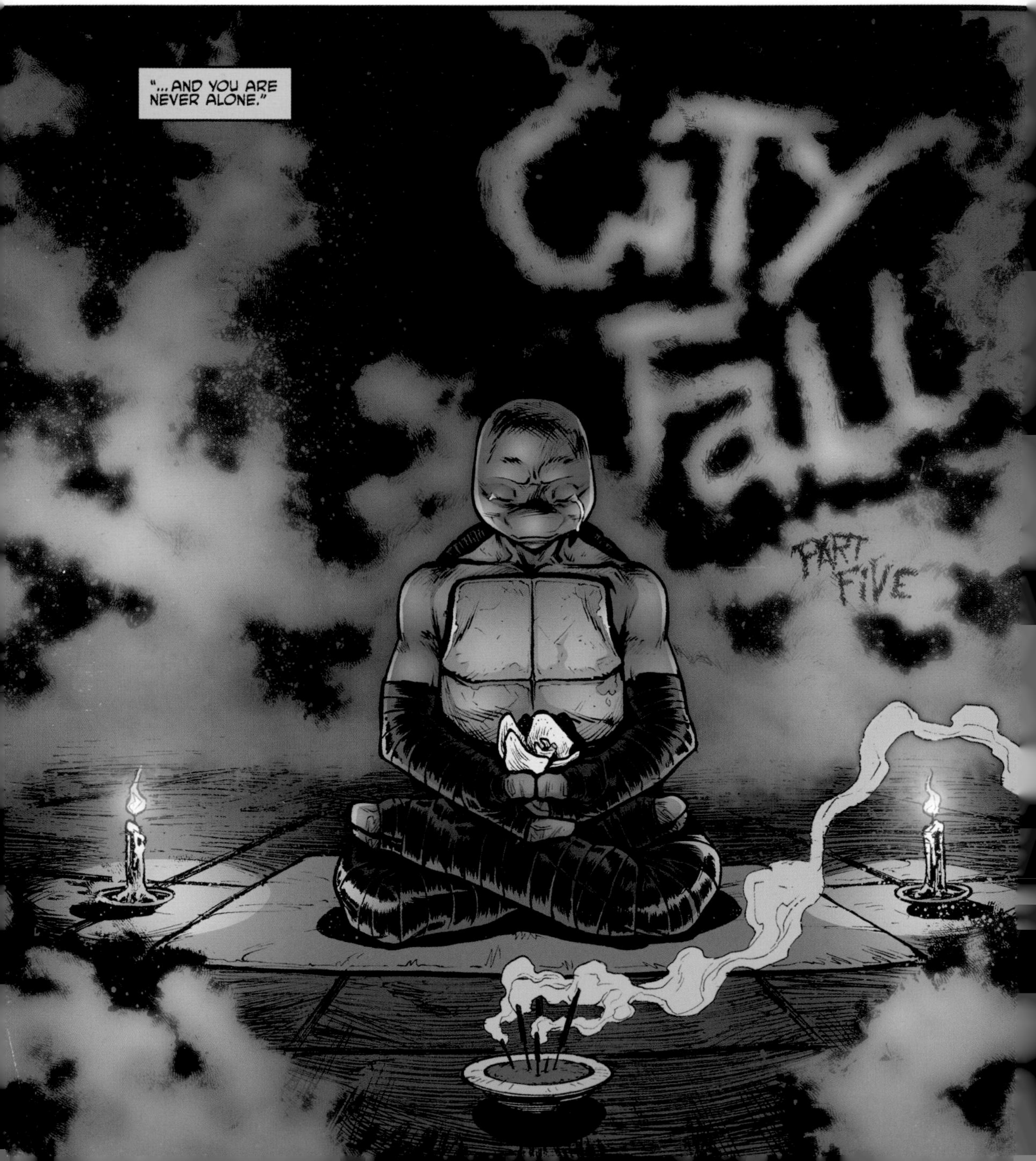
"...AND YOU ARE NEVER ALONE."
CITY FALL
PART FIVE

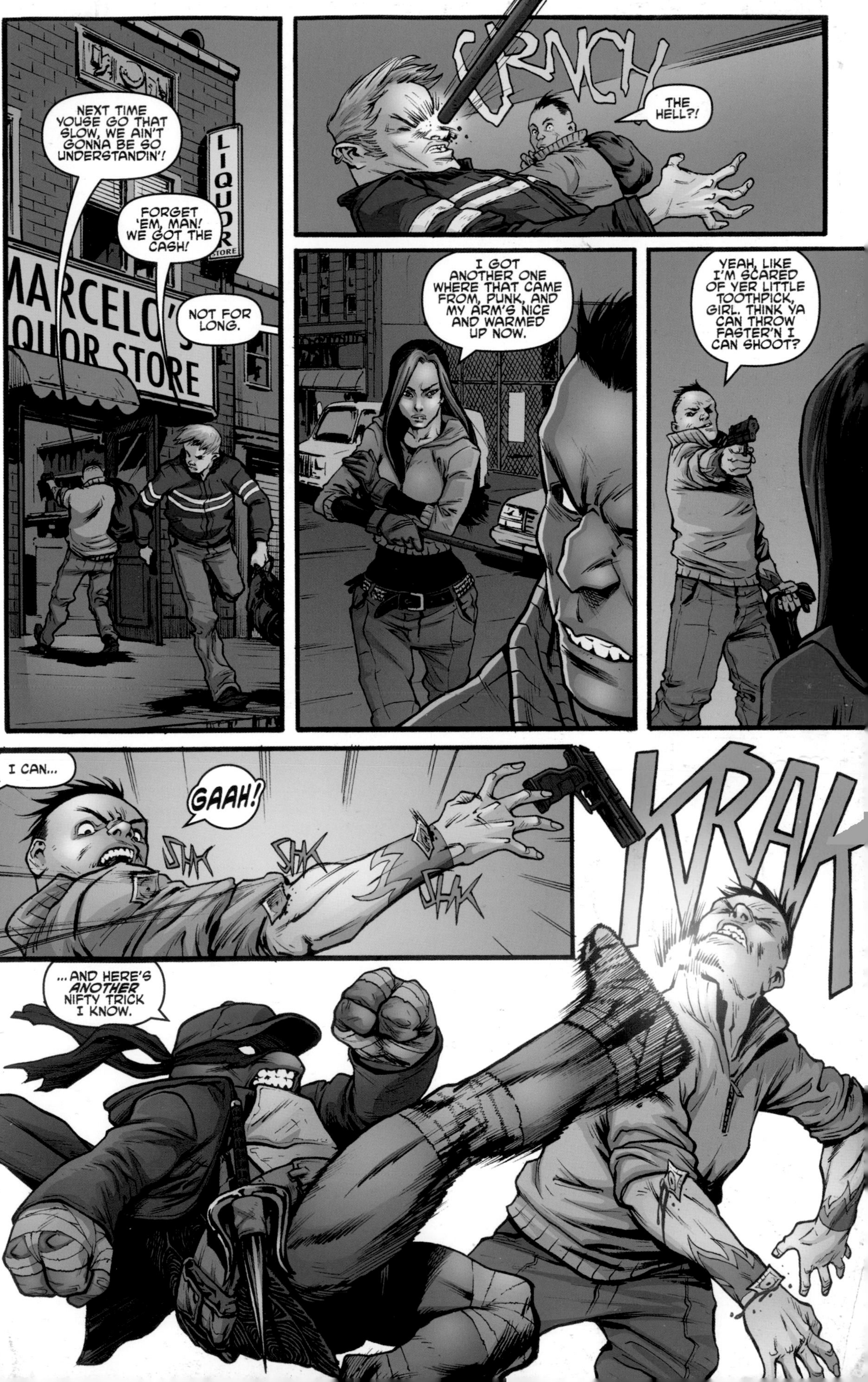
NEXT TIME YOUSE GO THAT SLOW, WE AIN'T GONNA BE SO UNDERSTANDIN'!
LIQUOR STORE
FORGET 'EM, MAN! WE GOT THE CASH!
MARCELO'S LIQUOR STORE
NOT FOR LONG.
CRNCH
THE HELL?!
I GOT ANOTHER ONE WHERE THAT CAME FROM, PUNK, AND MY ARM'S NICE AND WARMED UP NOW.
YEAH, LIKE I'M SCARED OF YER LITTLE TOOTHPICK, GIRL. THINK YA CAN THROW FASTER'N I CAN SHOOT?
I CAN...
GAAH!
SHK
SHK
SHK
KRAK
...AND HERE'S *ANOTHER* NIFTY TRICK I KNOW.

ANGEL, YOU GOT TIME TO TALK?

I DO NOW. THANKS FOR THE ASSIST.

NO BIGGIE. WHY AIN'T THE OTHER PURPLE DRAGONS WITH YOU?

UH... THE DRAGONS ARE DEALIN' WITH SOME, UM... *FUNNY BUSINESS* RIGHT NOW. WHAT YOU MIGHT CALL A FAMILY SQUABBLE.*

THAT SEEMS TO BE GOIN' ROUND THESE DAYS. MUST BE SOMETHIN' IN THE WATER.

*See the HUN micro-series for more info. – B.C.

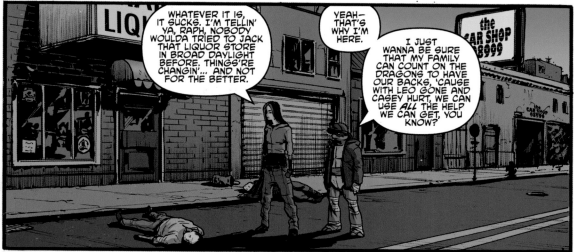

WHATEVER IT IS, IT SUCKS. I'M TELLIN' YA, RAPH, NOBODY WOULDA TRIED TO JACK THAT LIQUOR STORE IN BROAD DAYLIGHT BEFORE. THINGS'RE CHANGIN'... AND NOT FOR THE BETTER.

YEAH— THAT'S WHY I'M HERE.

I JUST WANNA BE SURE THAT MY FAMILY CAN COUNT ON THE DRAGONS TO HAVE OUR BACKS, 'CAUSE WITH LEO GONE AND CASEY HURT, WE CAN USE *ALL* THE HELP WE CAN GET, YOU KNOW?

YEAH, I KNOW. BUT SINCE THINGS IN THE DRAGONS AIN'T EXACTLY WHAT YOU'D CALL COPACETIC RIGHT NOW, I CAN'T GUARANTEE THE OTHERS WILL HELP YOU GUYS.

BUT YOU KNOW *I* GOT ALL YOUR BACKS...

...NO MATTER WHAT.

THANKS, ANGEL—THAT MEANS A LOT. REALLY.

OKAY, I'M OUTTA HERE. GOTTA MAKE ONE MORE STOP...

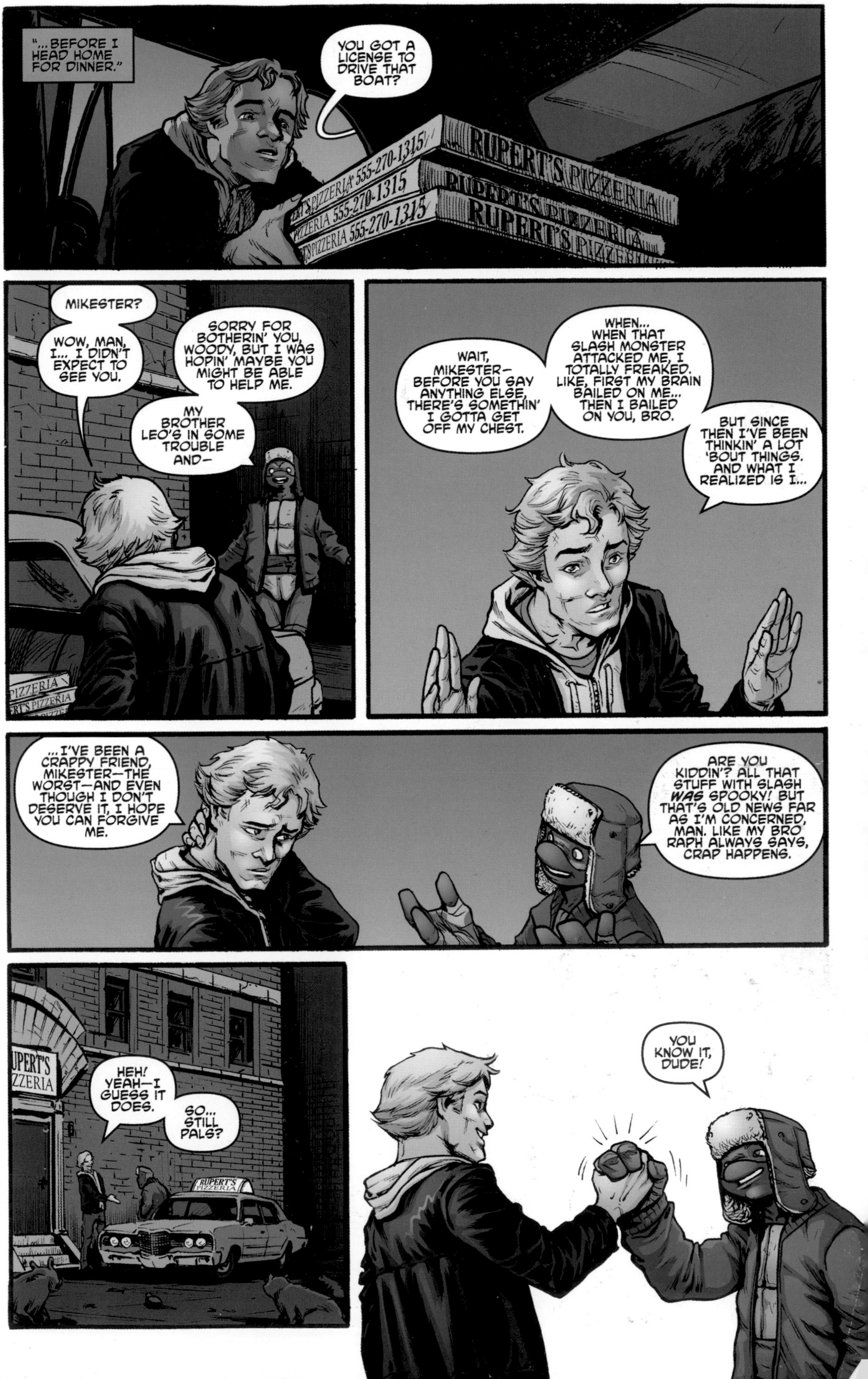
"...BEFORE I HEAD HOME FOR DINNER."
YOU GOT A LICENSE TO DRIVE THAT BOAT?
RUPERT'S PIZZERIA 555-270-1315
MIKESTER?
WOW, MAN, I... I DIDN'T EXPECT TO SEE YOU.
SORRY FOR BOTHERIN' YOU, WOODY, BUT I WAS HOPIN' MAYBE YOU MIGHT BE ABLE TO HELP ME.
MY BROTHER LEO'S IN SOME TROUBLE AND–
WAIT, MIKESTER–BEFORE YOU SAY ANYTHING ELSE, THERE'S SOMETHIN' I GOTTA GET OFF MY CHEST.
WHEN... WHEN THAT SLASH MONSTER ATTACKED ME, I TOTALLY FREAKED. LIKE, FIRST MY BRAIN BAILED ON ME... THEN I BAILED ON YOU, BRO.
BUT SINCE THEN I'VE BEEN THINKIN' A LOT 'BOUT THINGS. AND WHAT I REALIZED IS I...
...I'VE BEEN A CRAPPY FRIEND, MIKESTER–THE WORST–AND EVEN THOUGH I DON'T DESERVE IT, I HOPE YOU CAN FORGIVE ME.
ARE YOU KIDDIN'? ALL THAT STUFF WITH SLASH *WAS* SPOOKY! BUT THAT'S OLD NEWS FAR AS I'M CONCERNED, MAN. LIKE MY BRO RAPH ALWAYS SAYS, CRAP HAPPENS.
RUPERT'S PIZZERIA
HEH! YEAH–I GUESS IT DOES.
SO... STILL PALS?
YOU KNOW IT, DUDE!

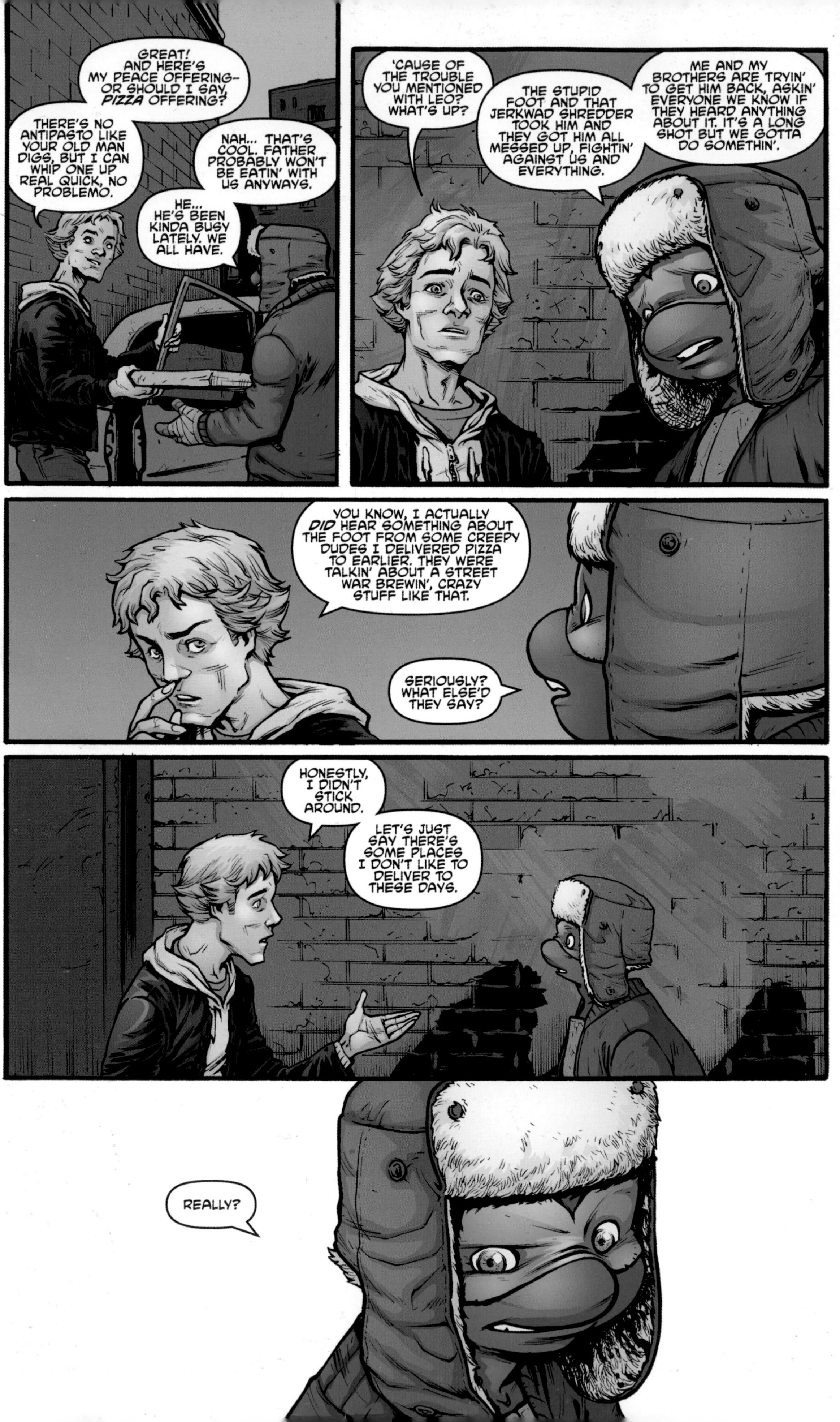
GREAT! AND HERE'S MY PEACE OFFERING-- OR SHOULD I SAY, *PIZZA* OFFERING?
THERE'S NO ANTIPASTO LIKE YOUR OLD MAN DIGS, BUT I CAN WHIP ONE UP REAL QUICK, NO PROBLEMO.
NAH... THAT'S COOL. FATHER PROBABLY WON'T BE EATIN' WITH US ANYWAYS.
HE... HE'S BEEN KINDA BUSY LATELY. WE ALL HAVE.
'CAUSE OF THE TROUBLE YOU MENTIONED WITH LEO? WHAT'S UP?
THE STUPID FOOT AND THAT JERKWAD SHREDDER TOOK HIM AND THEY GOT HIM ALL MESSED UP, FIGHTIN' AGAINST US AND EVERYTHING.
ME AND MY BROTHERS ARE TRYIN' TO GET HIM BACK, ASKIN' EVERYONE WE KNOW IF THEY HEARD ANYTHING ABOUT IT. IT'S A LONG SHOT BUT WE GOTTA DO SOMETHIN'.
YOU KNOW, I ACTUALLY *DID* HEAR SOMETHING ABOUT THE FOOT FROM SOME CREEPY DUDES I DELIVERED PIZZA TO EARLIER. THEY WERE TALKIN' ABOUT A STREET WAR BREWIN', CRAZY STUFF LIKE THAT.
SERIOUSLY? WHAT ELSE'D THEY SAY?
HONESTLY, I DIDN'T STICK AROUND.
LET'S JUST SAY THERE'S SOME PLACES I DON'T LIKE TO DELIVER TO THESE DAYS.
REALLY?

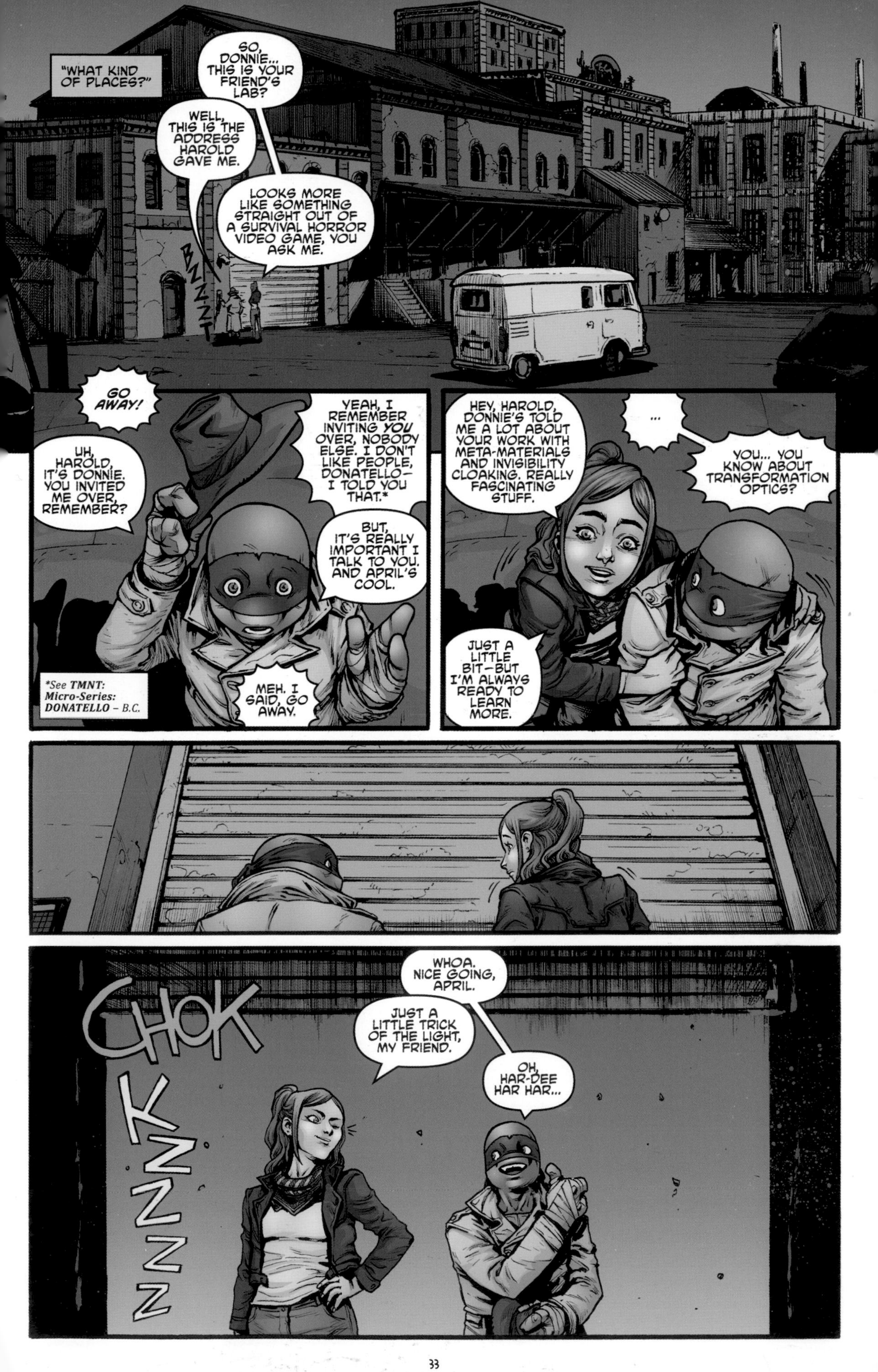
"WHAT KIND OF PLACES?"
SO, DONNIE... THIS IS YOUR FRIEND'S LAB?
WELL, THIS IS THE ADDRESS HAROLD GAVE ME.
LOOKS MORE LIKE SOMETHING STRAIGHT OUT OF A SURVIVAL HORROR VIDEO GAME, YOU ASK ME.
BZZZT
GO AWAY!
UH, HAROLD, IT'S DONNIE. YOU INVITED ME OVER, REMEMBER?
YEAH, I REMEMBER INVITING YOU OVER, NOBODY ELSE. I DON'T LIKE PEOPLE, DONATELLO—I TOLD YOU THAT.*
BUT, IT'S REALLY IMPORTANT I TALK TO YOU. AND APRIL'S COOL.
MEH. I SAID, GO AWAY.
*See TMNT: Micro-Series: DONATELLO – B.C.
HEY, HAROLD, DONNIE'S TOLD ME A LOT ABOUT YOUR WORK WITH META-MATERIALS AND INVISIBILITY CLOAKING. REALLY FASCINATING STUFF.
...
YOU... YOU KNOW ABOUT TRANSFORMATION OPTICS?
JUST A LITTLE BIT—BUT I'M ALWAYS READY TO LEARN MORE.
CHOK
KZZZZZ
WHOA. NICE GOING, APRIL.
JUST A LITTLE TRICK OF THE LIGHT, MY FRIEND.
OH, HAR-DEE HAR HAR...

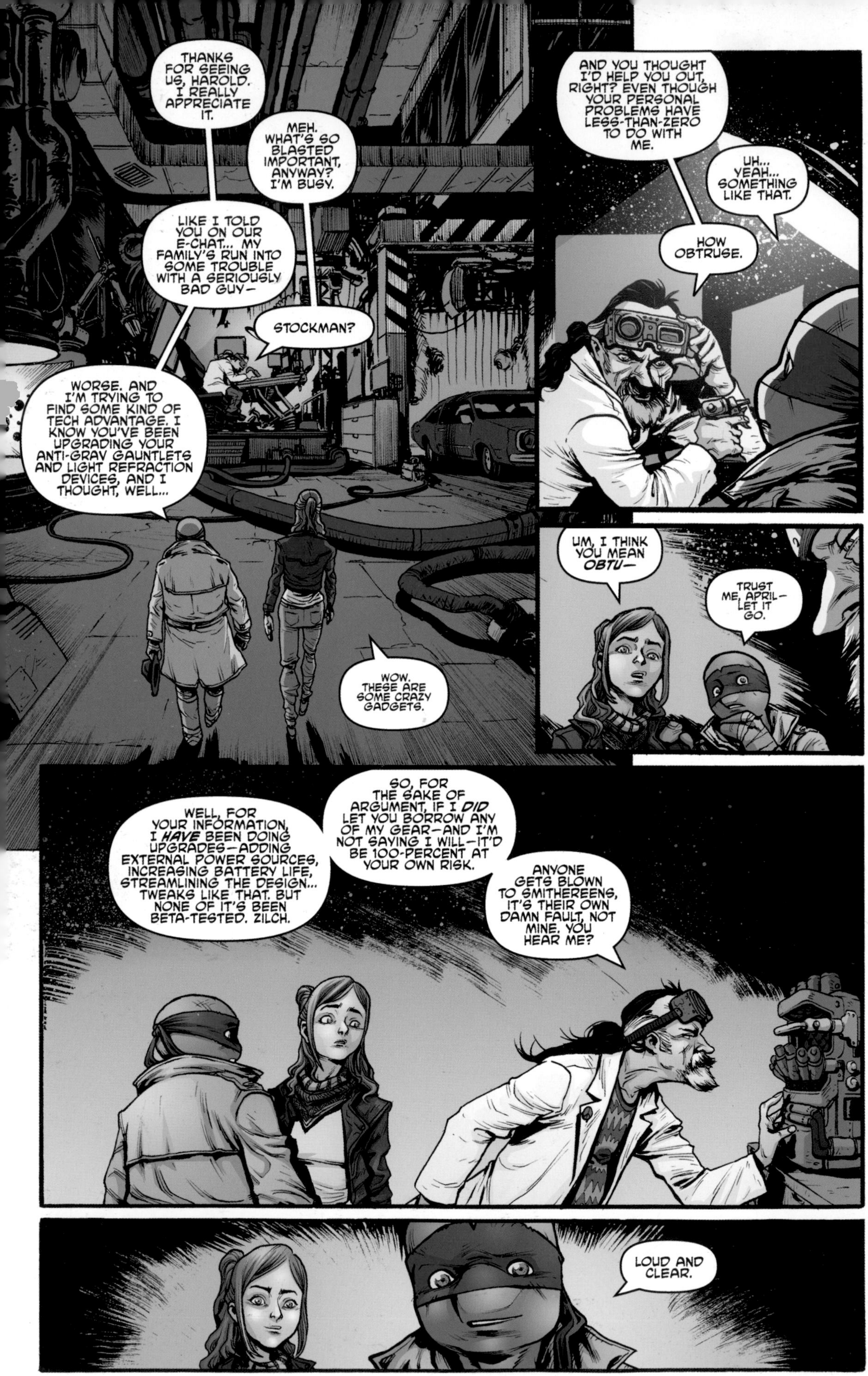
THANKS FOR SEEING US, HAROLD. I REALLY APPRECIATE IT.
MEH. WHAT'S SO BLASTED IMPORTANT, ANYWAY? I'M BUSY.
LIKE I TOLD YOU ON OUR E-CHAT... MY FAMILY'S RUN INTO SOME TROUBLE WITH A SERIOUSLY BAD GUY—
STOCKMAN?
WORSE. AND I'M TRYING TO FIND SOME KIND OF TECH ADVANTAGE. I KNOW YOU'VE BEEN UPGRADING YOUR ANTI-GRAV GAUNTLETS AND LIGHT REFRACTION DEVICES, AND I THOUGHT, WELL...
WOW. THESE ARE SOME CRAZY GADGETS.
AND YOU THOUGHT I'D HELP YOU OUT, RIGHT? EVEN THOUGH YOUR PERSONAL PROBLEMS HAVE LESS-THAN-ZERO TO DO WITH ME.
UH... YEAH... SOMETHING LIKE THAT.
HOW OBTRUSE.
UM, I THINK YOU MEAN *OBTU—*
TRUST ME, APRIL—LET IT GO.
WELL, FOR YOUR INFORMATION, I *HAVE* BEEN DOING UPGRADES—ADDING EXTERNAL POWER SOURCES, INCREASING BATTERY LIFE, STREAMLINING THE DESIGN... TWEAKS LIKE THAT. BUT NONE OF IT'S BEEN BETA-TESTED. ZILCH.
SO, FOR THE SAKE OF ARGUMENT, IF I *DID* LET YOU BORROW ANY OF MY GEAR—AND I'M NOT SAYING I WILL—IT'D BE 100-PERCENT AT YOUR OWN RISK.
ANYONE GETS BLOWN TO SMITHEREENS, IT'S THEIR OWN DAMN FAULT, NOT MINE. YOU HEAR ME?
LOUD AND CLEAR.

AND SO IT COMES TO THIS, MY FRIENDS...

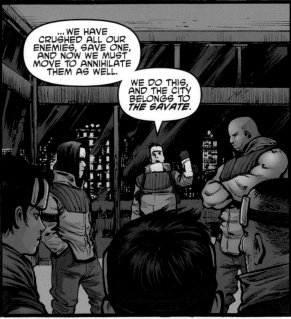

...WE HAVE CRUSHED ALL OUR ENEMIES, SAVE ONE, AND NOW WE MUST MOVE TO ANNIHILATE THEM AS WELL.

WE DO THIS, AND THE CITY BELONGS TO *THE SAVATE.*

YOU KNOW WE WILL FOLLOW YOU DOWN WHATEVER PATH YOU CHOOSE, VICTOR.

WHEN DO YOU WISH TO STRIKE AGAINST THE FOOT?

VERY SOON, PIERRE. WHEN THE CRETINS LEAST EXPECT IT.

I PROMISE YOU...

...THEY'LL NEVER SEE US COMING.

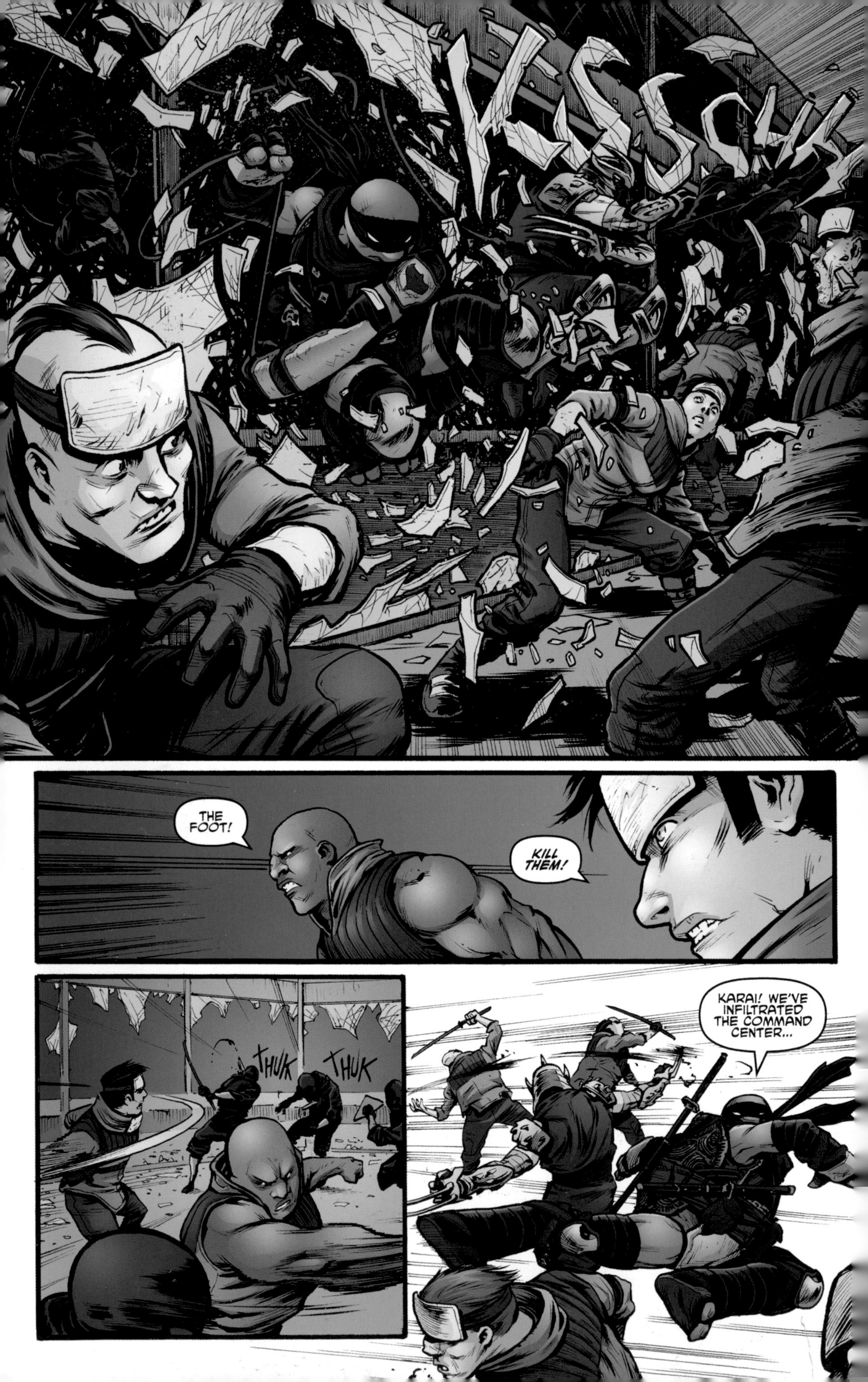
KSSSCHKK
THE FOOT!
KILL THEM!
THUK
THUK
KARAI! WE'VE INFILTRATED THE COMMAND CENTER...

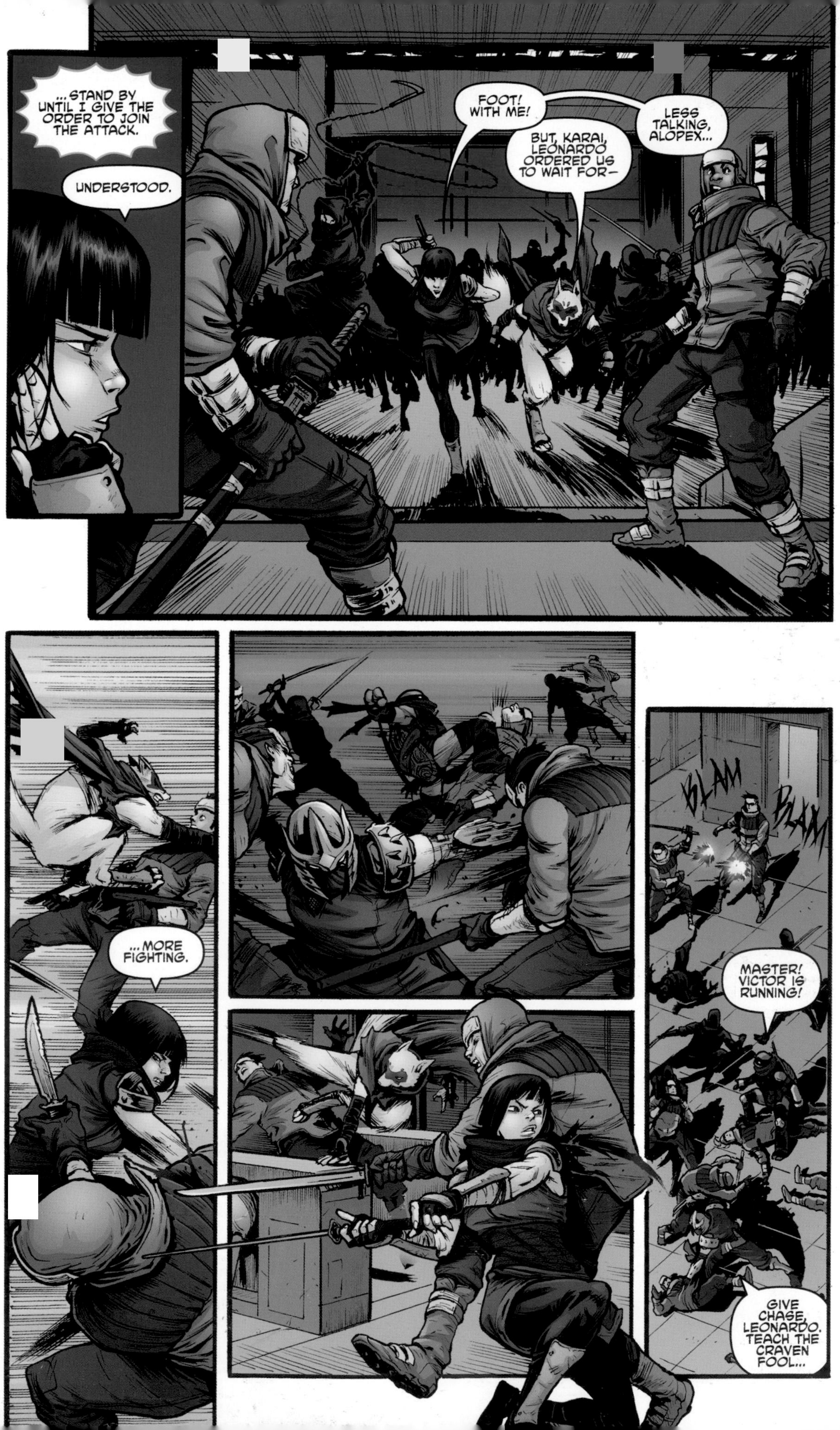
...STAND BY UNTIL I GIVE THE ORDER TO JOIN THE ATTACK.
UNDERSTOOD.
FOOT! WITH ME!
BUT, KARAI, LEONARDO ORDERED US TO WAIT FOR—
LESS TALKING, ALOPEX...
...MORE FIGHTING.
BLAM
BLAM
MASTER! VICTOR IS RUNNING!
GIVE CHASE, LEONARDO. TEACH THE CRAVEN FOOL...

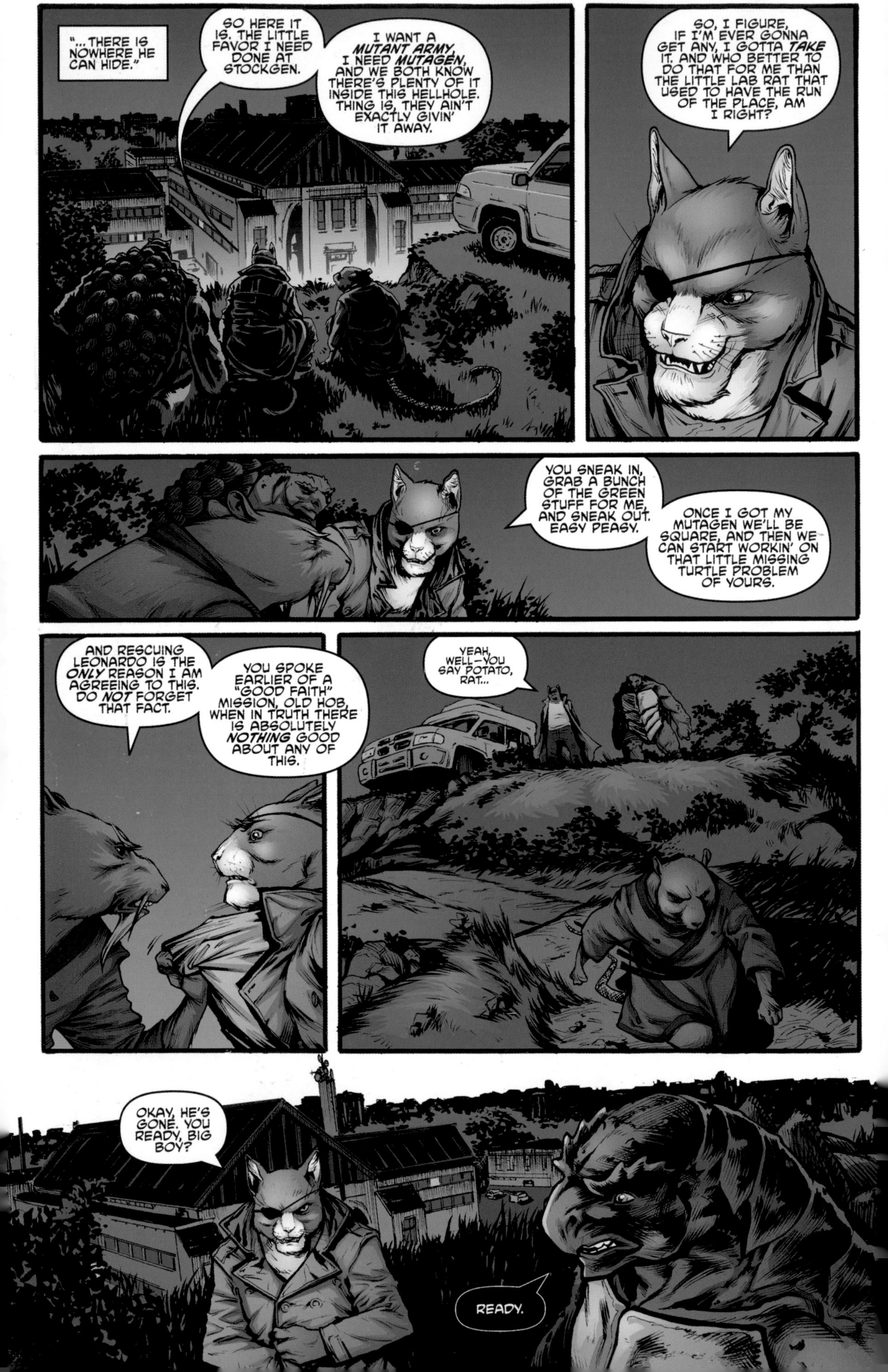
"...THERE IS NOWHERE HE CAN HIDE."
SO HERE IT IS. THE LITTLE FAVOR I NEED DONE AT STOCKGEN.
I WANT A MUTANT ARMY, I NEED MUTAGEN, AND WE BOTH KNOW THERE'S PLENTY OF IT INSIDE THIS HELLHOLE. THING IS, THEY AIN'T EXACTLY GIVIN' IT AWAY.
SO, I FIGURE, IF I'M EVER GONNA GET ANY, I GOTTA TAKE IT. AND WHO BETTER TO DO THAT FOR ME THAN THE LITTLE LAB RAT THAT USED TO HAVE THE RUN OF THE PLACE, AM I RIGHT?
YOU SNEAK IN, GRAB A BUNCH OF THE GREEN STUFF FOR ME, AND SNEAK OUT. EASY PEASY.
ONCE I GOT MY MUTAGEN WE'LL BE SQUARE, AND THEN WE CAN START WORKIN' ON THAT LITTLE MISSING TURTLE PROBLEM OF YOURS.
AND RESCUING LEONARDO IS THE ONLY REASON I AM AGREEING TO THIS. DO NOT FORGET THAT FACT.
YOU SPOKE EARLIER OF A "GOOD FAITH" MISSION, OLD HOB, WHEN IN TRUTH THERE IS ABSOLUTELY NOTHING GOOD ABOUT ANY OF THIS.
YEAH, WELL—YOU SAY POTATO, RAT...
OKAY, HE'S GONE. YOU READY, BIG BOY?
READY.

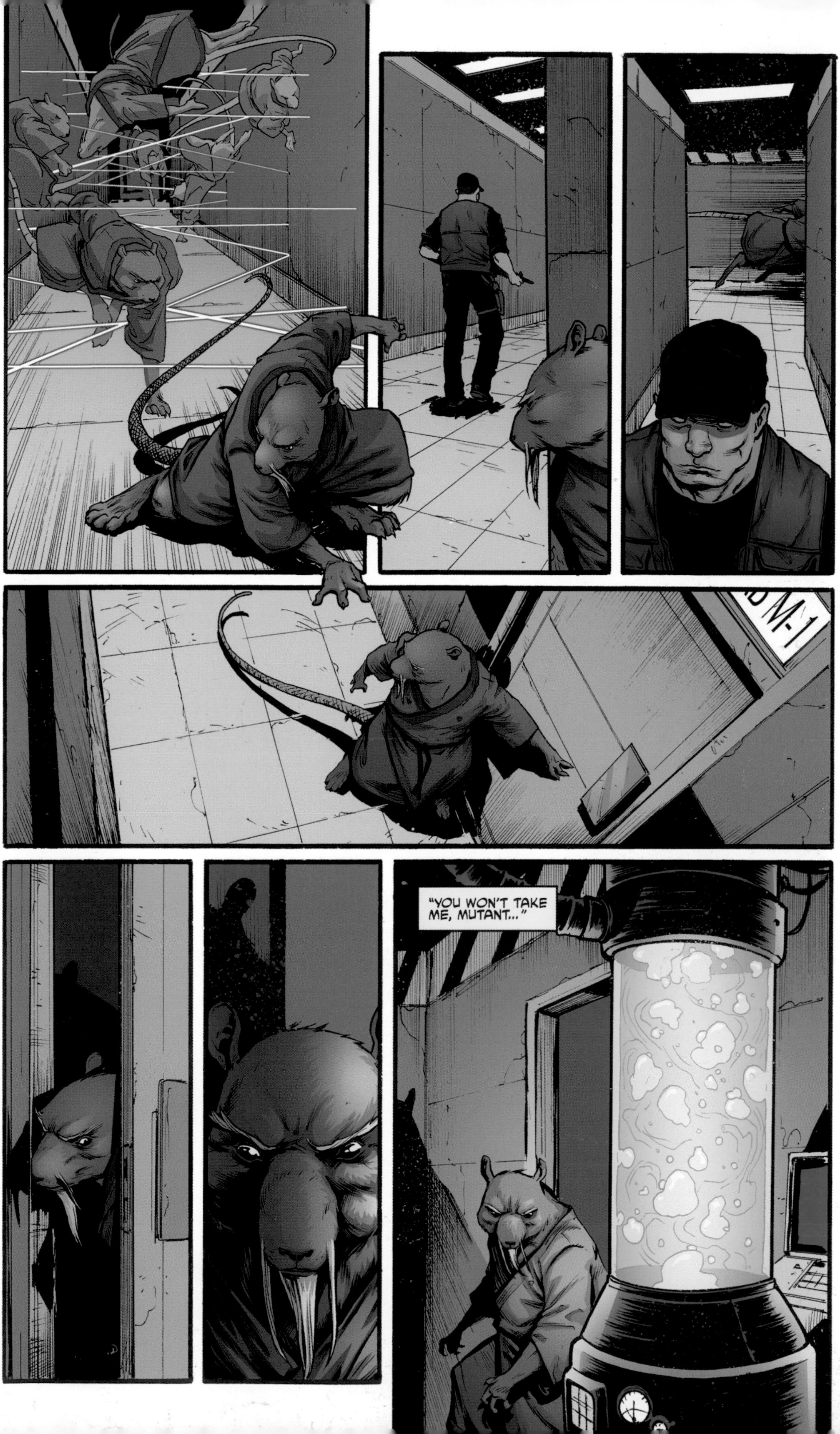

M-1
"YOU WON'T TAKE ME, MUTANT..."

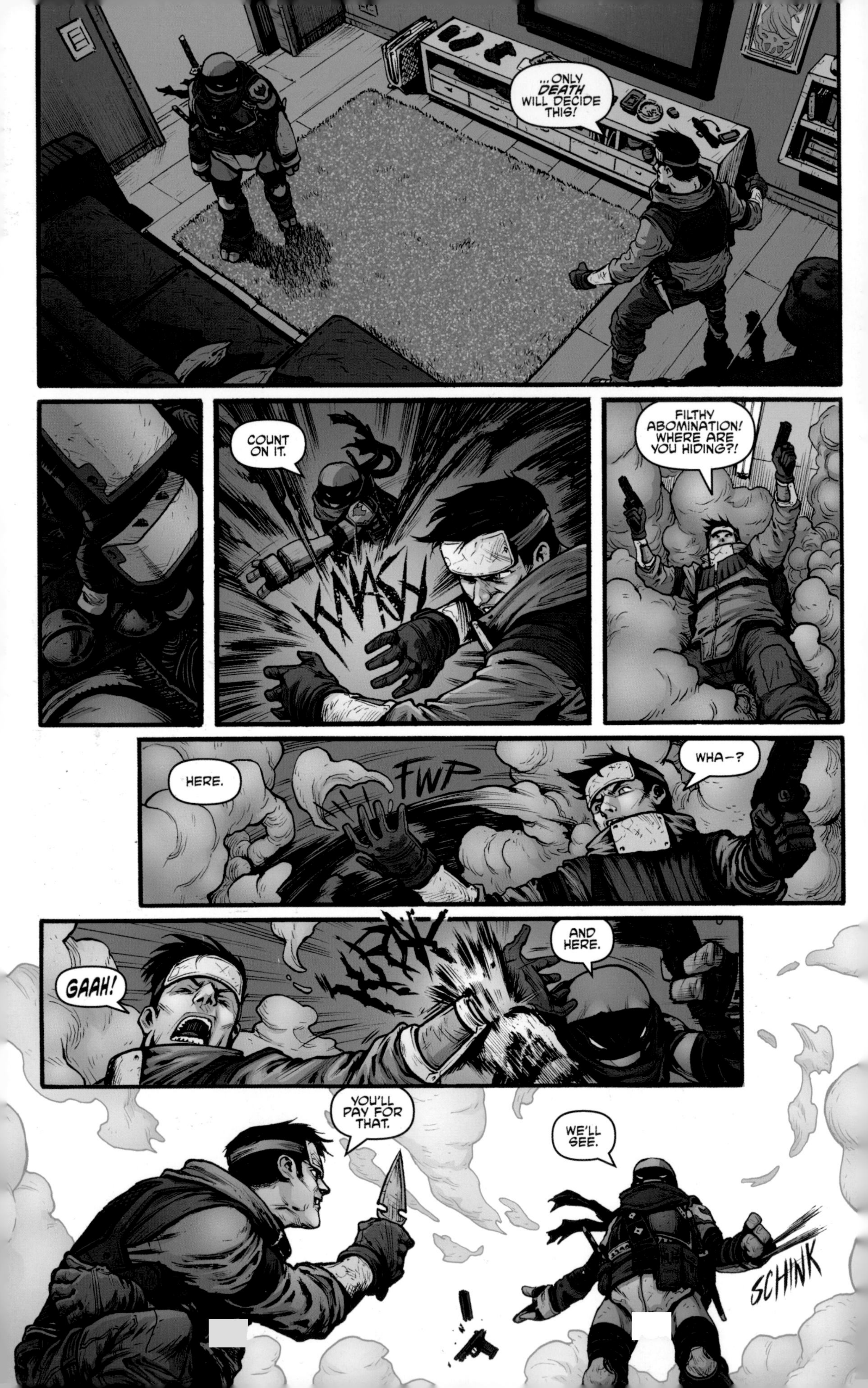
...ONLY DEATH WILL DECIDE THIS!
COUNT ON IT.
KNASH
FILTHY ABOMINATION! WHERE ARE YOU HIDING?!
HERE.
FWP
WHA-?
GAAH!
AND HERE.
YOU'LL PAY FOR THAT.
WE'LL SEE.
SCHINK

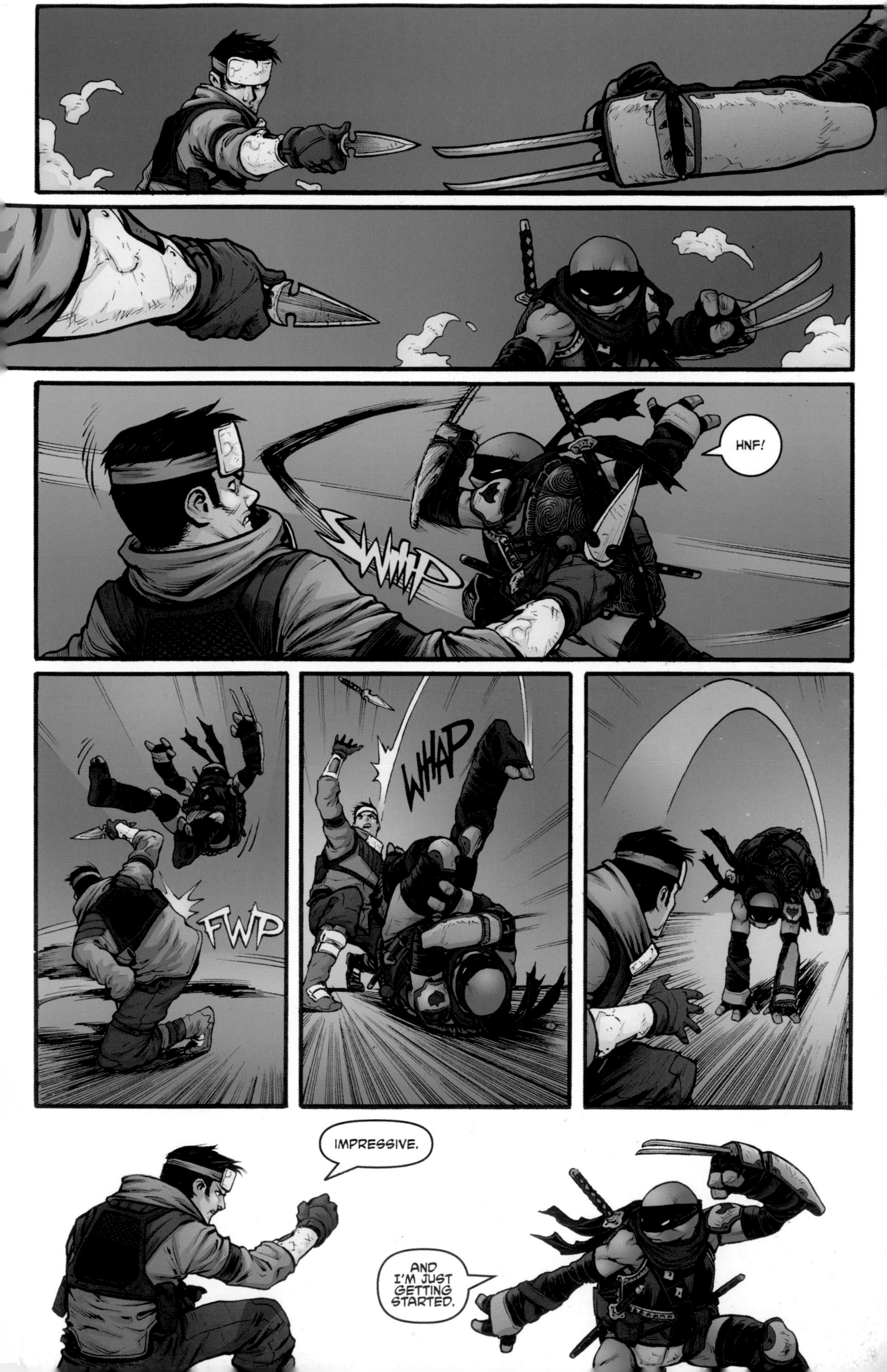
HNF!
SWHIP
FWP
WHAP
IMPRESSIVE.
AND I'M JUST GETTING STARTED.

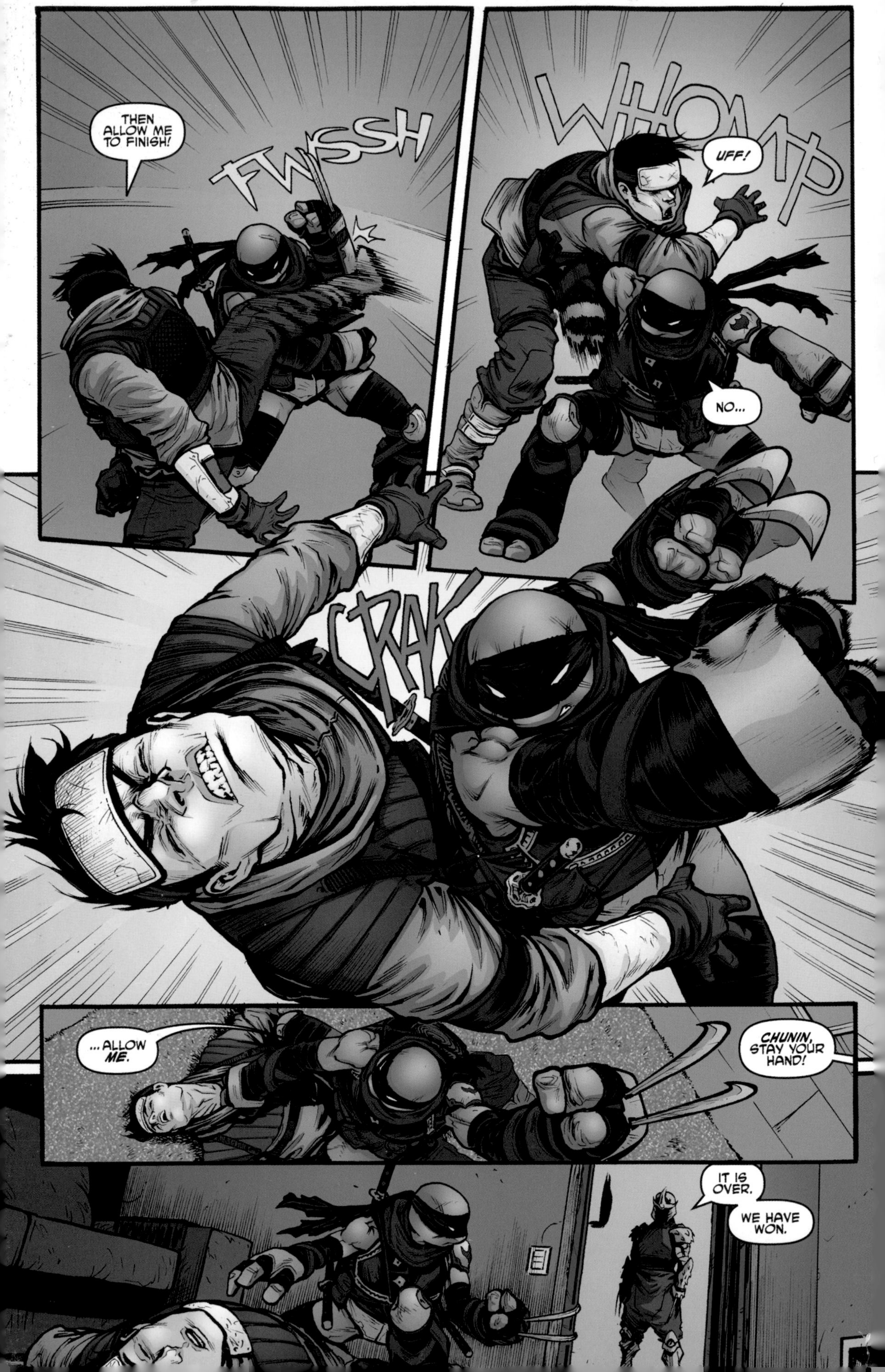
THEN ALLOW ME TO FINISH!
FWSSH
WHOMP
UFF!
NO...
CRAK
...ALLOW *ME*.
CHUNIN, STAY YOUR HAND!
IT IS OVER.
WE HAVE WON.

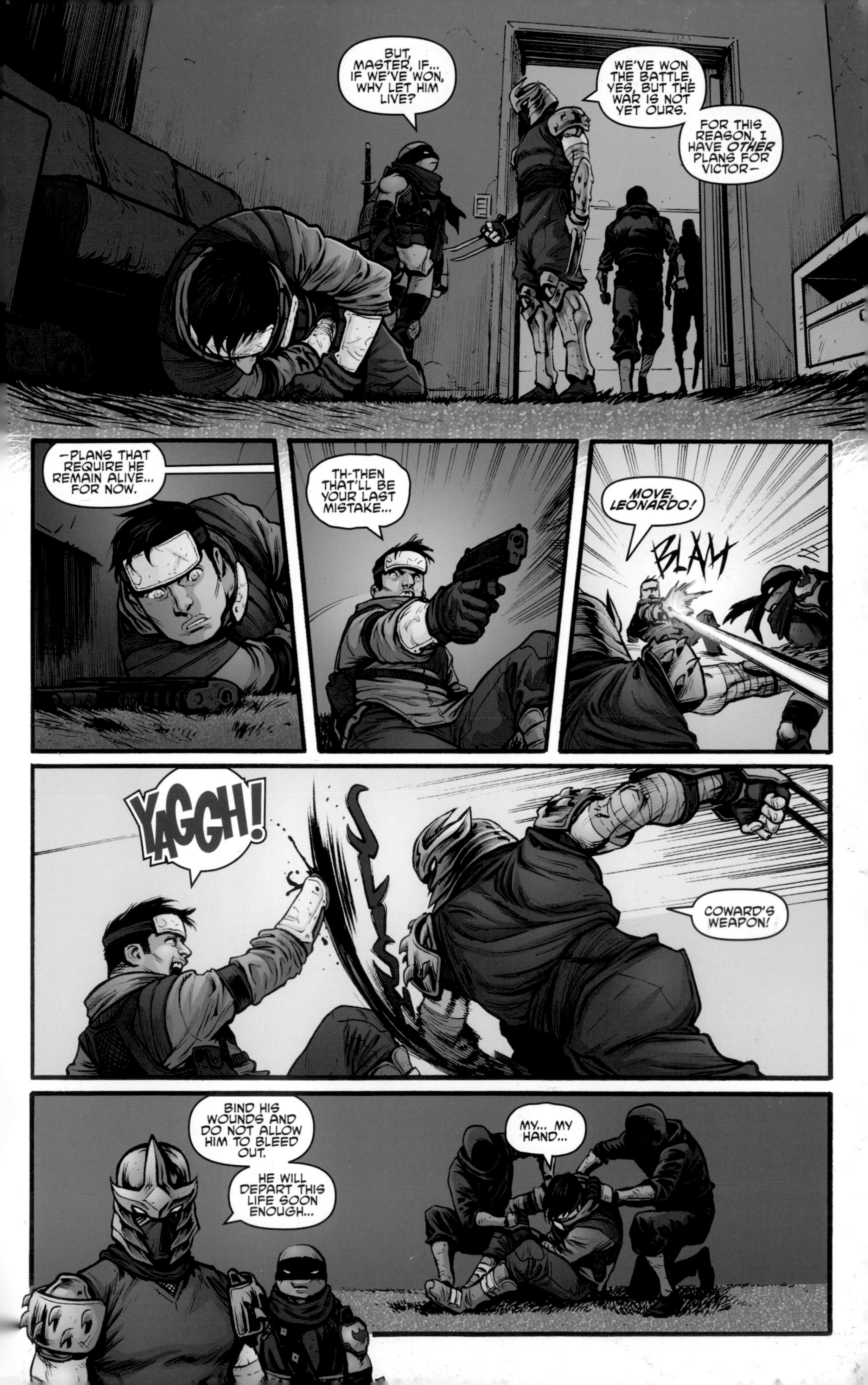
BUT, MASTER, IF... IF WE'VE WON, WHY LET HIM LIVE?
WE'VE WON THE BATTLE, YES, BUT THE WAR IS NOT YET OURS.
FOR THIS REASON, I HAVE *OTHER* PLANS FOR VICTOR—
—PLANS THAT REQUIRE HE REMAIN ALIVE... FOR NOW.
TH-THEN THAT'LL BE YOUR LAST MISTAKE...
MOVE, LEONARDO!
BLAM
YAGGH!
COWARD'S WEAPON!
BIND HIS WOUNDS AND DO NOT ALLOW HIM TO BLEED OUT.
HE WILL DEPART THIS LIFE SOON ENOUGH...
MY... MY HAND...

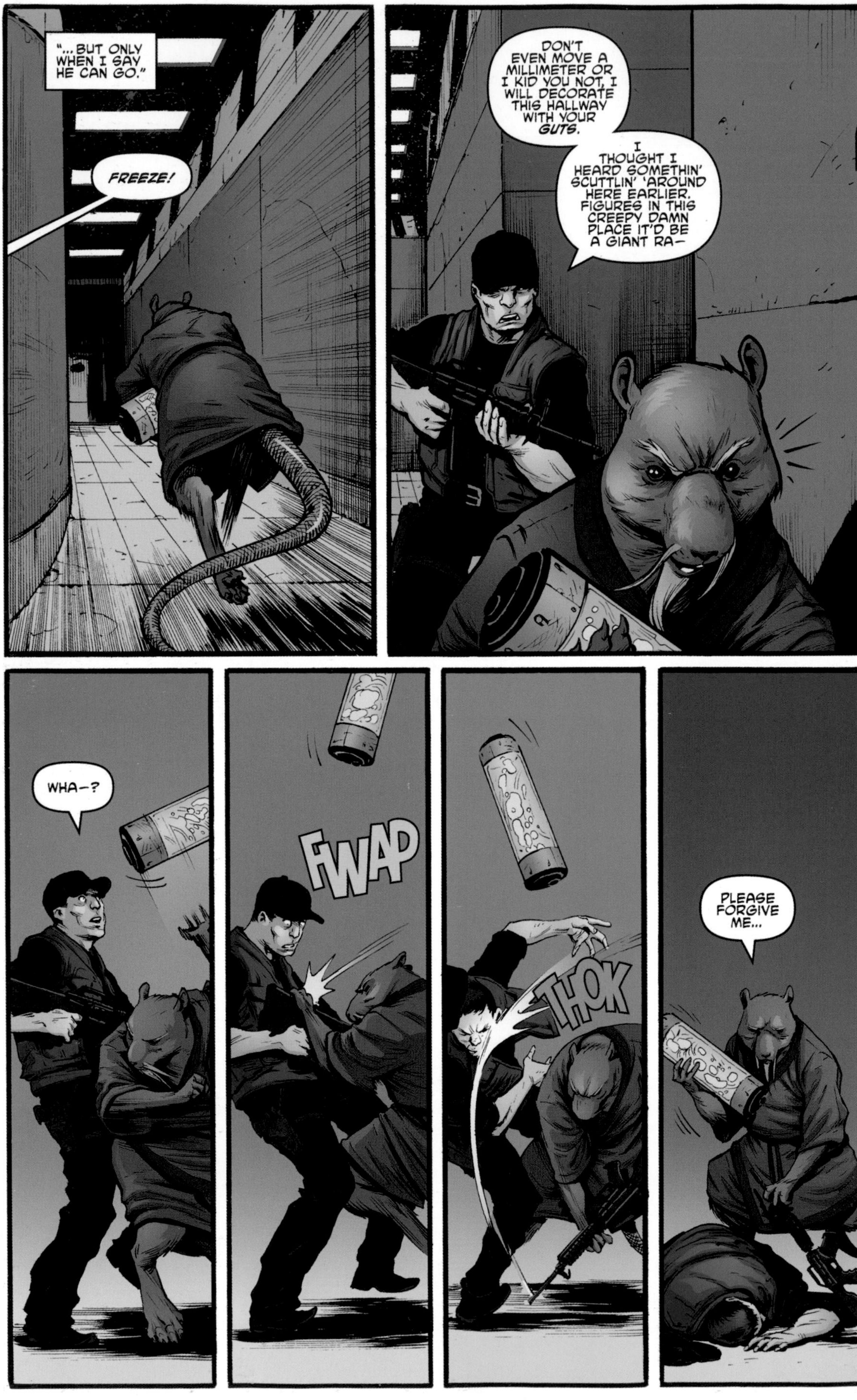
"...BUT ONLY WHEN I SAY HE CAN GO."
FREEZE!
DON'T EVEN MOVE A MILLIMETER OR I KID YOU NOT, I WILL DECORATE THIS HALLWAY WITH YOUR GUTS.
I THOUGHT I HEARD SOMETHIN' SCUTTLIN' 'AROUND HERE EARLIER. FIGURES IN THIS CREEPY DAMN PLACE IT'D BE A GIANT RA—
WHA—?
FWAP
THOK
PLEASE FORGIVE ME...

"...I DID NOT WISH FOR THIS TO HAPPEN."

SO, YOU GONNA MOPE IN THAT WINDOW ALL NIGHT, OR YOU GONNA COME IN ALREADY?

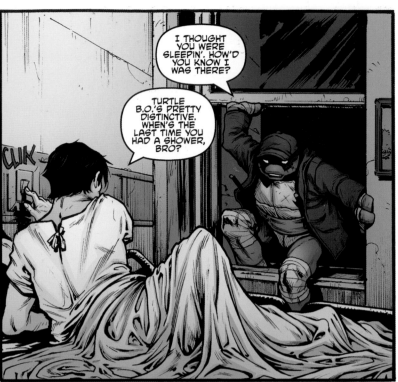

I THOUGHT YOU WERE SLEEPIN'. HOW'D YOU KNOW I WAS THERE?

TURTLE B.O.'S PRETTY DISTINCTIVE. WHEN'S THE LAST TIME YOU HAD A SHOWER, BRO?

CLIK

GOTTA SAY, WITH ALL I'M HEARIN' 'BOUT LEO, I'M SURPRISED TO SEE YOU HERE.

UM... YEAH, I BEEN PRETTY BUSY, BUT I... I WANTED TO STOP BY AND...

...AND TELL YOU I'M SORRY, MAN—SORRY FOR GETTIN' YOU HURT AND ALL THE BAD STUFF THAT'S HAPPENED.

IF... IF I COULD CHANGE PLACES WITH YOU, I'D DO IT IN A SECOND— I SWEAR I WOULD.

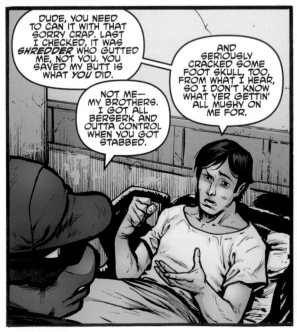

DUDE, YOU NEED TO CAN IT WITH THAT SORRY CRAP. LAST I CHECKED, IT WAS *SHREDDER* WHO GUTTED ME, NOT YOU. YOU SAVED MY BUTT IS WHAT *YOU* DID.

AND SERIOUSLY CRACKED SOME FOOT SKULL, TOO, FROM WHAT I HEAR, SO I DON'T KNOW WHAT YER GETTIN' ALL MUSHY ON ME FOR.

NOT ME— MY BROTHERS. I GOT ALL BERSERK AND OUTTA CONTROL WHEN YOU GOT STABBED.

THANKS, CASE.

THAT'S WHAT LEO ALWAYS SAYS. OR... SAID.

AIN'T NOTHIN' TO THANK—WE'RE FAMILY AND WE GOT EACH OTHER'S BACKS, NO MATTER WHAT.

WE'RE ALL TRYIN' TO FIGURE OUT HOW TO GET HIM BACK. MIKEY'S OUT TALKIN' TO ANYONE ON THE STREET WHO MIGHT KNOW SOMETHIN' AND DONNIE'S TRYIN' TO HOOK US UP WITH SOME HIGH-TECH GEAR FOR... WHO KNOWS WHAT.

HELL, I EVEN TALKED TO ANGEL TODAY, HOPIN' SHE COULD HELP. SHE PROMISED TO DO HER BEST.

AIN'T SURPRISED— ANGEL'S GOOD PEOPLE. AND SPLINTER? HOW'S HE HOLDIN' UP?

YEAH, FATHER...

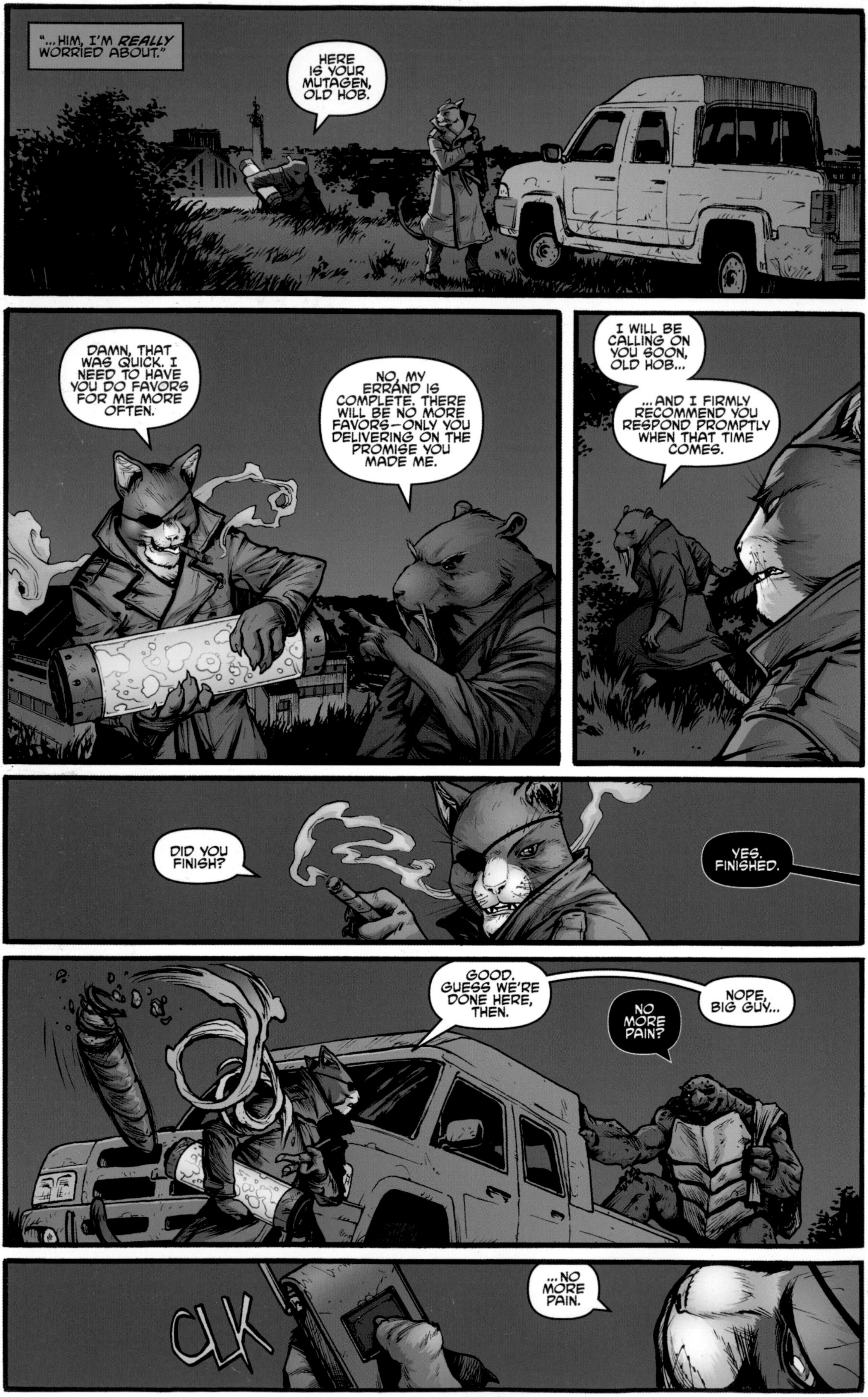
"...HIM, I'M *REALLY* WORRIED ABOUT."
HERE IS YOUR MUTAGEN, OLD HOB.
DAMN, THAT WAS QUICK. I NEED TO HAVE YOU DO FAVORS FOR ME MORE OFTEN.
NO, MY ERRAND IS COMPLETE. THERE WILL BE NO MORE FAVORS—ONLY YOU DELIVERING ON THE PROMISE YOU MADE ME.
I WILL BE CALLING ON YOU SOON, OLD HOB...
...AND I FIRMLY RECOMMEND YOU RESPOND PROMPTLY WHEN THAT TIME COMES.
DID YOU FINISH?
YES. FINISHED.
GOOD. GUESS WE'RE DONE HERE, THEN.
NO MORE PAIN?
NOPE, BIG GUY...
CLK
...NO MORE PAIN.

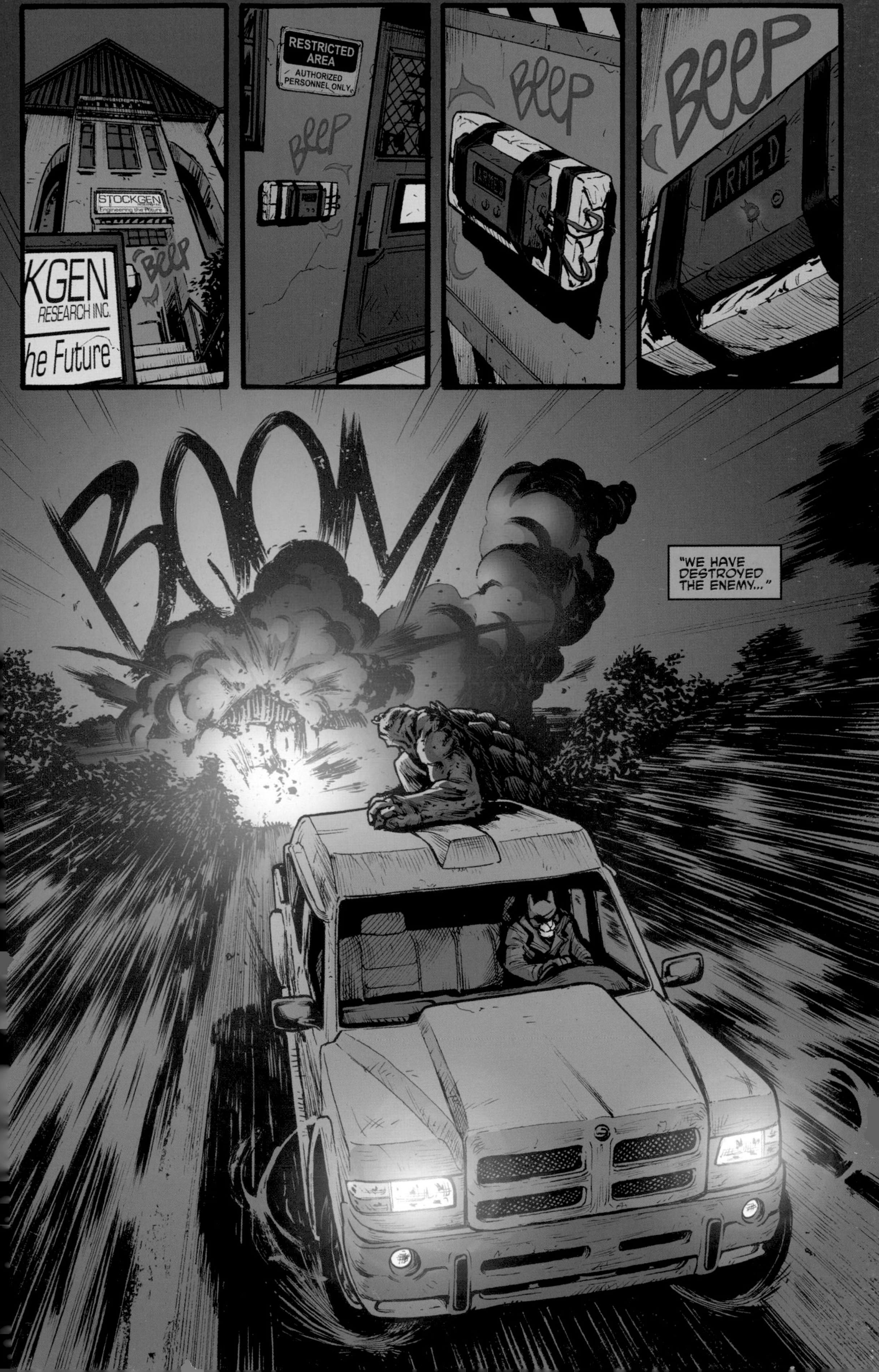
STOCKGEN
Engineering the Future
KGEN
RESEARCH INC.
he Future
BEEP
RESTRICTED AREA
AUTHORIZED PERSONNEL ONLY
BEEP
BEEP
ARMED
BEEP
ARMED
BOOM
"WE HAVE DESTROYED THE ENEMY..."

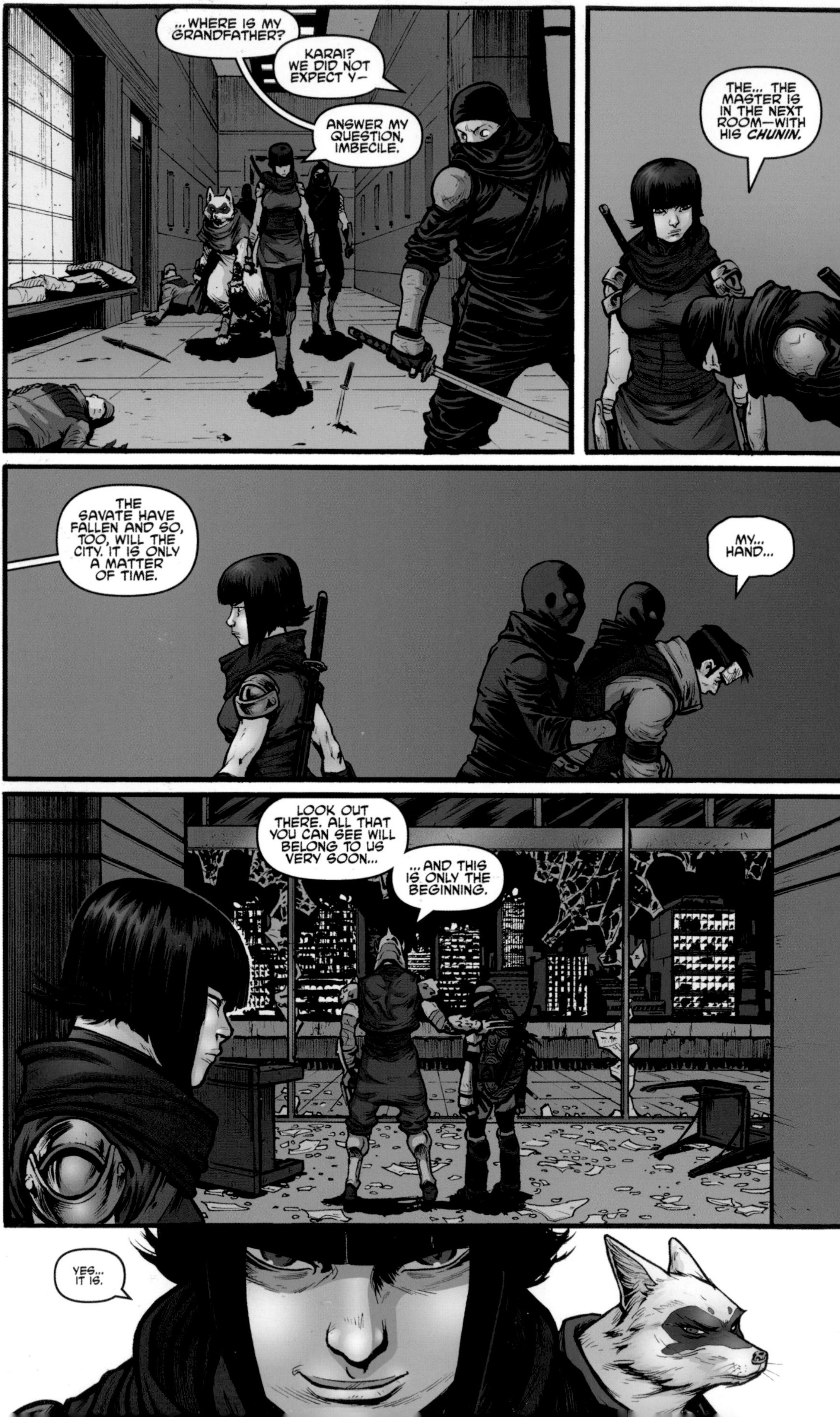
...WHERE IS MY GRANDFATHER?
KARAI? WE DID NOT EXPECT Y—
ANSWER MY QUESTION, IMBECILE.
THE... THE MASTER IS IN THE NEXT ROOM—WITH HIS CHUNIN.
THE SAVATE HAVE FALLEN AND SO, TOO, WILL THE CITY. IT IS ONLY A MATTER OF TIME.
MY... HAND...
LOOK OUT THERE. ALL THAT YOU CAN SEE WILL BELONG TO US VERY SOON...
...AND THIS IS ONLY THE BEGINNING.
YES... IT IS.

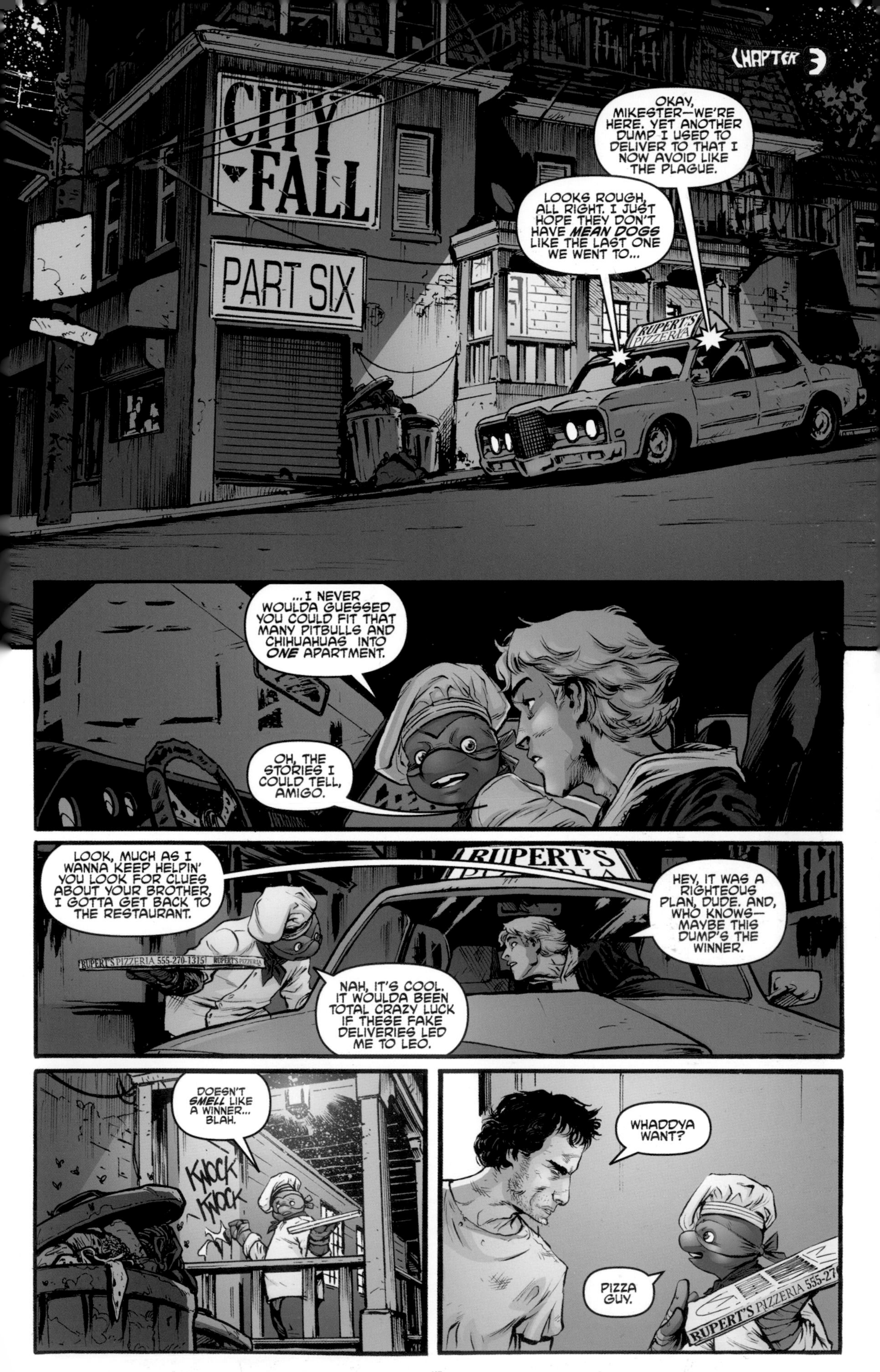
CHAPTER 3
CITY FALL
PART SIX
OKAY, MIKESTER—WE'RE HERE. YET ANOTHER DUMP I USED TO DELIVER TO THAT I NOW AVOID LIKE THE PLAGUE.
LOOKS ROUGH, ALL RIGHT. I JUST HOPE THEY DON'T HAVE MEAN DOGS LIKE THE LAST ONE WE WENT TO...
RUPERT'S PIZZERIA
...I NEVER WOULDA GUESSED YOU COULD FIT THAT MANY PITBULLS AND CHIHUAHUAS INTO ONE APARTMENT.
OH, THE STORIES I COULD TELL, AMIGO.
RUPERT'S
LOOK, MUCH AS I WANNA KEEP HELPIN' YOU LOOK FOR CLUES ABOUT YOUR BROTHER, I GOTTA GET BACK TO THE RESTAURANT.
HEY, IT WAS A RIGHTEOUS PLAN, DUDE. AND, WHO KNOWS—MAYBE THIS DUMP'S THE WINNER.
RUPERT'S PIZZERIA 555-270-1315! RUPERT'S PIZZERIA
NAH, IT'S COOL. IT WOULDA BEEN TOTAL CRAZY LUCK IF THESE FAKE DELIVERIES LED ME TO LEO.
DOESN'T SMELL LIKE A WINNER... BLAH.
KNOCK KNOCK
WHADDYA WANT?
PIZZA GUY.
RUPERT'S PIZZERIA 555-27

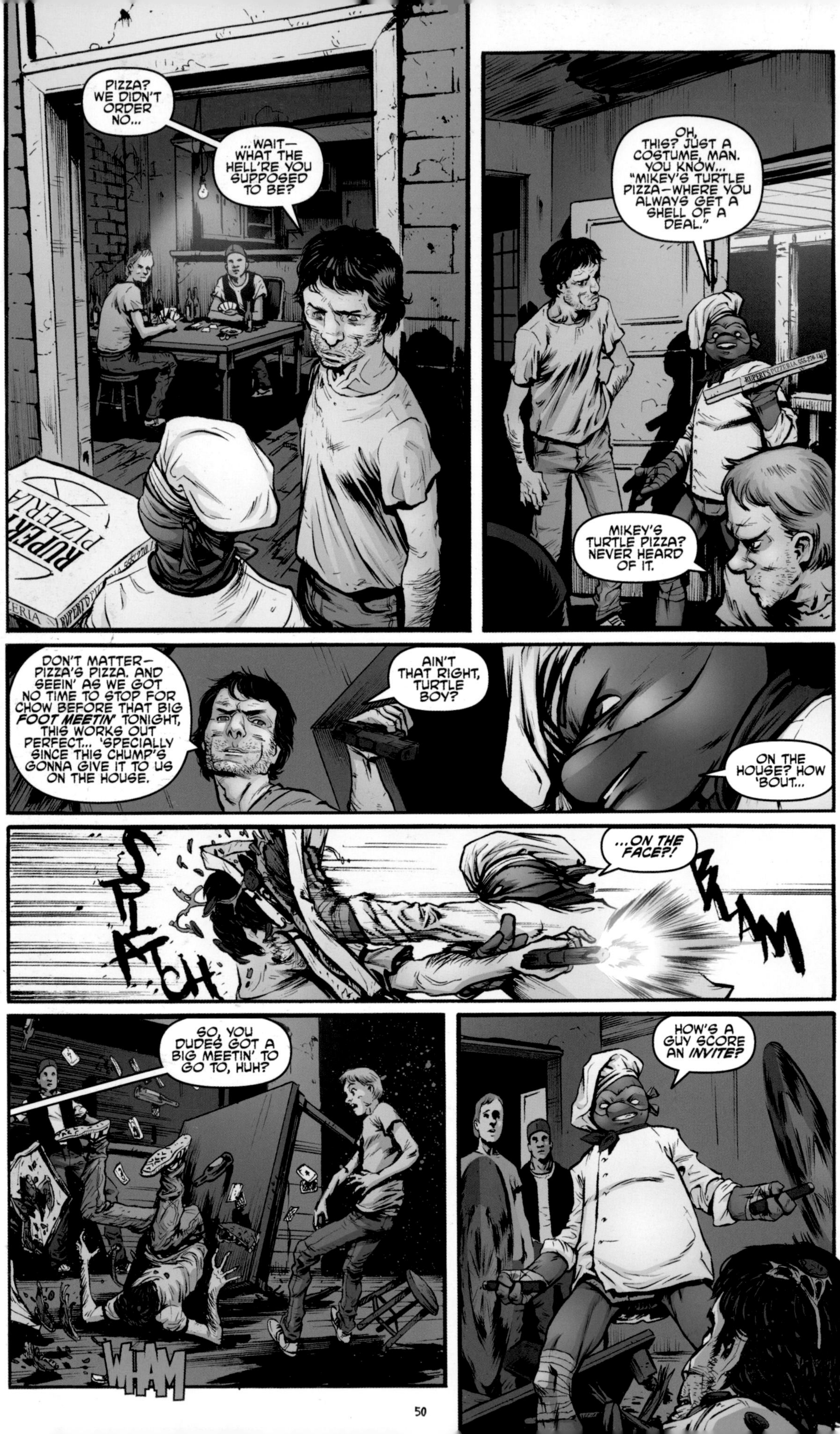
PIZZA? WE DIDN'T ORDER NO...
...WAIT— WHAT THE HELL'RE YOU SUPPOSED TO BE?
RUPERT'S PIZZERIA
OH, THIS? JUST A COSTUME, MAN. YOU KNOW... "MIKEY'S TURTLE PIZZA—WHERE YOU ALWAYS GET A SHELL OF A DEAL."
MIKEY'S TURTLE PIZZA? NEVER HEARD OF IT.
DON'T MATTER— PIZZA'S PIZZA. AND SEEIN' AS WE GOT NO TIME TO STOP FOR CHOW BEFORE THAT BIG *FOOT MEETIN'* TONIGHT, THIS WORKS OUT PERFECT... 'SPECIALLY SINCE THIS CHUMP'S GONNA GIVE IT TO US ON THE HOUSE.
AIN'T THAT RIGHT, TURTLE BOY?
ON THE HOUSE? HOW 'BOUT...
...*ON THE FACE?!*
SPLATCH
BLAM
SO, YOU DUDES GOT A BIG MEETIN' TO GO TO, HUH?
WHAM
HOW'S A GUY SCORE AN *INVITE?*

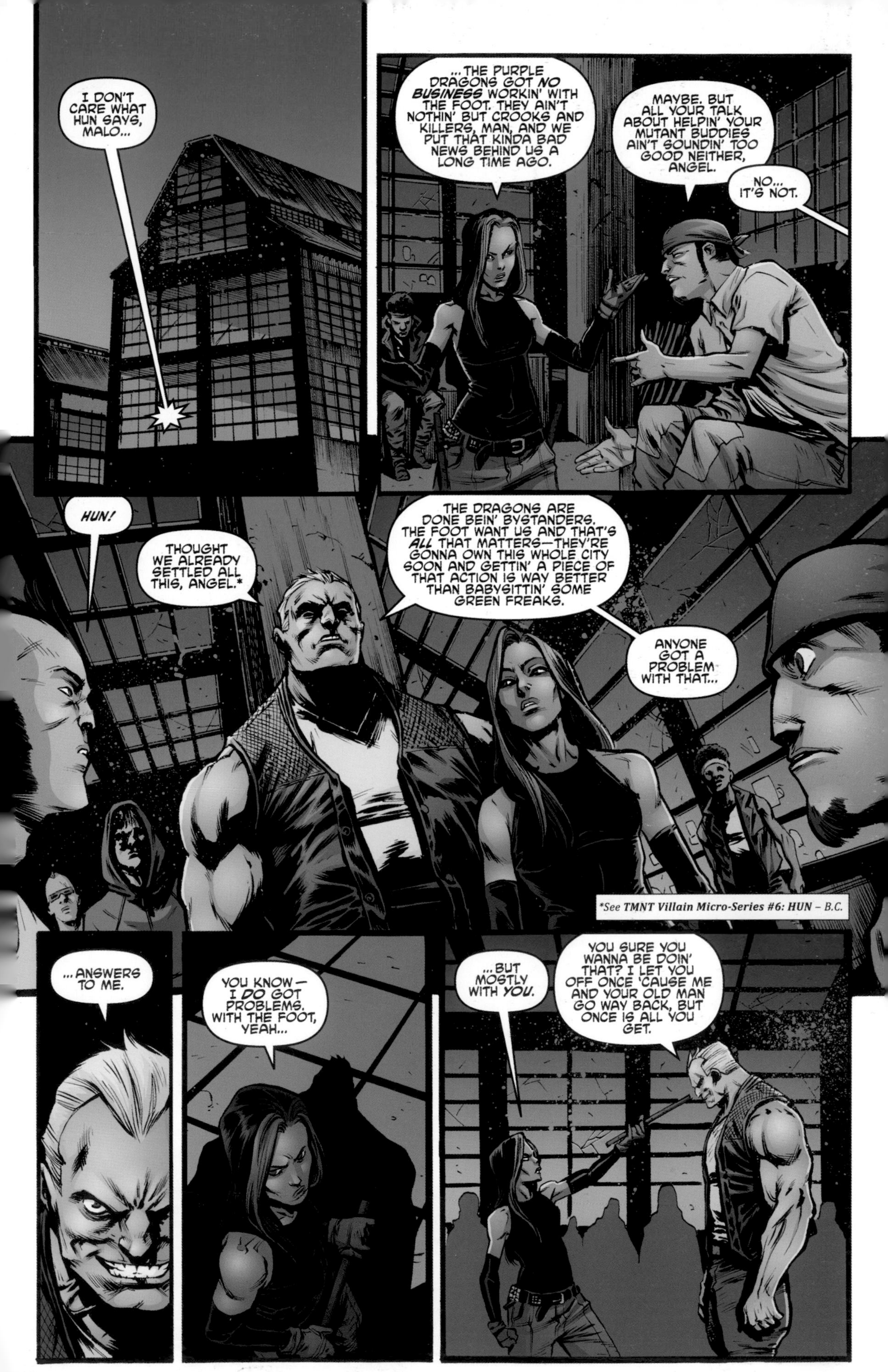
I DON'T CARE WHAT HUN SAYS, MALO...
...THE PURPLE DRAGONS GOT NO BUSINESS WORKIN' WITH THE FOOT. THEY AIN'T NOTHIN' BUT CROOKS AND KILLERS, MAN, AND WE PUT THAT KINDA BAD NEWS BEHIND US A LONG TIME AGO.
MAYBE. BUT ALL YOUR TALK ABOUT HELPIN' YOUR MUTANT BUDDIES AIN'T SOUNDIN' TOO GOOD NEITHER, ANGEL.
NO... IT'S NOT.
HUN!
THOUGHT WE ALREADY SETTLED ALL THIS, ANGEL.*
THE DRAGONS ARE DONE BEIN' BYSTANDERS. THE FOOT WANT US AND THAT'S ALL THAT MATTERS—THEY'RE GONNA OWN THIS WHOLE CITY SOON AND GETTIN' A PIECE OF THAT ACTION IS WAY BETTER THAN BABYSITTIN' SOME GREEN FREAKS.
ANYONE GOT A PROBLEM WITH THAT...
*See TMNT Villain Micro-Series #6: HUN – B.C.
...ANSWERS TO ME.
YOU KNOW— I DO GOT PROBLEMS. WITH THE FOOT, YEAH...
...BUT MOSTLY WITH YOU.
YOU SURE YOU WANNA BE DOIN' THAT? I LET YOU OFF ONCE 'CAUSE ME AND YOUR OLD MAN GO WAY BACK, BUT ONCE IS ALL YOU GET.

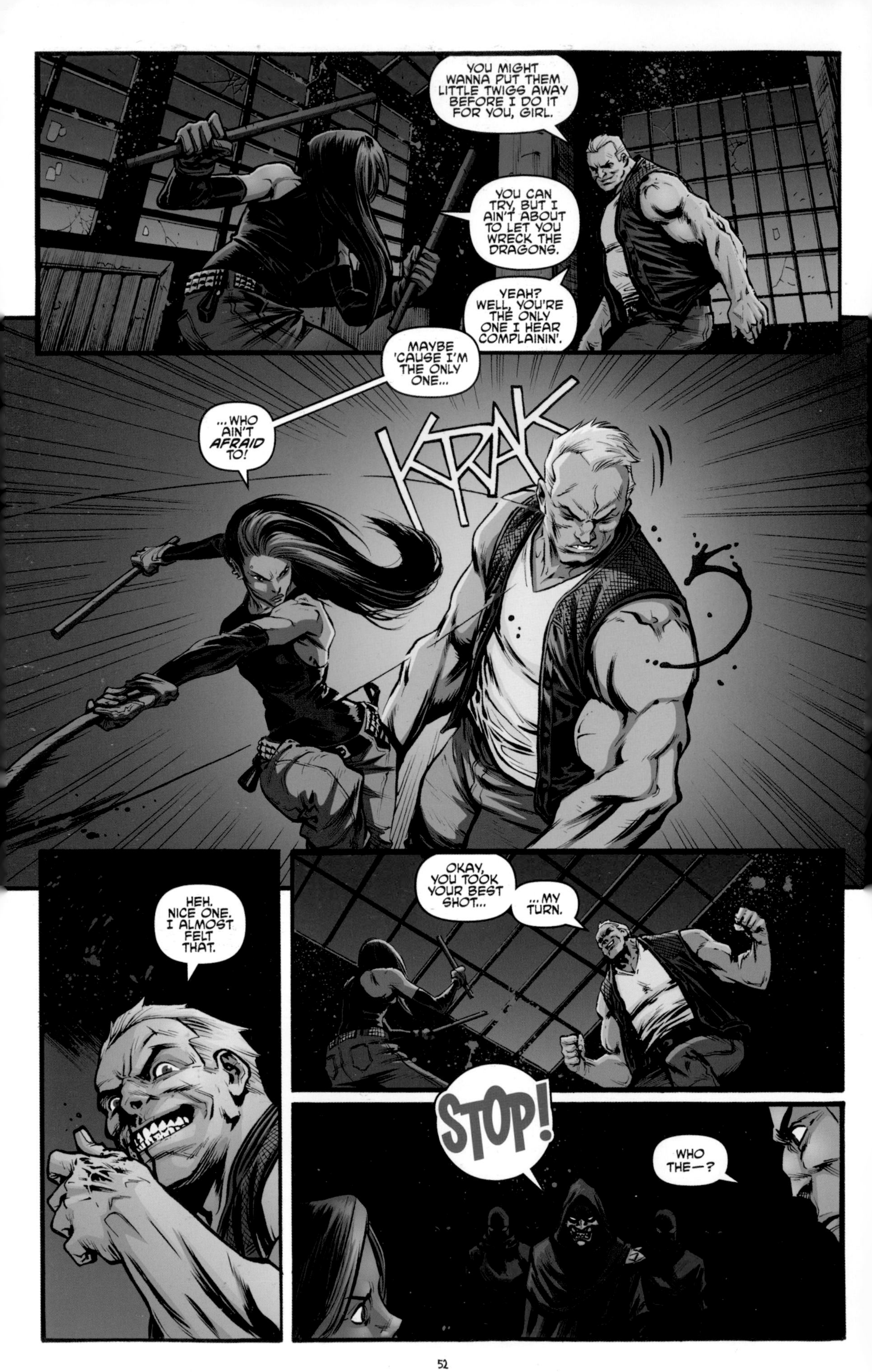
YOU MIGHT WANNA PUT THEM LITTLE TWIGS AWAY BEFORE I DO IT FOR YOU, GIRL.
YOU CAN TRY, BUT I AIN'T ABOUT TO LET YOU WRECK THE DRAGONS.
YEAH? WELL, YOU'RE THE ONLY ONE I HEAR COMPLAININ'.
MAYBE 'CAUSE I'M THE ONLY ONE...
...WHO AIN'T AFRAID TO!
KRAK
HEH. NICE ONE. I ALMOST FELT THAT.
OKAY, YOU TOOK YOUR BEST SHOT...
...MY TURN.
STOP!
WHO THE—?

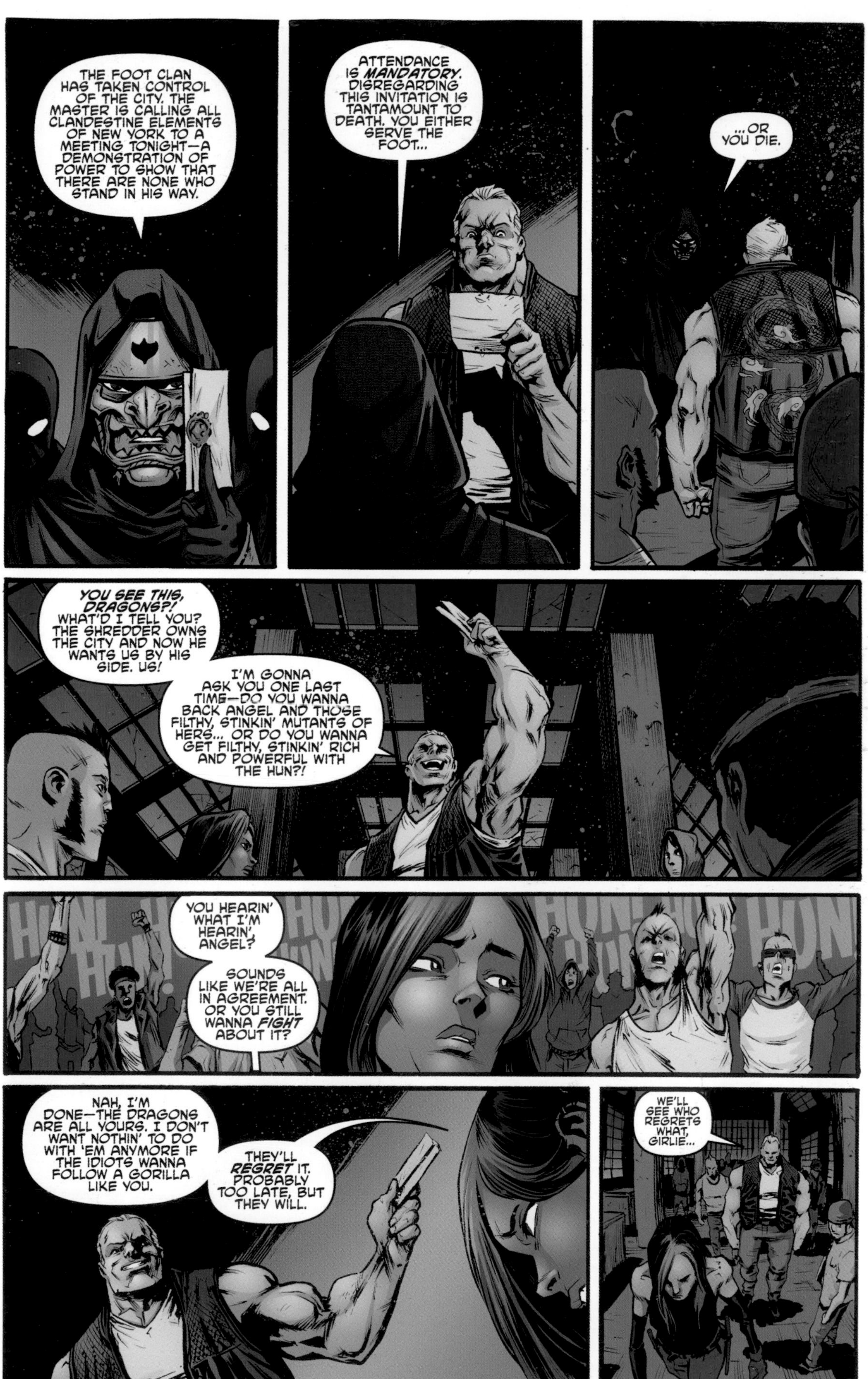
THE FOOT CLAN HAS TAKEN CONTROL OF THE CITY. THE MASTER IS CALLING ALL CLANDESTINE ELEMENTS OF NEW YORK TO A MEETING TONIGHT—A DEMONSTRATION OF POWER TO SHOW THAT THERE ARE NONE WHO STAND IN HIS WAY.
ATTENDANCE IS MANDATORY. DISREGARDING THIS INVITATION IS TANTAMOUNT TO DEATH. YOU EITHER SERVE THE FOOT...
...OR YOU DIE.
YOU SEE THIS, DRAGONS?! WHAT'D I TELL YOU? THE SHREDDER OWNS THE CITY AND NOW HE WANTS US BY HIS SIDE. US!
I'M GONNA ASK YOU ONE LAST TIME—DO YOU WANNA BACK ANGEL AND THOSE FILTHY, STINKIN' MUTANTS OF HERS... OR DO YOU WANNA GET FILTHY, STINKIN' RICH AND POWERFUL WITH THE HUN?!
YOU HEARIN' WHAT I'M HEARIN', ANGEL?
SOUNDS LIKE WE'RE ALL IN AGREEMENT. OR YOU STILL WANNA FIGHT ABOUT IT?
NAH, I'M DONE—THE DRAGONS ARE ALL YOURS. I DON'T WANT NOTHIN' TO DO WITH 'EM ANYMORE IF THE IDIOTS WANNA FOLLOW A GORILLA LIKE YOU.
THEY'LL REGRET IT. PROBABLY TOO LATE, BUT THEY WILL.
WE'LL SEE WHO REGRETS WHAT, GIRLIE...

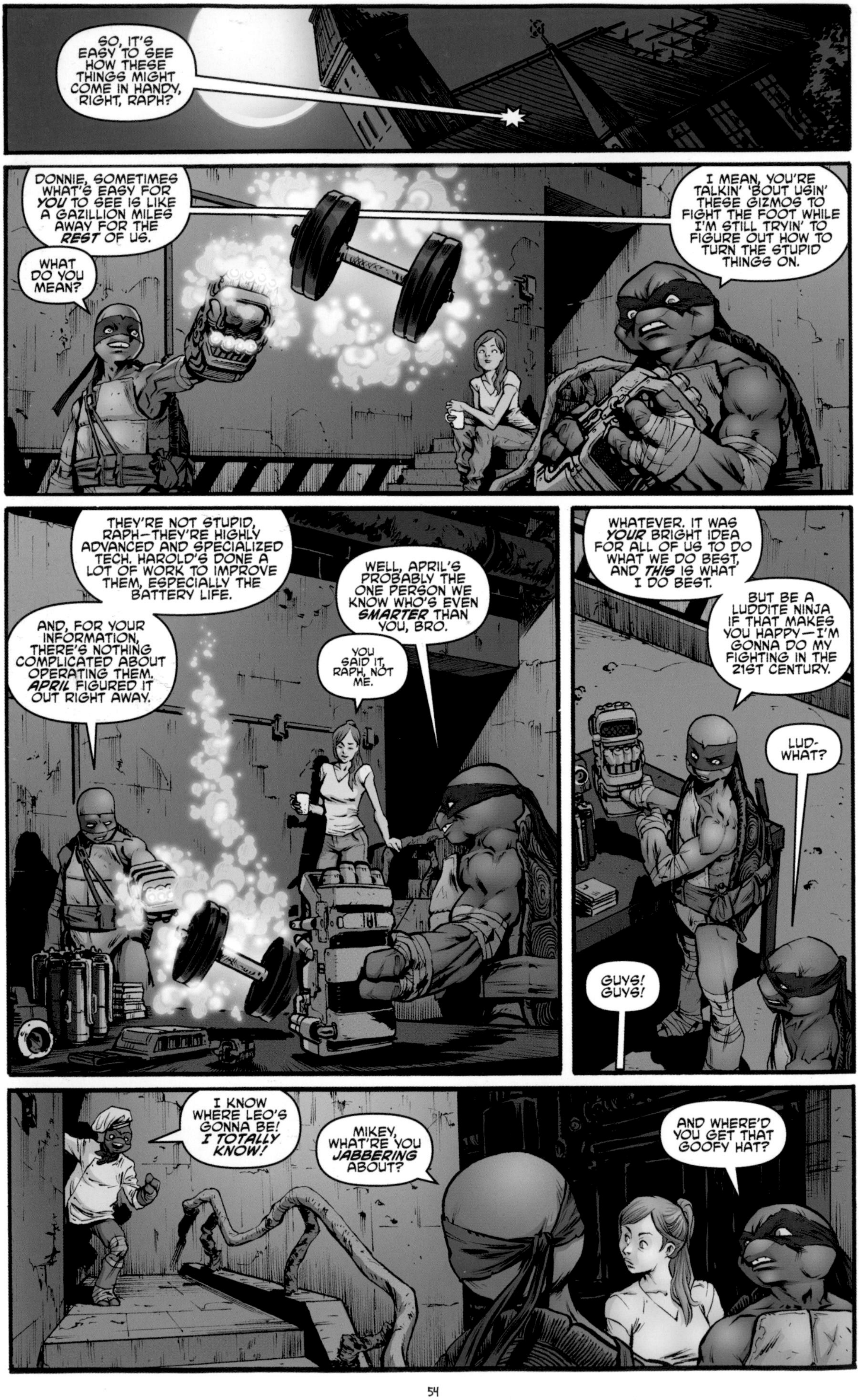
SO, IT'S EASY TO SEE HOW THESE THINGS MIGHT COME IN HANDY, RIGHT, RAPH?
DONNIE, SOMETIMES WHAT'S EASY FOR YOU TO SEE IS LIKE A GAZILLION MILES AWAY FOR THE REST OF US.
WHAT DO YOU MEAN?
I MEAN, YOU'RE TALKIN' 'BOUT USIN' THESE GIZMOS TO FIGHT THE FOOT WHILE I'M STILL TRYIN' TO FIGURE OUT HOW TO TURN THE STUPID THINGS ON.
THEY'RE NOT STUPID, RAPH—THEY'RE HIGHLY ADVANCED AND SPECIALIZED TECH. HAROLD'S DONE A LOT OF WORK TO IMPROVE THEM, ESPECIALLY THE BATTERY LIFE.
AND, FOR YOUR INFORMATION, THERE'S NOTHING COMPLICATED ABOUT OPERATING THEM. APRIL FIGURED IT OUT RIGHT AWAY.
WELL, APRIL'S PROBABLY THE ONE PERSON WE KNOW WHO'S EVEN SMARTER THAN YOU, BRO.
YOU SAID IT, RAPH, NOT ME.
WHATEVER. IT WAS YOUR BRIGHT IDEA FOR ALL OF US TO DO WHAT WE DO BEST, AND THIS IS WHAT I DO BEST.
BUT BE A LUDDITE NINJA IF THAT MAKES YOU HAPPY—I'M GONNA DO MY FIGHTING IN THE 21ST CENTURY.
LUD-WHAT?
GUYS! GUYS!
I KNOW WHERE LEO'S GONNA BE! I TOTALLY KNOW!
MIKEY, WHAT'RE YOU JABBERING ABOUT?
AND WHERE'D YOU GET THAT GOOFY HAT?

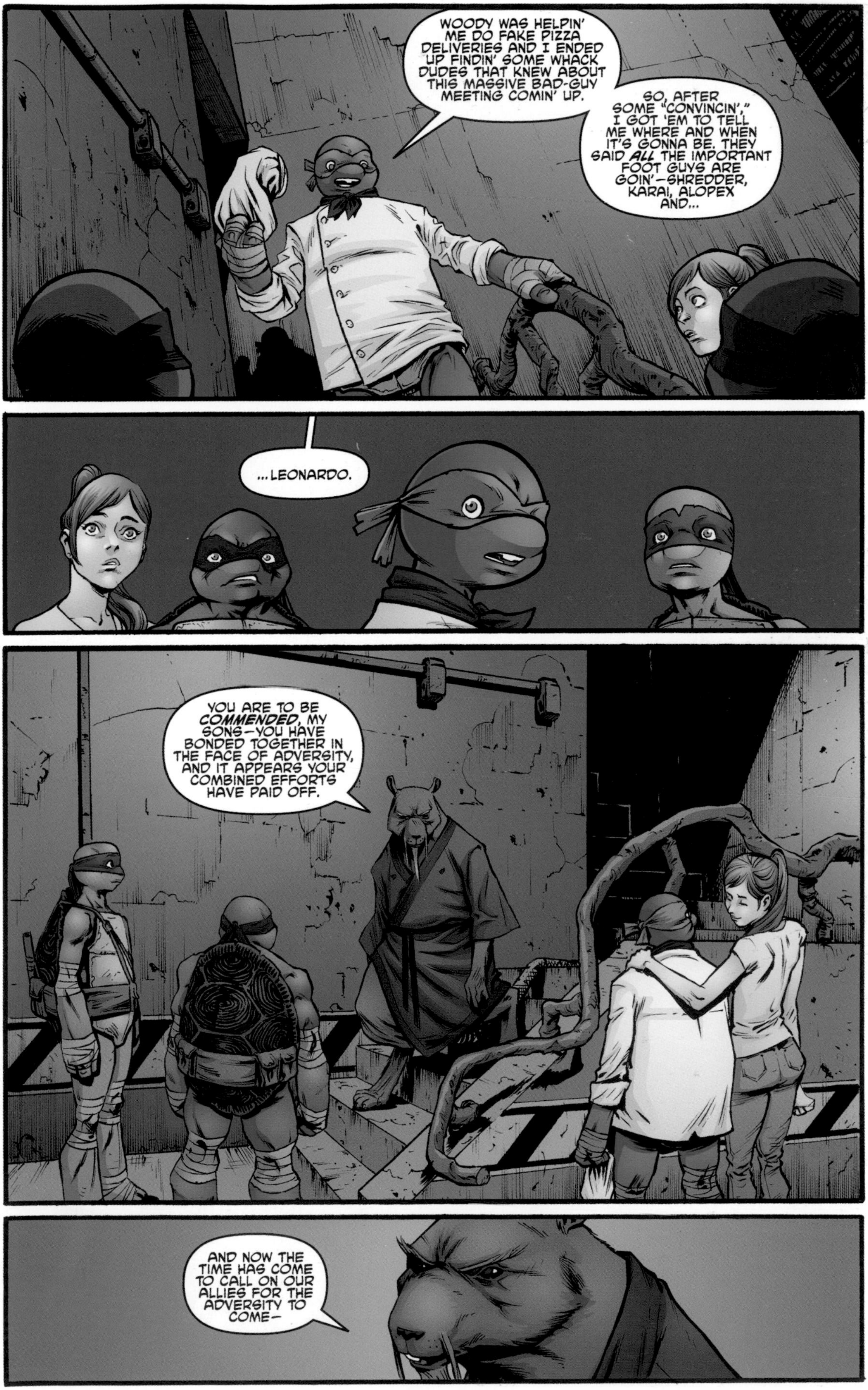
WOODY WAS HELPIN' ME DO FAKE PIZZA DELIVERIES AND I ENDED UP FINDIN' SOME WHACK DUDES THAT KNEW ABOUT THIS MASSIVE BAD-GUY MEETING COMIN' UP.
SO, AFTER SOME "CONVINCIN'," I GOT 'EM TO TELL ME WHERE AND WHEN IT'S GONNA BE. THEY SAID *ALL* THE IMPORTANT FOOT GUYS ARE GOIN'—SHREDDER, KARAI, ALOPEX AND...
...LEONARDO.
YOU ARE TO BE **COMMENDED**, MY SONS—YOU HAVE BONDED TOGETHER IN THE FACE OF ADVERSITY, AND IT APPEARS YOUR COMBINED EFFORTS HAVE PAID OFF.
AND NOW THE TIME HAS COME TO CALL ON OUR ALLIES FOR THE ADVERSITY TO COME—

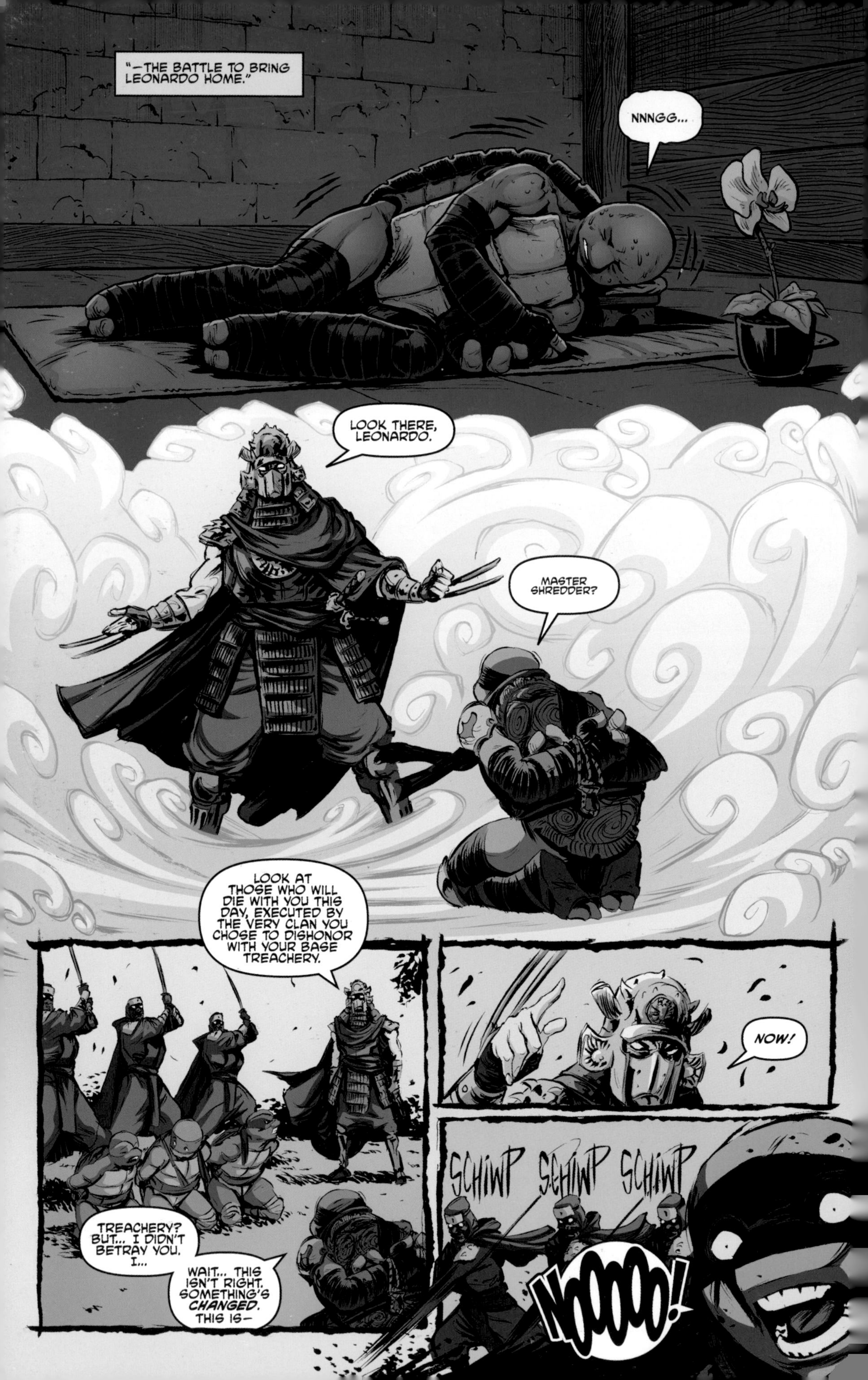
"—THE BATTLE TO BRING LEONARDO HOME."
NNNGG...
LOOK THERE, LEONARDO.
MASTER SHREDDER?
LOOK AT THOSE WHO WILL DIE WITH YOU THIS DAY, EXECUTED BY THE VERY CLAN YOU CHOSE TO DISHONOR WITH YOUR BASE TREACHERY.
TREACHERY? BUT... I DIDN'T BETRAY YOU. I...
WAIT... THIS ISN'T RIGHT. SOMETHING'S *CHANGED*. THIS IS—
NOW!
SCHWP SCHWP SCHWP
NOOOOO!

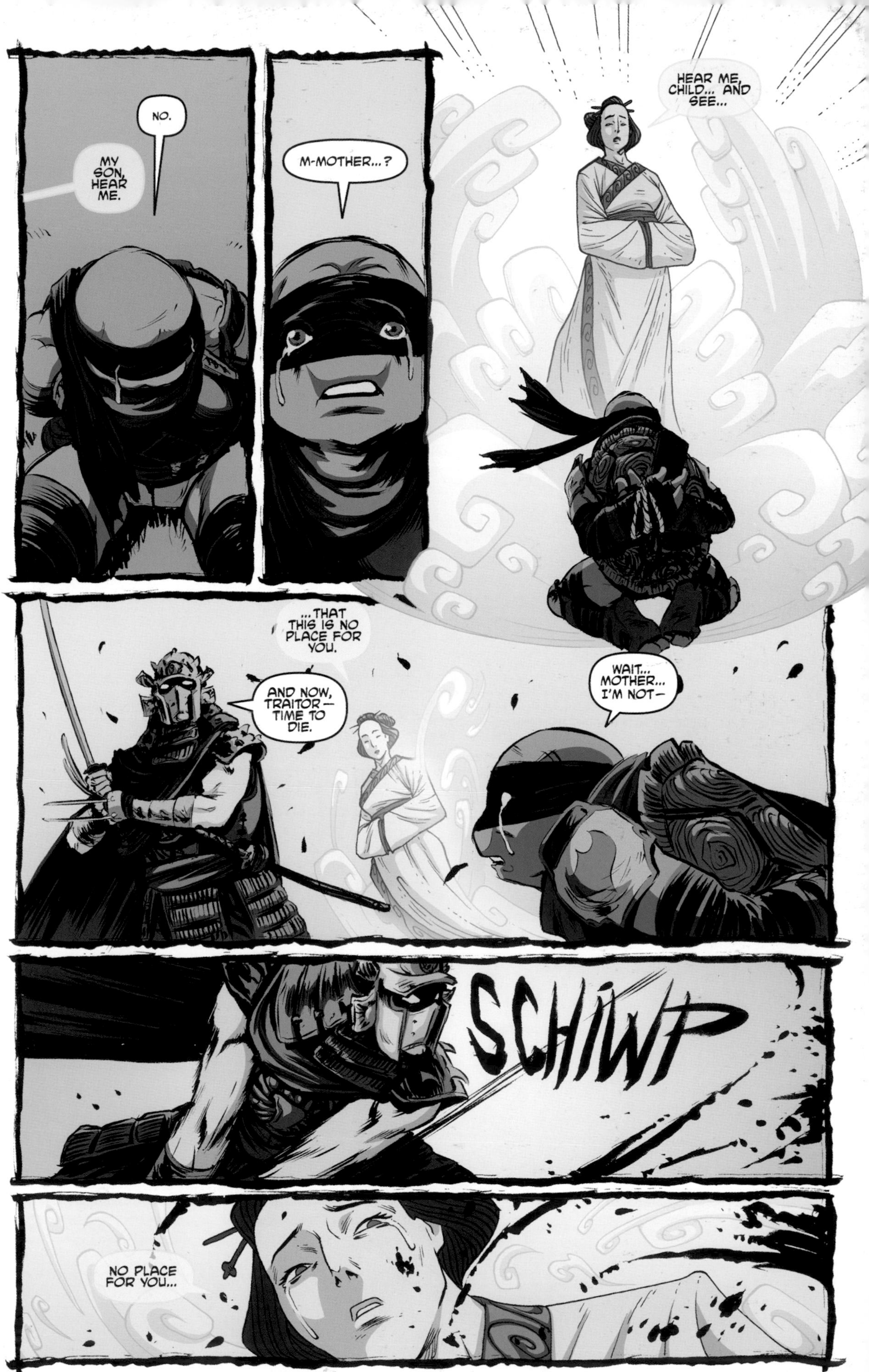
NO.
MY SON, HEAR ME.
M-MOTHER...?
HEAR ME, CHILD... AND SEE...
...THAT THIS IS NO PLACE FOR YOU.
AND NOW, TRAITOR— TIME TO DIE.
WAIT... MOTHER... I'M NOT—
SCHWP
NO PLACE FOR YOU...

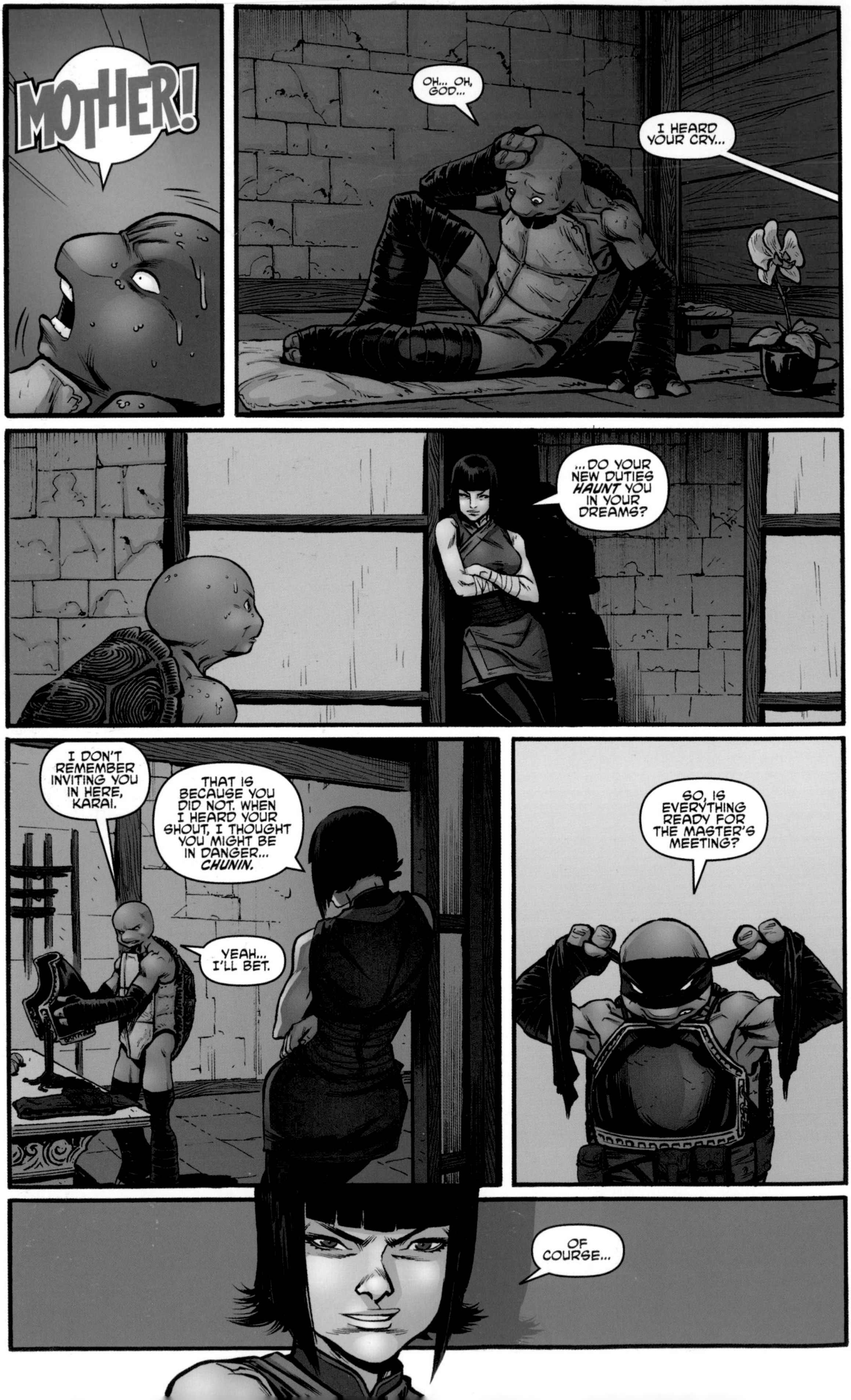
MOTHER!
OH... OH, GOD...
I HEARD YOUR CRY...
...DO YOUR NEW DUTIES HAUNT YOU IN YOUR DREAMS?
I DON'T REMEMBER INVITING YOU IN HERE, KARAI.
THAT IS BECAUSE YOU DID NOT. WHEN I HEARD YOUR SHOUT, I THOUGHT YOU MIGHT BE IN DANGER... CHUNIN.
YEAH... I'LL BET.
SO, IS EVERYTHING READY FOR THE MASTER'S MEETING?
OF COURSE...

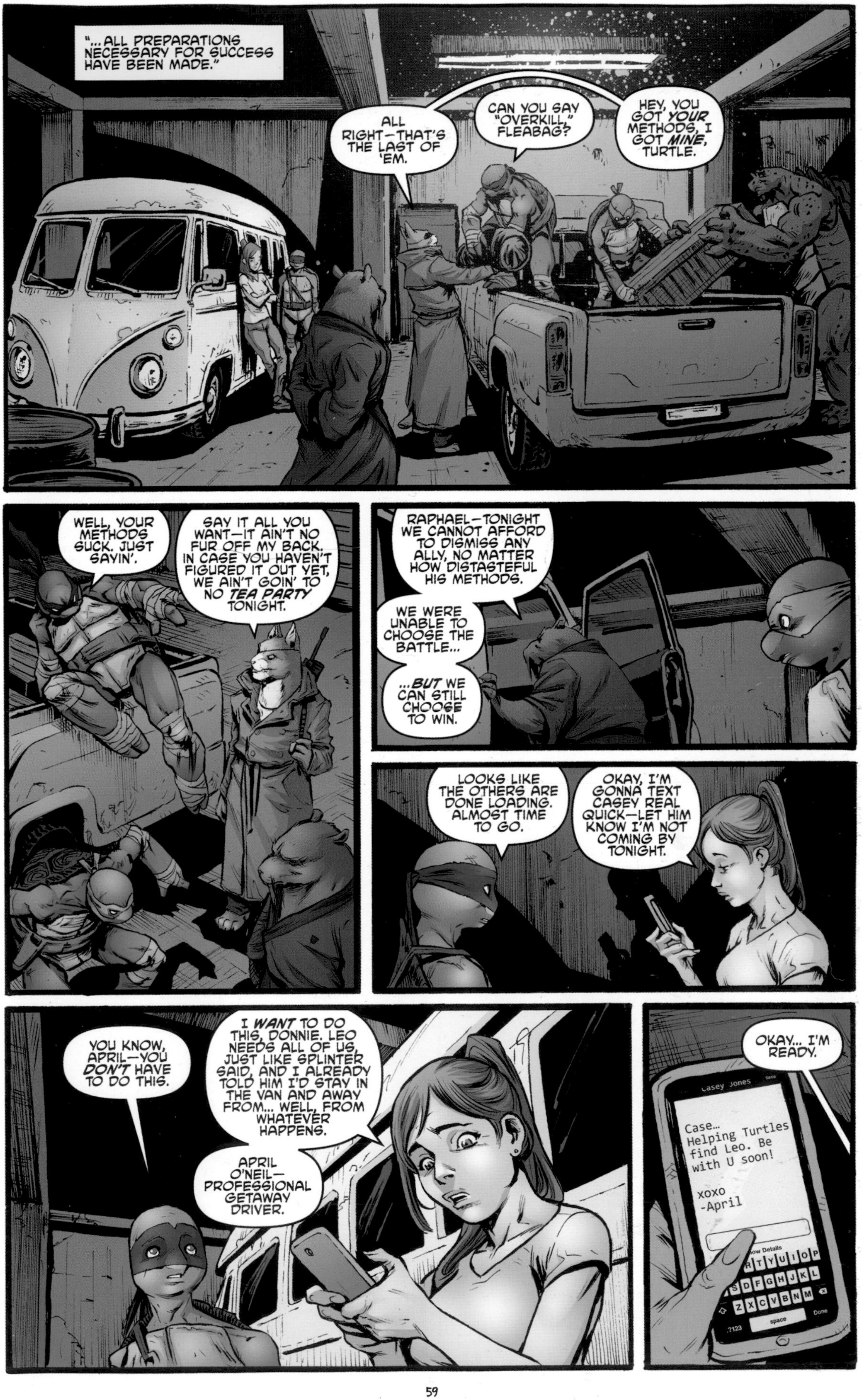
"...ALL PREPARATIONS NECESSARY FOR SUCCESS HAVE BEEN MADE."
ALL RIGHT—THAT'S THE LAST OF 'EM.
CAN YOU SAY "OVERKILL," FLEABAG?
HEY, YOU GOT YOUR METHODS, I GOT MINE, TURTLE.
WELL, YOUR METHODS SUCK. JUST SAYIN'.
SAY IT ALL YOU WANT—IT AIN'T NO FUR OFF MY BACK. IN CASE YOU HAVEN'T FIGURED IT OUT YET, WE AIN'T GOIN' TO NO TEA PARTY TONIGHT.
RAPHAEL—TONIGHT WE CANNOT AFFORD TO DISMISS ANY ALLY, NO MATTER HOW DISTASTEFUL HIS METHODS.
WE WERE UNABLE TO CHOOSE THE BATTLE...
...BUT WE CAN STILL CHOOSE TO WIN.
LOOKS LIKE THE OTHERS ARE DONE LOADING. ALMOST TIME TO GO.
OKAY, I'M GONNA TEXT CASEY REAL QUICK—LET HIM KNOW I'M NOT COMING BY TONIGHT.
YOU KNOW, APRIL—YOU DON'T HAVE TO DO THIS.
I WANT TO DO THIS, DONNIE. LEO NEEDS ALL OF US, JUST LIKE SPLINTER SAID, AND I ALREADY TOLD HIM I'D STAY IN THE VAN AND AWAY FROM... WELL, FROM WHATEVER HAPPENS.
APRIL O'NEIL—PROFESSIONAL GETAWAY DRIVER.
OKAY... I'M READY.
Casey Jones
Case... Helping Turtles find Leo. Be with U soon!
xoxo
-April

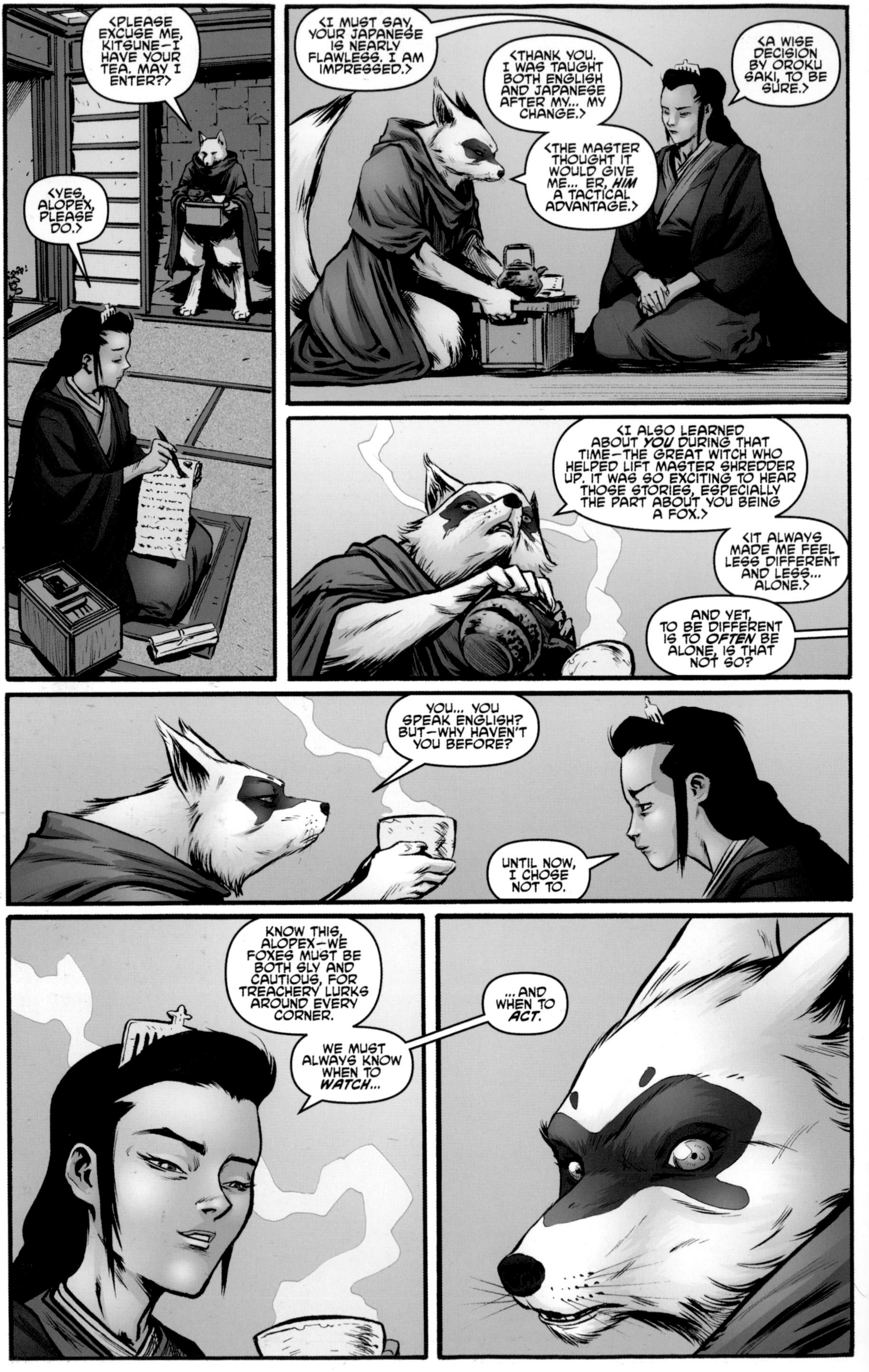
<PLEASE EXCUSE ME, KITSUNE—I HAVE YOUR TEA. MAY I ENTER?>
<YES, ALOPEX, PLEASE DO.>
<I MUST SAY, YOUR JAPANESE IS NEARLY FLAWLESS. I AM IMPRESSED.>
<THANK YOU. I WAS TAUGHT BOTH ENGLISH AND JAPANESE AFTER MY... MY CHANGE.>
<THE MASTER THOUGHT IT WOULD GIVE ME... ER, *HIM* A TACTICAL ADVANTAGE.>
<A WISE DECISION BY OROKU SAKI, TO BE SURE.>
<I ALSO LEARNED ABOUT *YOU* DURING THAT TIME—THE GREAT WITCH WHO HELPED LIFT MASTER SHREDDER UP. IT WAS SO EXCITING TO HEAR THOSE STORIES, ESPECIALLY THE PART ABOUT YOU BEING A FOX.>
<IT ALWAYS MADE ME FEEL LESS DIFFERENT AND LESS... ALONE.>
AND YET, TO BE DIFFERENT IS TO *OFTEN* BE ALONE, IS THAT NOT SO?
YOU... YOU SPEAK ENGLISH? BUT—WHY HAVEN'T YOU BEFORE?
UNTIL NOW, I CHOSE NOT TO.
KNOW THIS, ALOPEX—WE FOXES MUST BE BOTH SLY AND CAUTIOUS, FOR TREACHERY LURKS AROUND EVERY CORNER.
WE MUST ALWAYS KNOW WHEN TO *WATCH*...
...AND WHEN TO *ACT*.

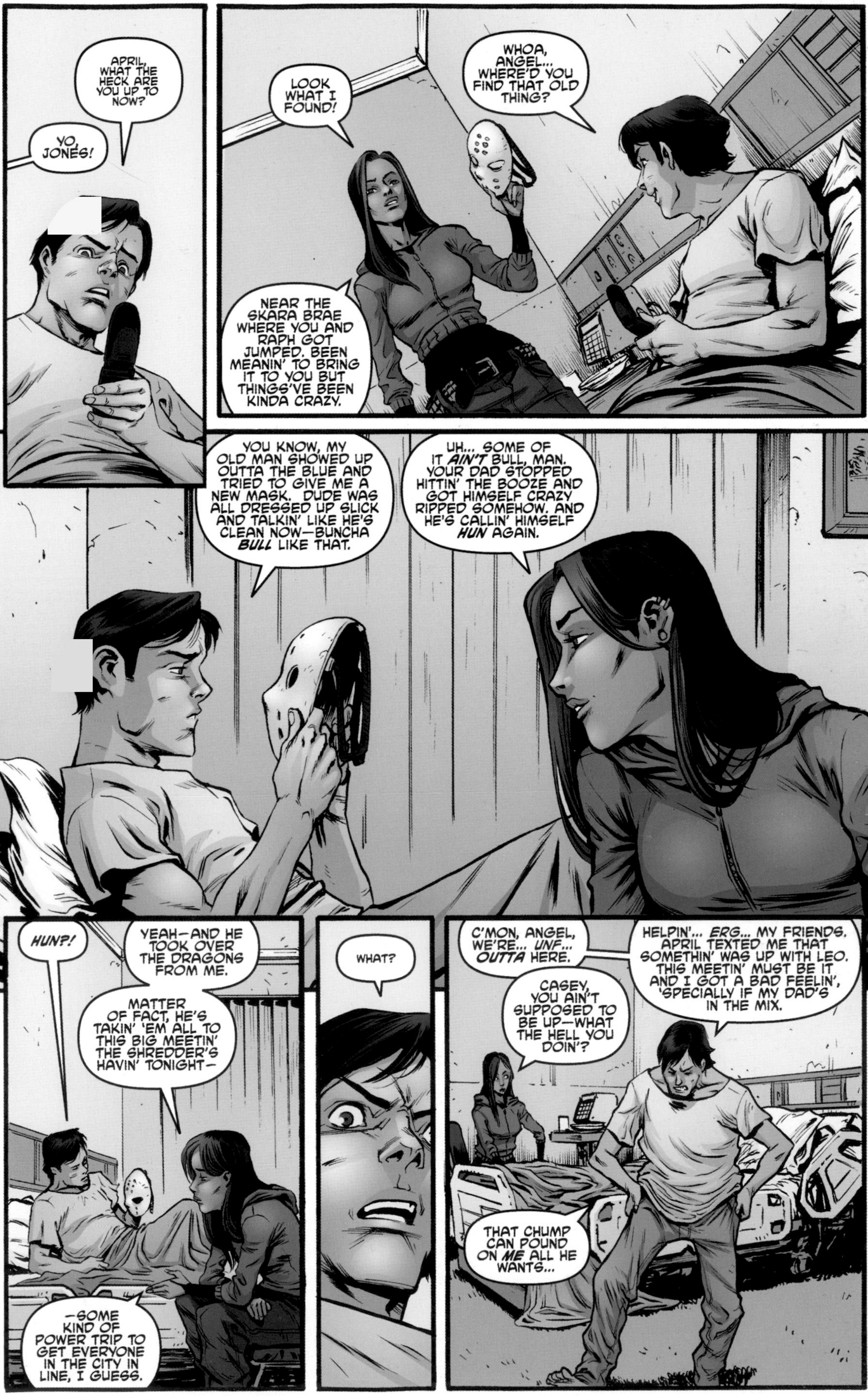
YO, JONES!
APRIL, WHAT THE HECK ARE YOU UP TO NOW?
LOOK WHAT I FOUND!
WHOA, ANGEL... WHERE'D YOU FIND THAT OLD THING?
NEAR THE SKARA BRAE WHERE YOU AND RAPH GOT JUMPED. BEEN MEANIN' TO BRING IT TO YOU BUT THINGS'VE BEEN KINDA CRAZY.
YOU KNOW, MY OLD MAN SHOWED UP OUTTA THE BLUE AND TRIED TO GIVE ME A NEW MASK. DUDE WAS ALL DRESSED UP SLICK AND TALKIN' LIKE HE'S CLEAN NOW—BUNCHA BULL LIKE THAT.
UH... SOME OF IT AIN'T BULL, MAN. YOUR DAD STOPPED HITTIN' THE BOOZE AND GOT HIMSELF CRAZY RIPPED SOMEHOW. AND HE'S CALLIN' HIMSELF HUN AGAIN.
HUN?!
YEAH—AND HE TOOK OVER THE DRAGONS FROM ME.
MATTER OF FACT, HE'S TAKIN' 'EM ALL TO THIS BIG MEETIN' THE SHREDDER'S HAVIN' TONIGHT—
—SOME KIND OF POWER TRIP TO GET EVERYONE IN THE CITY IN LINE, I GUESS.
WHAT?
C'MON, ANGEL, WE'RE... UNF... OUTTA HERE.
CASEY, YOU AIN'T SUPPOSED TO BE UP—WHAT THE HELL YOU DOIN'?
HELPIN'... ERG... MY FRIENDS. APRIL TEXTED ME THAT SOMETHIN' WAS UP WITH LEO. THIS MEETIN' MUST BE IT AND I GOT A BAD FEELIN', 'SPECIALLY IF MY DAD'S IN THE MIX.
THAT CHUMP CAN POUND ON ME ALL HE WANTS...

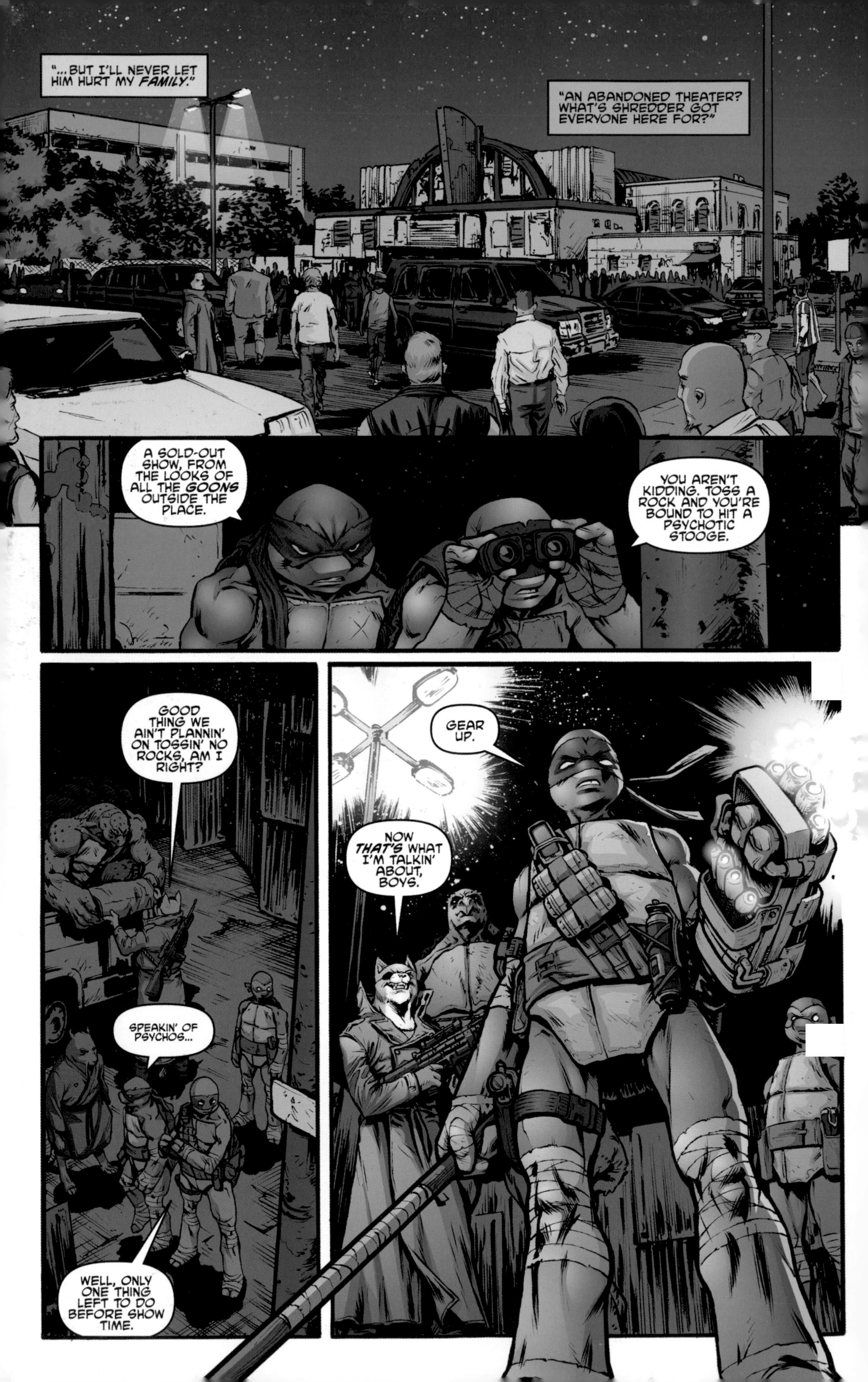
"...BUT I'LL NEVER LET HIM HURT MY FAMILY."
"AN ABANDONED THEATER? WHAT'S SHREDDER GOT EVERYONE HERE FOR?"
A SOLD-OUT SHOW, FROM THE LOOKS OF ALL THE GOONS OUTSIDE THE PLACE.
YOU AREN'T KIDDING. TOSS A ROCK AND YOU'RE BOUND TO HIT A PSYCHOTIC STOOGE.
GOOD THING WE AIN'T PLANNIN' ON TOSSIN' NO ROCKS, AM I RIGHT?
SPEAKIN' OF PSYCHOS...
WELL, ONLY ONE THING LEFT TO DO BEFORE SHOW TIME.
GEAR UP.
NOW THAT'S WHAT I'M TALKIN' ABOUT, BOYS.

LADIES AND GENTLEMEN. YOU WERE *WISE* TO ACCEPT MY INVITATION.

I AM *THE SHREDDER,* LEADER OF THE FOOT CLAN.

AND, AS OF TONIGHT...

...MASTER OF YOU ALL.

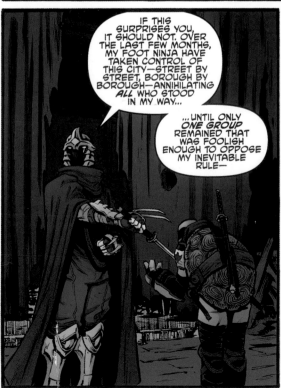

IF THIS SURPRISES YOU, IT SHOULD NOT. OVER THE LAST FEW MONTHS, MY FOOT NINJA HAVE TAKEN CONTROL OF THIS CITY—STREET BY STREET, BOROUGH BY BOROUGH—ANNIHILATING *ALL* WHO STOOD IN MY WAY...

...UNTIL ONLY *ONE GROUP* REMAINED THAT WAS FOOLISH ENOUGH TO OPPOSE MY INEVITABLE RULE—

THE *SAVATE.*

YOU... YOU BASTARD...

63

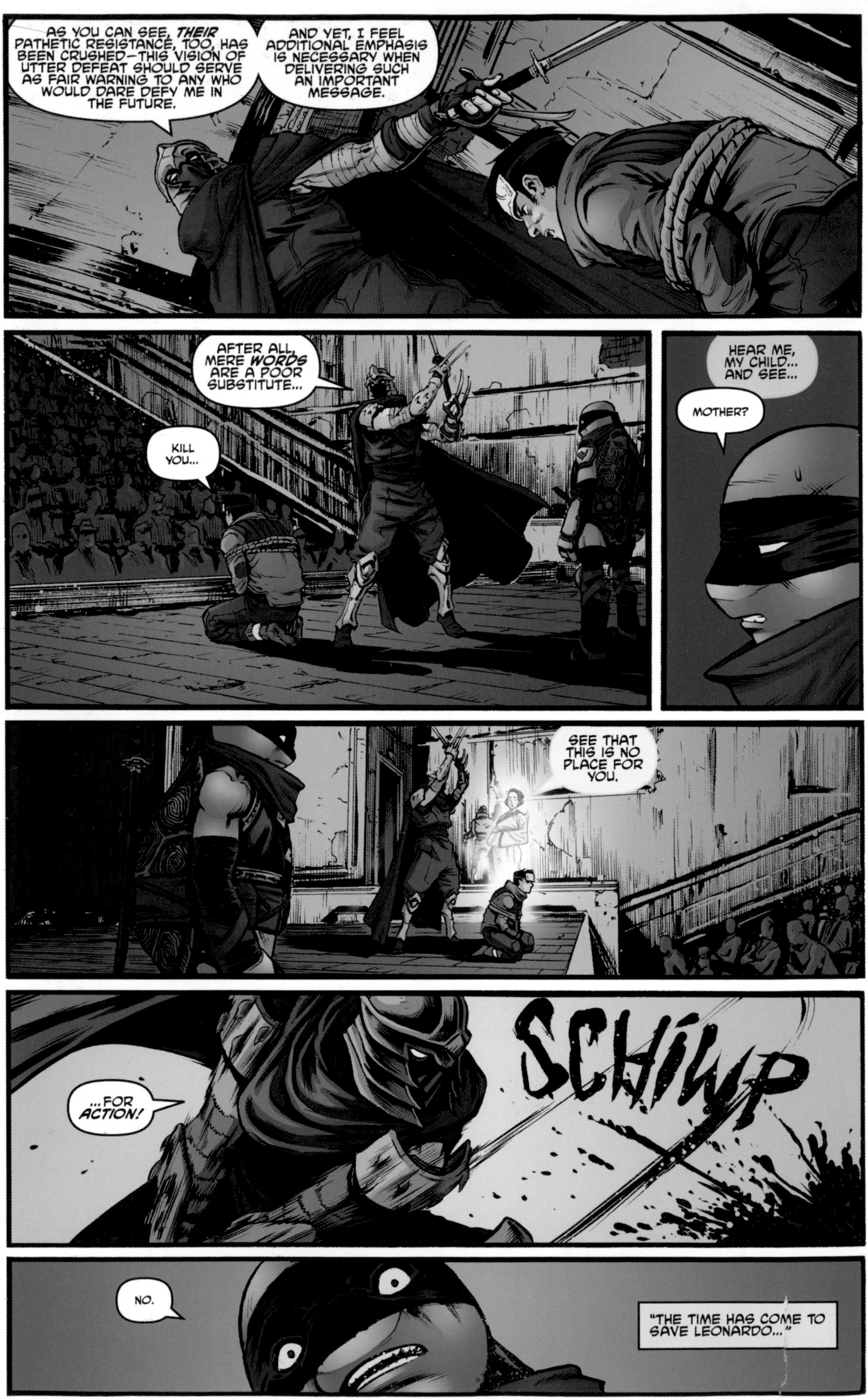
AS YOU CAN SEE, *THEIR* PATHETIC RESISTANCE, TOO, HAS BEEN CRUSHED—THIS VISION OF UTTER DEFEAT SHOULD SERVE AS FAIR WARNING TO ANY WHO WOULD DARE DEFY ME IN THE FUTURE.
AND YET, I FEEL ADDITIONAL EMPHASIS IS NECESSARY WHEN DELIVERING SUCH AN IMPORTANT MESSAGE.
AFTER ALL, MERE *WORDS* ARE A POOR SUBSTITUTE...
KILL YOU...
HEAR ME, MY CHILD... AND SEE...
MOTHER?
SEE THAT THIS IS NO PLACE FOR YOU.
...FOR *ACTION!*
SCHWP
NO.
"THE TIME HAS COME TO SAVE LEONARDO..."

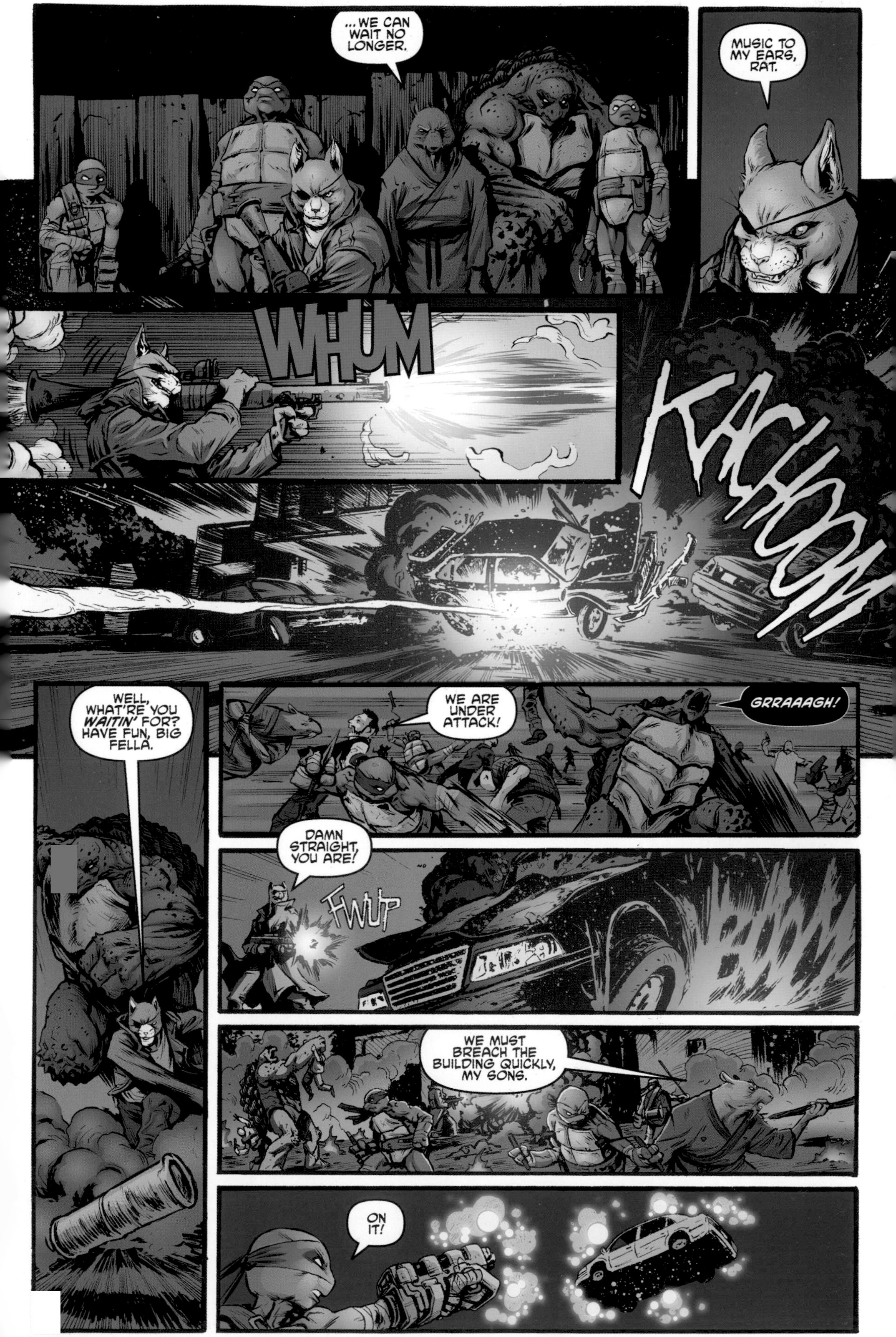
...WE CAN WAIT NO LONGER.
MUSIC TO MY EARS, RAT.
WHUM
KACHOOM
WELL, WHAT'RE YOU *WAITIN'* FOR? HAVE FUN, BIG FELLA.
WE ARE UNDER ATTACK!
GRRAAAGH!
DAMN STRAIGHT, YOU ARE!
FWUP
WE MUST BREACH THE BUILDING QUICKLY, MY SONS.
ON IT!

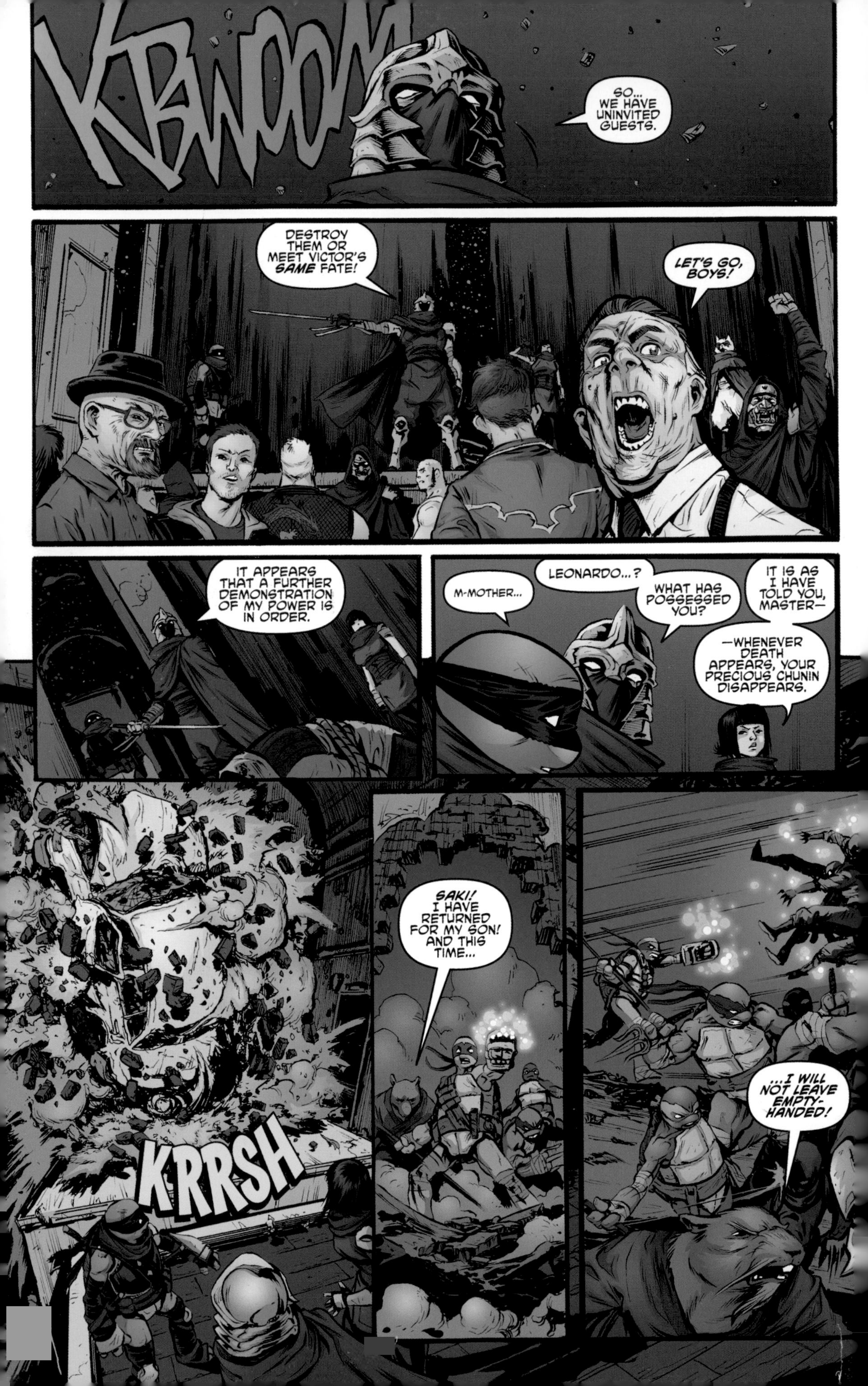
KRAWOOM
SO... WE HAVE UNINVITED GUESTS.
DESTROY THEM OR MEET VICTOR'S SAME FATE!
LET'S GO, BOYS!
IT APPEARS THAT A FURTHER DEMONSTRATION OF MY POWER IS IN ORDER.
M-MOTHER...
LEONARDO...?
WHAT HAS POSSESSED YOU?
IT IS AS I HAVE TOLD YOU, MASTER—
—WHENEVER DEATH APPEARS, YOUR PRECIOUS CHUNIN DISAPPEARS.
KRRSH
SAKI! I HAVE RETURNED FOR MY SON! AND THIS TIME...
...I WILL NOT LEAVE EMPTY-HANDED!

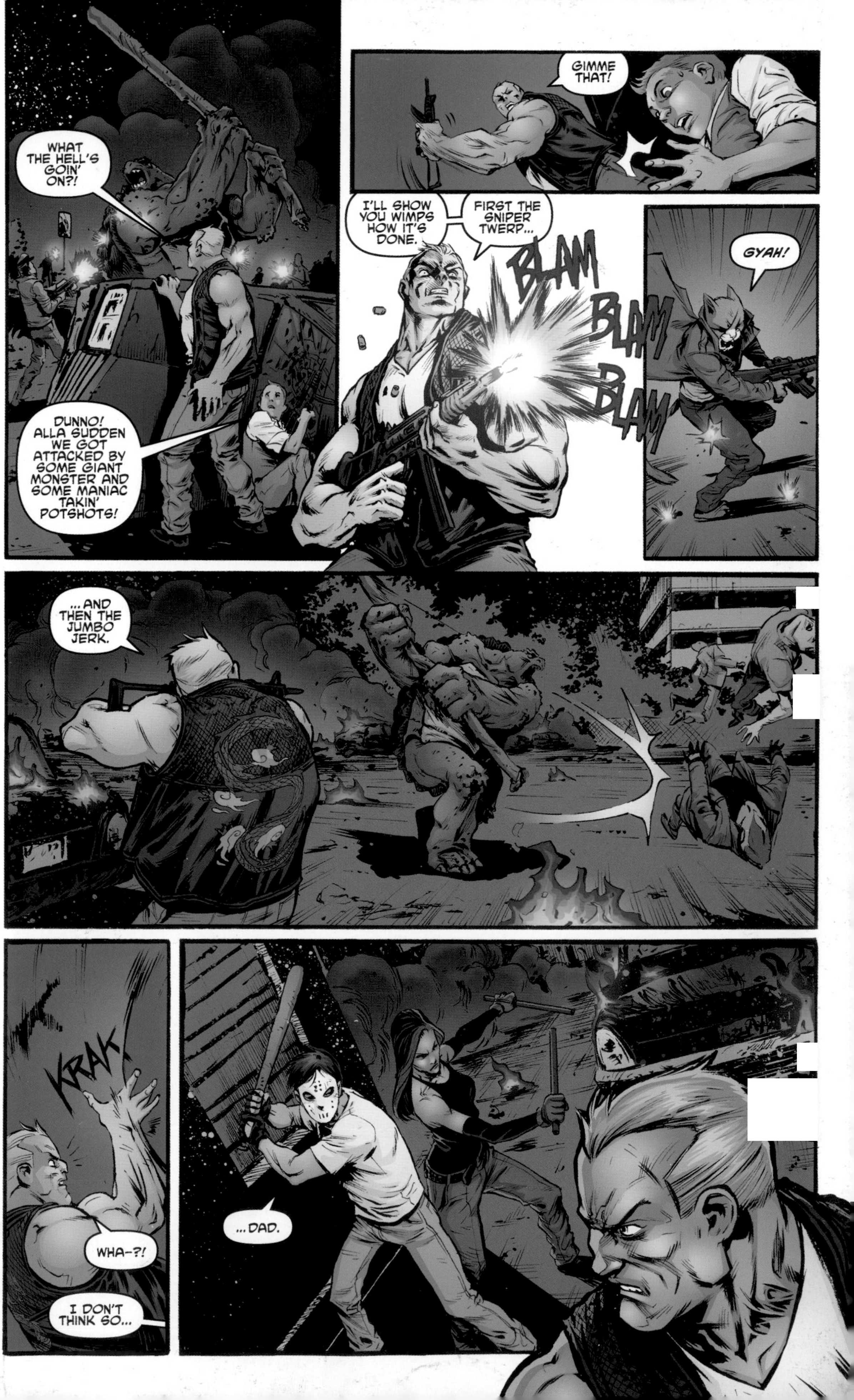
WHAT THE HELL'S GOIN' ON?!
DUNNO! ALLA SUDDEN WE GOT ATTACKED BY SOME GIANT MONSTER AND SOME MANIAC TAKIN' POTSHOTS!
GIMME THAT!
I'LL SHOW YOU WIMPS HOW IT'S DONE.
FIRST THE SNIPER TWERP...
BLAM
BLAM
BLAM
GYAH!
...AND THEN THE JUMBO JERK.
KRAK
WHA-?!
I DON'T THINK SO...
...DAD.

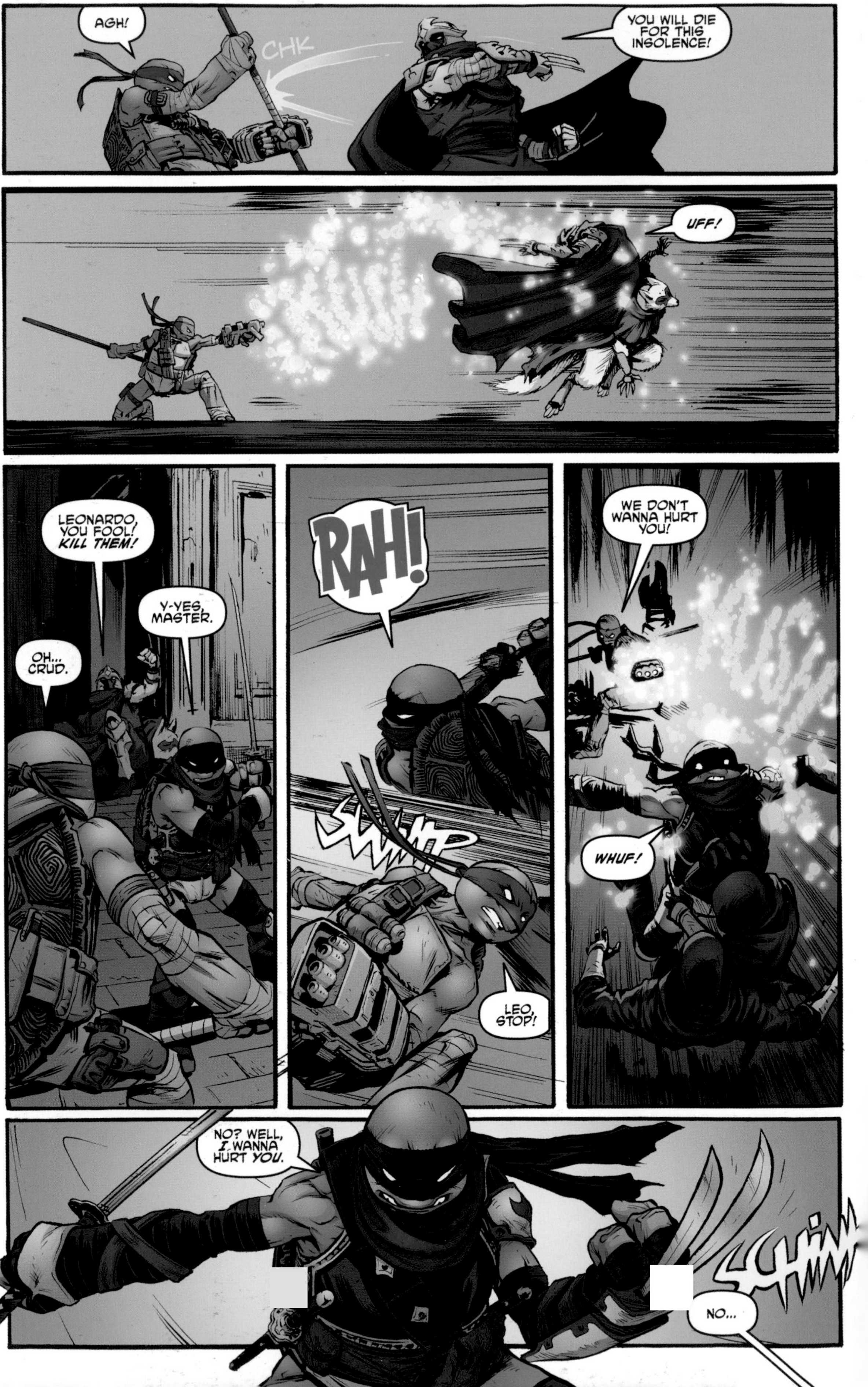
AGH!
CHK
YOU WILL DIE FOR THIS INSOLENCE!
UFF!
LEONARDO, YOU FOOL! KILL THEM!
Y-YES, MASTER.
OH... CRUD.
RAH!
LEO, STOP!
WE DON'T WANNA HURT YOU!
WHUF!
NO? WELL, I WANNA HURT YOU.
NO...

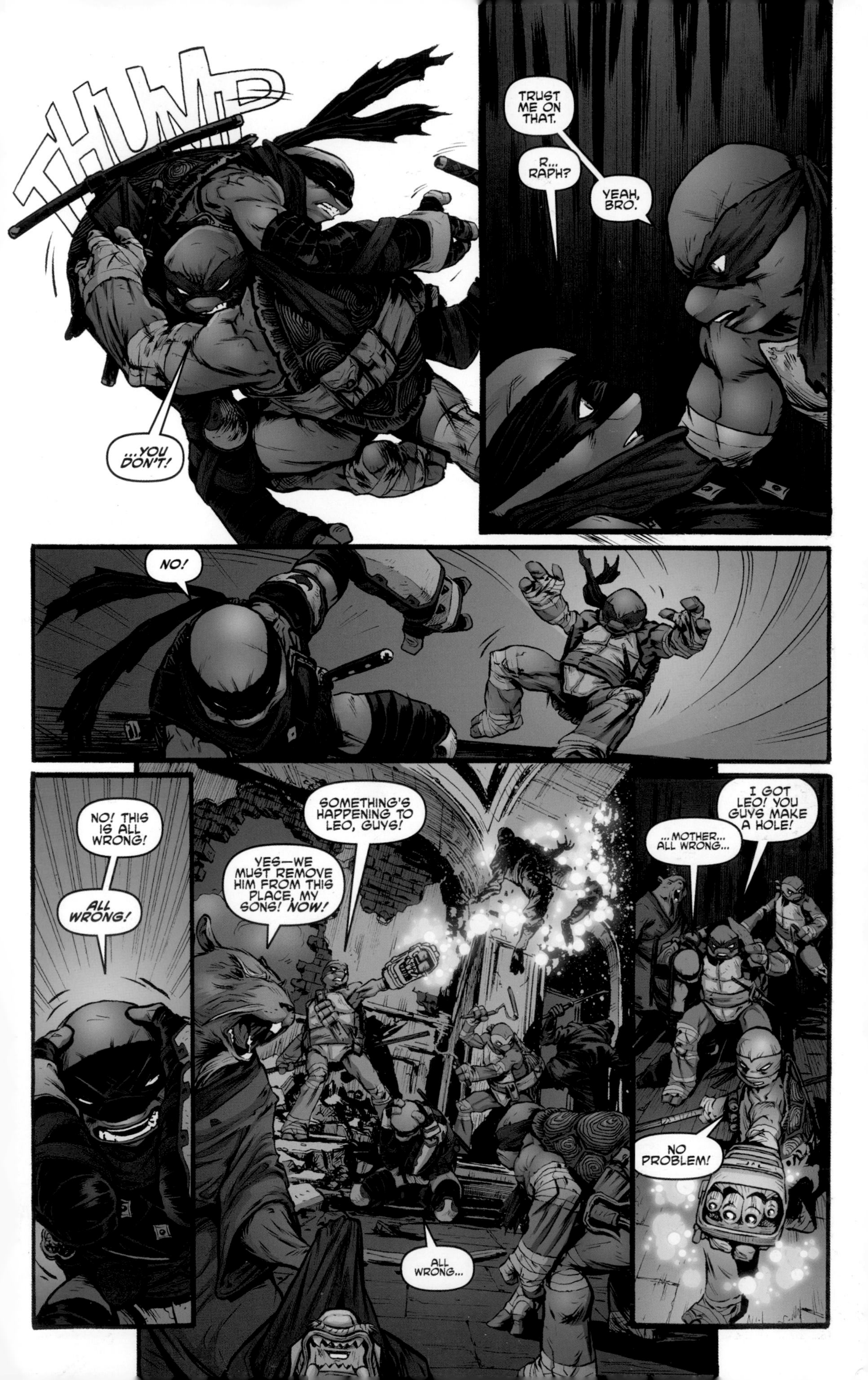
THUMP
...YOU DON'T!
TRUST ME ON THAT.
R... RAPH?
YEAH, BRO.
NO!
NO! THIS IS ALL WRONG!
ALL WRONG!
SOMETHING'S HAPPENING TO LEO, GUYS!
YES—WE MUST REMOVE HIM FROM THIS PLACE, MY SONS! NOW!
ALL WRONG...
...MOTHER... ALL WRONG...
I GOT LEO! YOU GUYS MAKE A HOLE!
NO PROBLEM!

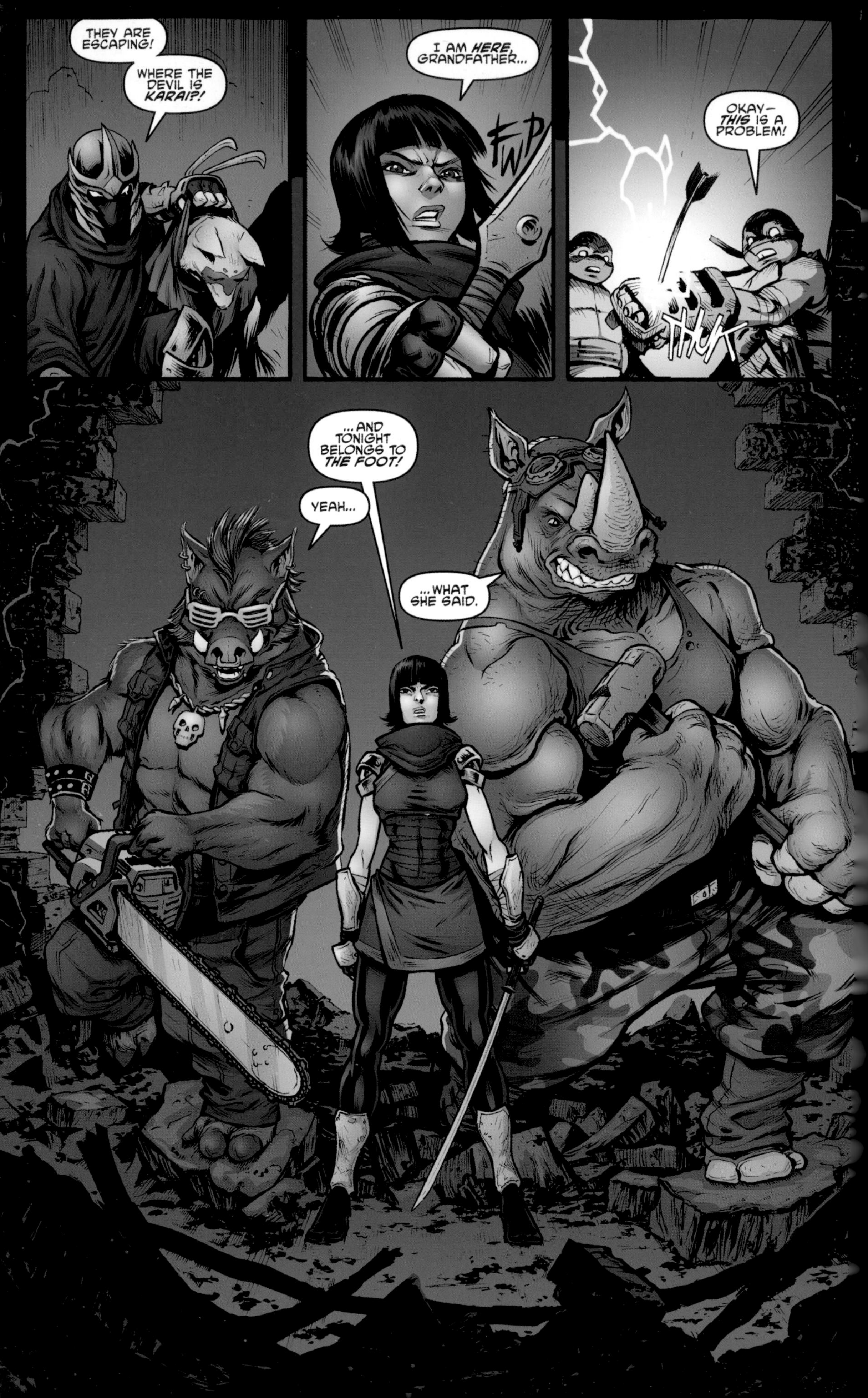
THEY ARE ESCAPING!
WHERE THE DEVIL IS KARAI?!
I AM HERE, GRANDFATHER...
FWP
OKAY— THIS IS A PROBLEM!
THUK
...AND TONIGHT BELONGS TO THE FOOT!
YEAH...
...WHAT SHE SAID.

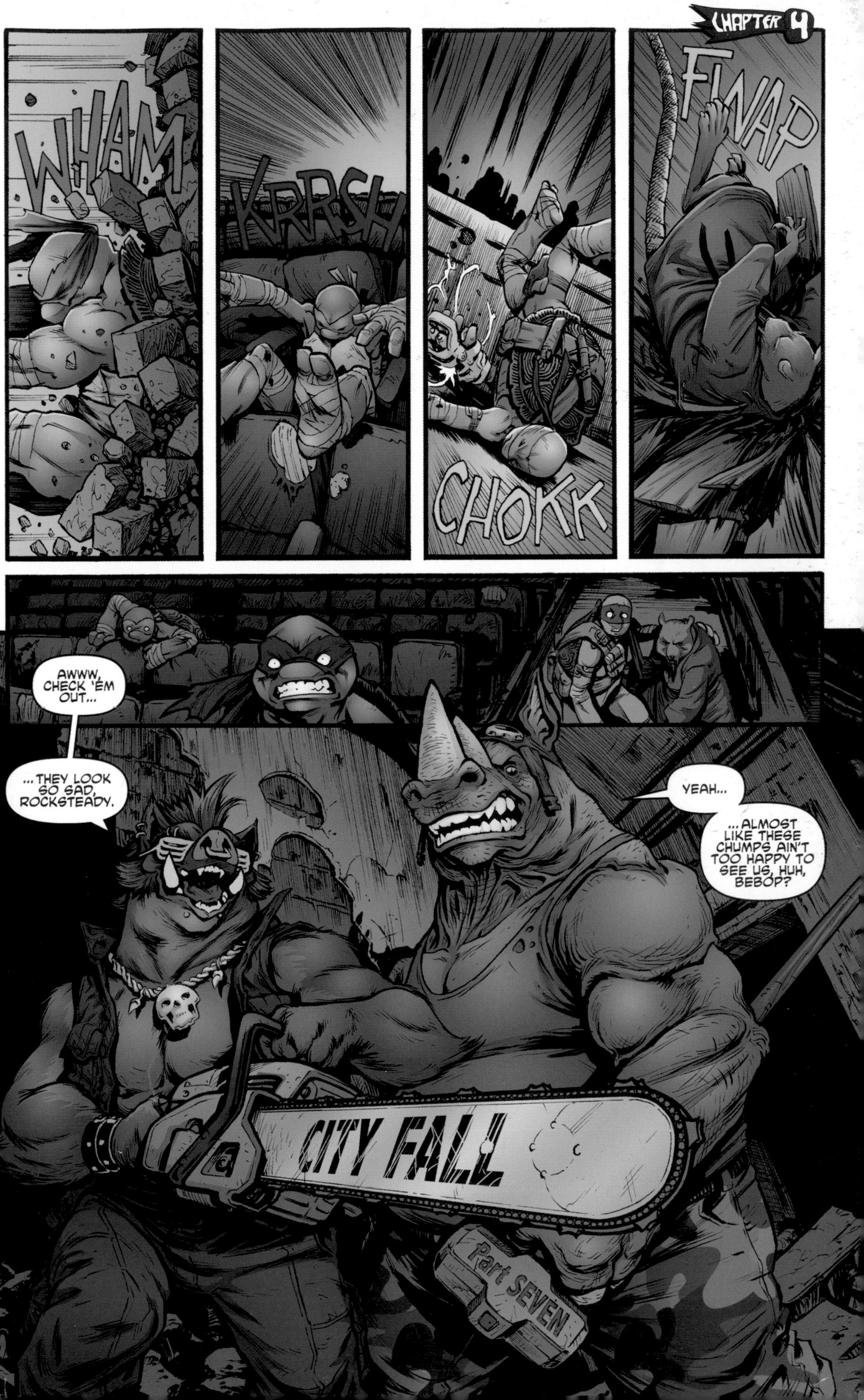
CHAPTER 4
WHAM
KRRSH
CHOKK
FWAP
AWWW, CHECK 'EM OUT...
...THEY LOOK SO SAD, ROCKSTEADY.
YEAH...
...ALMOST LIKE THESE CHUMPS AIN'T TOO HAPPY TO SEE US, HUH, BEBOP?
CITY FALL
Part SEVEN

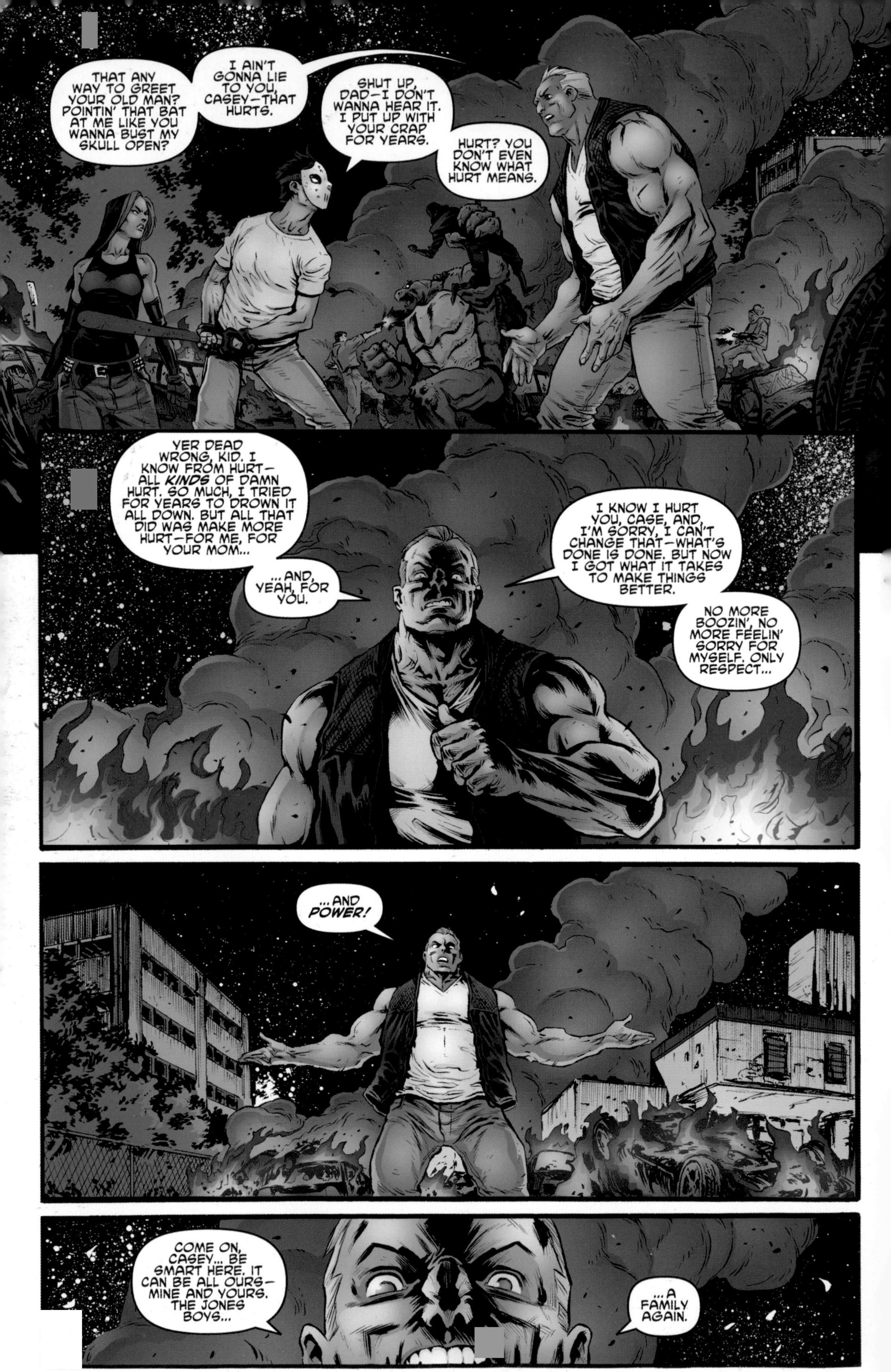
THAT ANY WAY TO GREET YOUR OLD MAN? POINTIN' THAT BAT AT ME LIKE YOU WANNA BUST MY SKULL OPEN?
I AIN'T GONNA LIE TO YOU, CASEY—THAT HURTS.
SHUT UP, DAD—I DON'T WANNA HEAR IT. I PUT UP WITH YOUR CRAP FOR YEARS.
HURT? YOU DON'T EVEN KNOW WHAT HURT MEANS.
YER DEAD WRONG, KID. I KNOW FROM HURT—ALL *KINDS* OF DAMN HURT. SO MUCH, I TRIED FOR YEARS TO DROWN IT ALL DOWN. BUT ALL THAT DID WAS MAKE MORE HURT—FOR ME, FOR YOUR MOM...
...AND, YEAH, FOR YOU.
I KNOW I HURT YOU, CASE, AND, I'M SORRY, I CAN'T CHANGE THAT—WHAT'S DONE IS DONE. BUT NOW I GOT WHAT IT TAKES TO MAKE THINGS BETTER.
NO MORE BOOZIN', NO MORE FEELIN' SORRY FOR MYSELF. ONLY RESPECT...
...AND *POWER!*
COME ON, CASEY... BE SMART HERE. IT CAN BE ALL OURS—MINE AND YOURS. THE JONES BOYS...
...A FAMILY AGAIN.

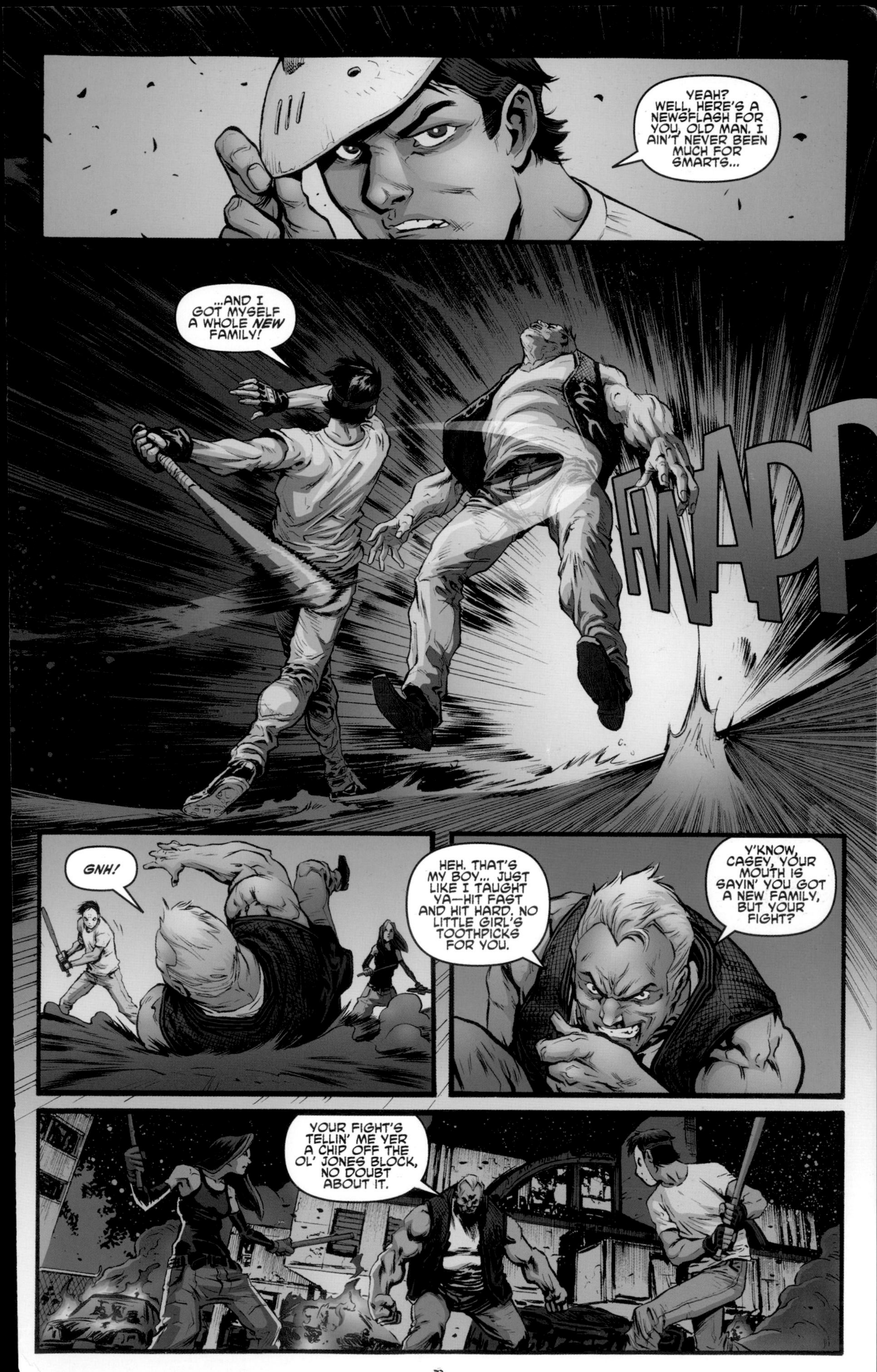

YEAH? WELL, HERE'S A NEWSFLASH FOR YOU, OLD MAN. I AIN'T NEVER BEEN MUCH FOR SMARTS...
...AND I GOT MYSELF A WHOLE *NEW* FAMILY!
FWAP
GNH!
HEH. THAT'S MY BOY... JUST LIKE I TAUGHT YA--HIT FAST AND HIT HARD. NO LITTLE GIRL'S TOOTHPICKS FOR YOU.
Y'KNOW, CASEY, YOUR MOUTH IS SAYIN' YOU GOT A NEW FAMILY, BUT YOUR FIGHT?
YOUR FIGHT'S TELLIN' ME YER A CHIP OFF THE OL' JONES BLOCK, NO DOUBT ABOUT IT.

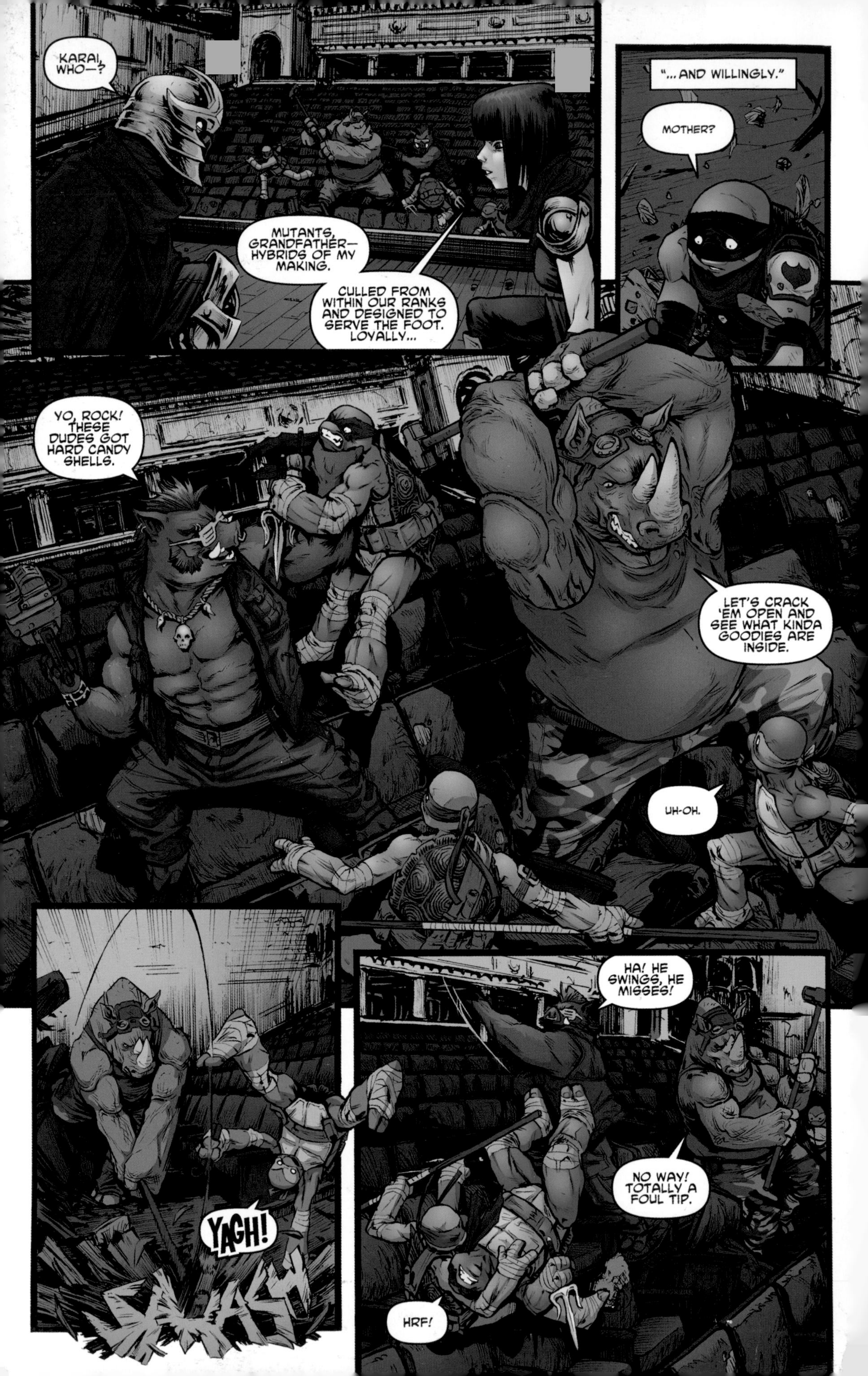
KARAI, WHO—?
MUTANTS, GRANDFATHER— HYBRIDS OF MY MAKING.
CULLED FROM WITHIN OUR RANKS AND DESIGNED TO SERVE THE FOOT. LOYALLY...
"... AND WILLINGLY."
MOTHER?
YO, ROCK! THESE DUDES GOT HARD CANDY SHELLS.
LET'S CRACK 'EM OPEN AND SEE WHAT KINDA GOODIES ARE INSIDE.
UH-OH.
YAGH!
HA! HE SWINGS, HE MISSES!
NO WAY! TOTALLY A FOUL TIP.
HRF!

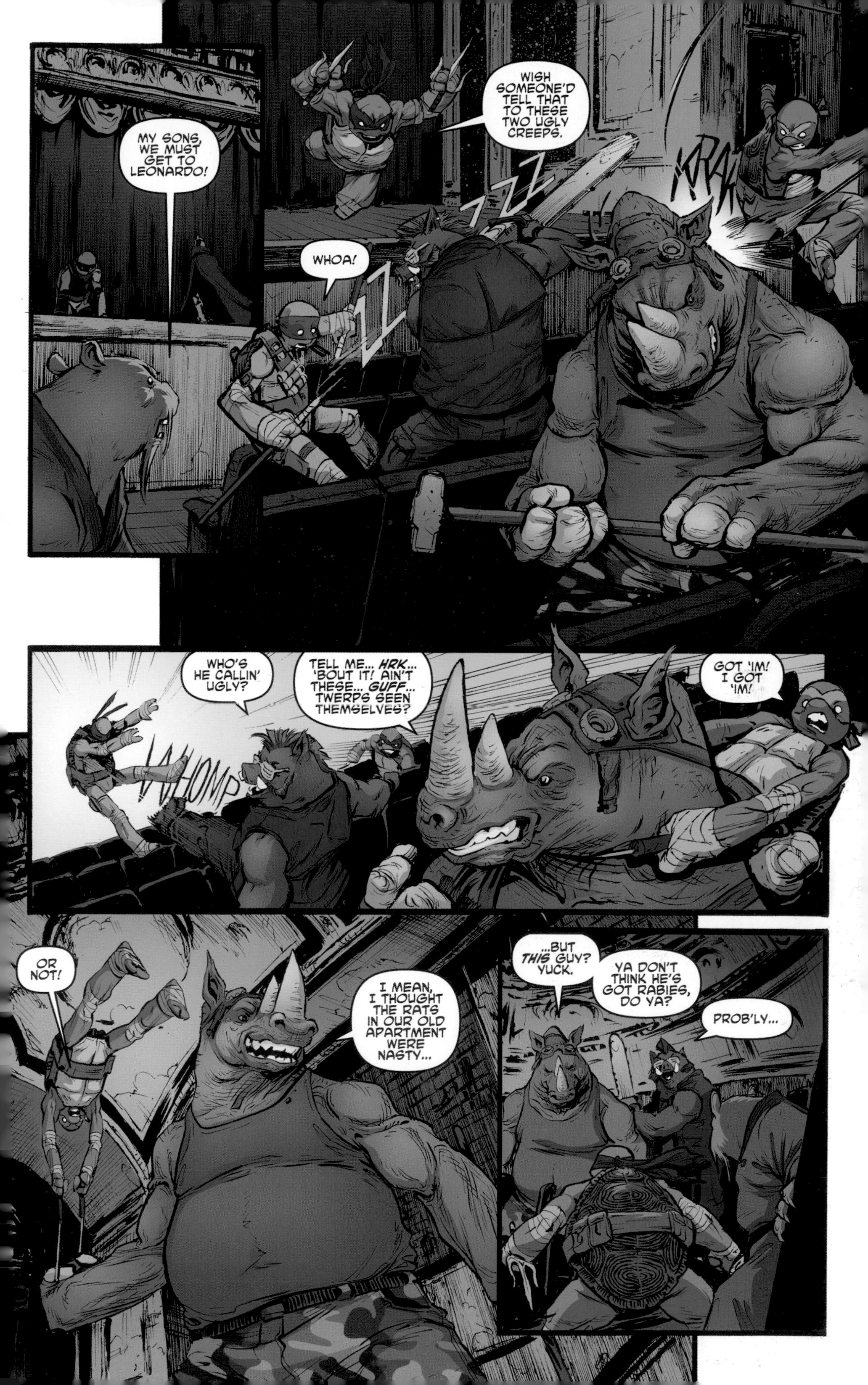
MY SONS, WE MUST GET TO LEONARDO!
WISH SOMEONE'D TELL THAT TO THESE TWO UGLY CREEPS.
WHOA!
WHO'S HE CALLIN' UGLY?
TELL ME... HRK... 'BOUT IT! AIN'T THESE... GUFF... TWERPS SEEN THEMSELVES?
GOT 'IM! I GOT 'IM!
OR NOT!
I MEAN, I THOUGHT THE RATS IN OUR OLD APARTMENT WERE NASTY...
...BUT THIS GUY? YUCK.
YA DON'T THINK HE'S GOT RABIES, DO YA?
PROB'LY...

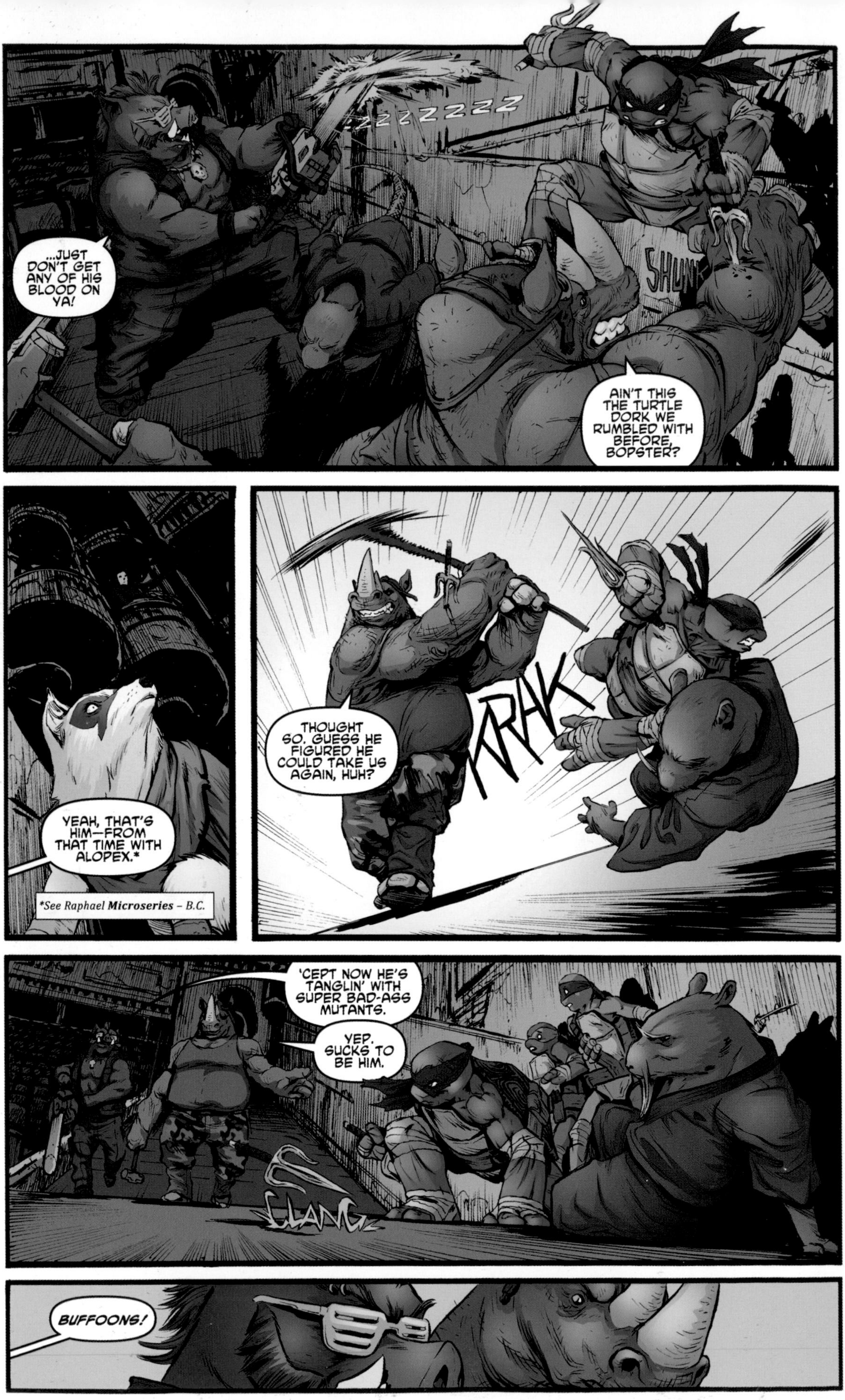

ZZZZZZZZZ
...JUST DON'T GET ANY OF HIS BLOOD ON YA!
SHUNK
AIN'T THIS THE TURTLE DORK WE RUMBLED WITH BEFORE, BOPSTER?
YEAH, THAT'S HIM—FROM THAT TIME WITH ALOPEX.*
*See Raphael Microseries – B.C.
THOUGHT SO. GUESS HE FIGURED HE COULD TAKE US AGAIN, HUH?
KRAK
'CEPT NOW HE'S TANGLIN' WITH SUPER BAD-ASS MUTANTS.
YEP. SUCKS TO BE HIM.
CLANG
BUFFOONS!

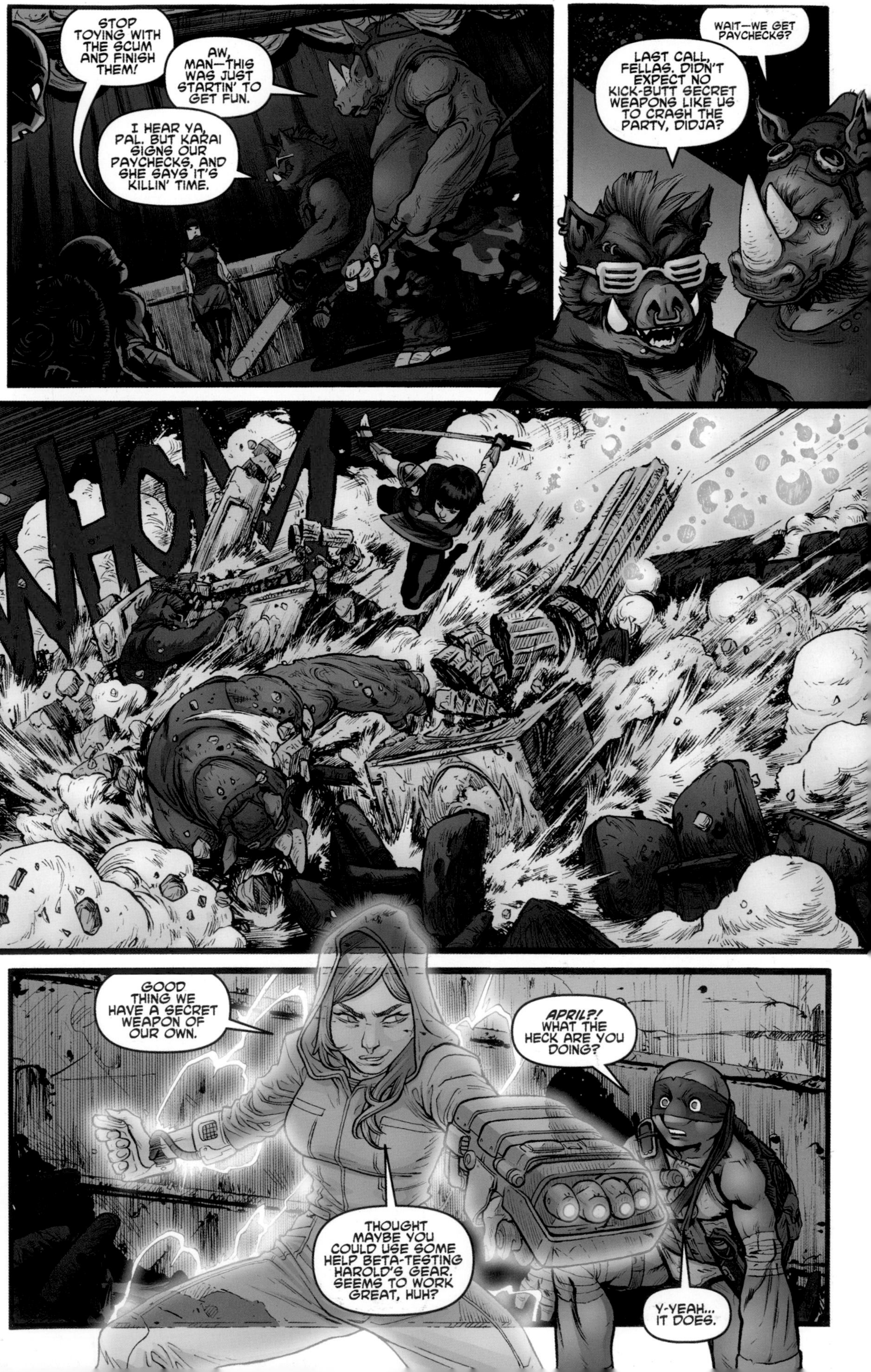
STOP TOYING WITH THE SCUM AND FINISH THEM!
AW, MAN—THIS WAS JUST STARTIN' TO GET FUN.
I HEAR YA, PAL. BUT KARAI SIGNS OUR PAYCHECKS, AND SHE SAYS IT'S KILLIN' TIME.
WAIT—WE GET PAYCHECKS?
LAST CALL, FELLAS. DIDN'T EXPECT NO KICK-BUTT SECRET WEAPONS LIKE US TO CRASH THE PARTY, DIDJA?
WHOM
GOOD THING WE HAVE A SECRET WEAPON OF OUR OWN.
APRIL?! WHAT THE HECK ARE YOU DOING?
THOUGHT MAYBE YOU COULD USE SOME HELP BETA-TESTING HAROLD'S GEAR. SEEMS TO WORK GREAT, HUH?
Y-YEAH... IT DOES.

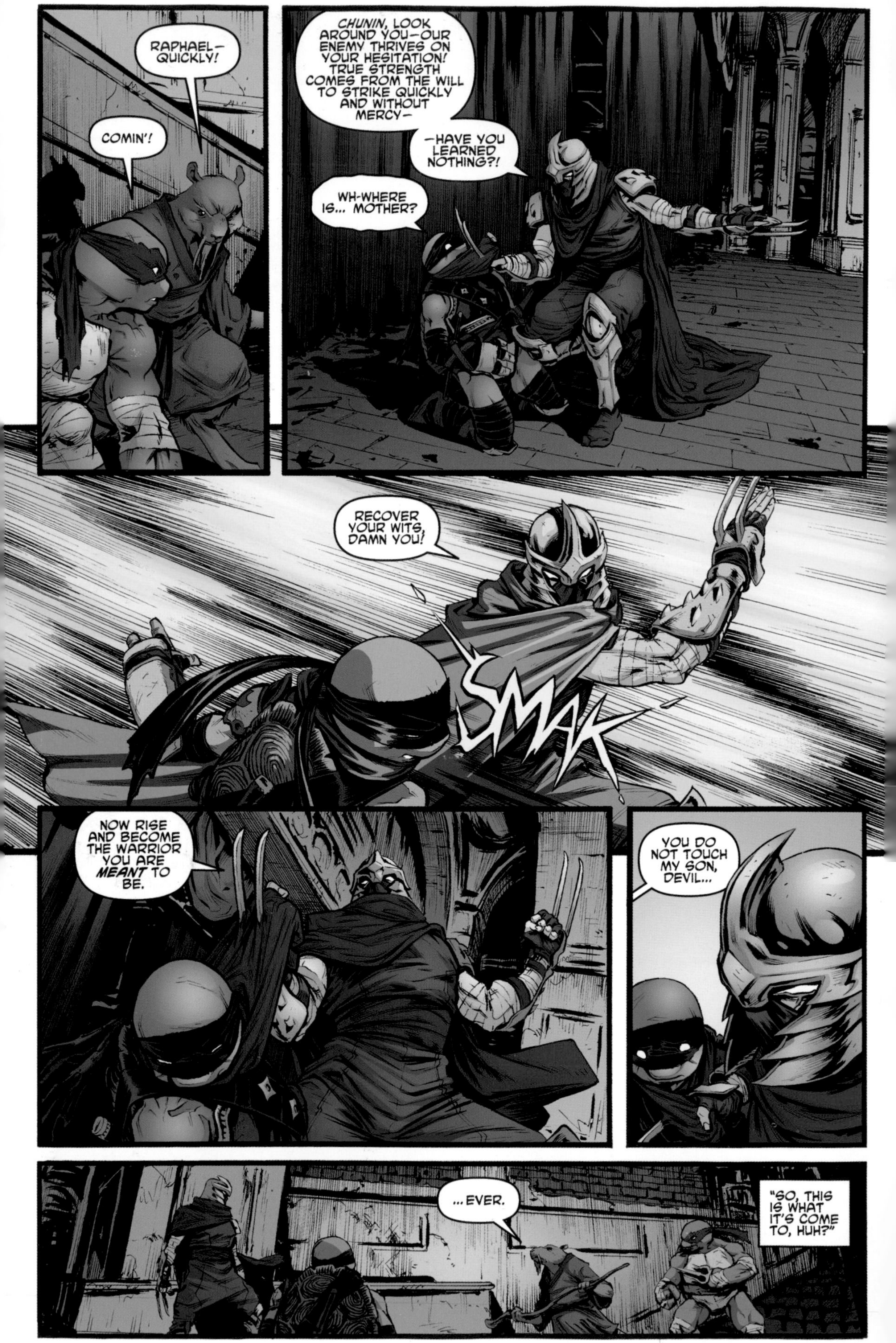
RAPHAEL— QUICKLY!
COMIN'!
CHUNIN, LOOK AROUND YOU—OUR ENEMY THRIVES ON YOUR HESITATION! TRUE STRENGTH COMES FROM THE WILL TO STRIKE QUICKLY AND WITHOUT MERCY—
—HAVE YOU LEARNED NOTHING?!
WH-WHERE IS... MOTHER?
RECOVER YOUR WITS, DAMN YOU!
SMAK
NOW RISE AND BECOME THE WARRIOR YOU ARE MEANT TO BE.
YOU DO NOT TOUCH MY SON, DEVIL...
...EVER.
"SO, THIS IS WHAT IT'S COME TO, HUH?"

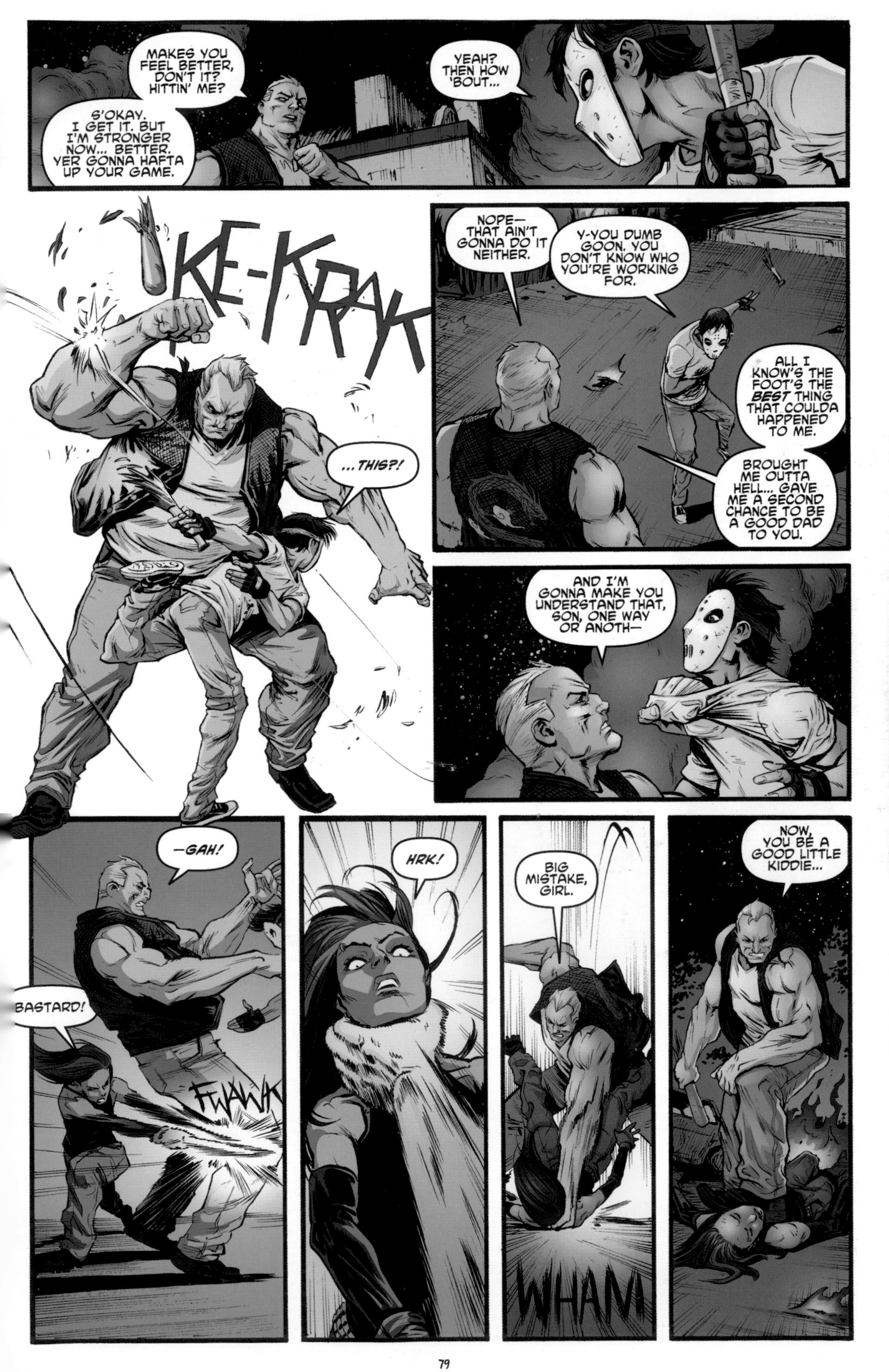
MAKES YOU FEEL BETTER, DON'T IT? HITTIN' ME?
S'OKAY. I GET IT. BUT I'M STRONGER NOW... BETTER. YER GONNA HAFTA UP YOUR GAME.
YEAH? THEN HOW 'BOUT...
KE-KRAK
...THIS?!
NOPE— THAT AIN'T GONNA DO IT NEITHER.
Y-YOU DUMB GOON. YOU DON'T KNOW WHO YOU'RE WORKING FOR.
ALL I KNOW'S THE FOOT'S THE BEST THING THAT COULDA HAPPENED TO ME.
BROUGHT ME OUTTA HELL... GAVE ME A SECOND CHANCE TO BE A GOOD DAD TO YOU.
AND I'M GONNA MAKE YOU UNDERSTAND THAT, SON, ONE WAY OR ANOTH—
—GAH!
BASTARD!
FWAWK
HRK!
BIG MISTAKE, GIRL.
WHAM
NOW, YOU BE A GOOD LITTLE KIDDIE...

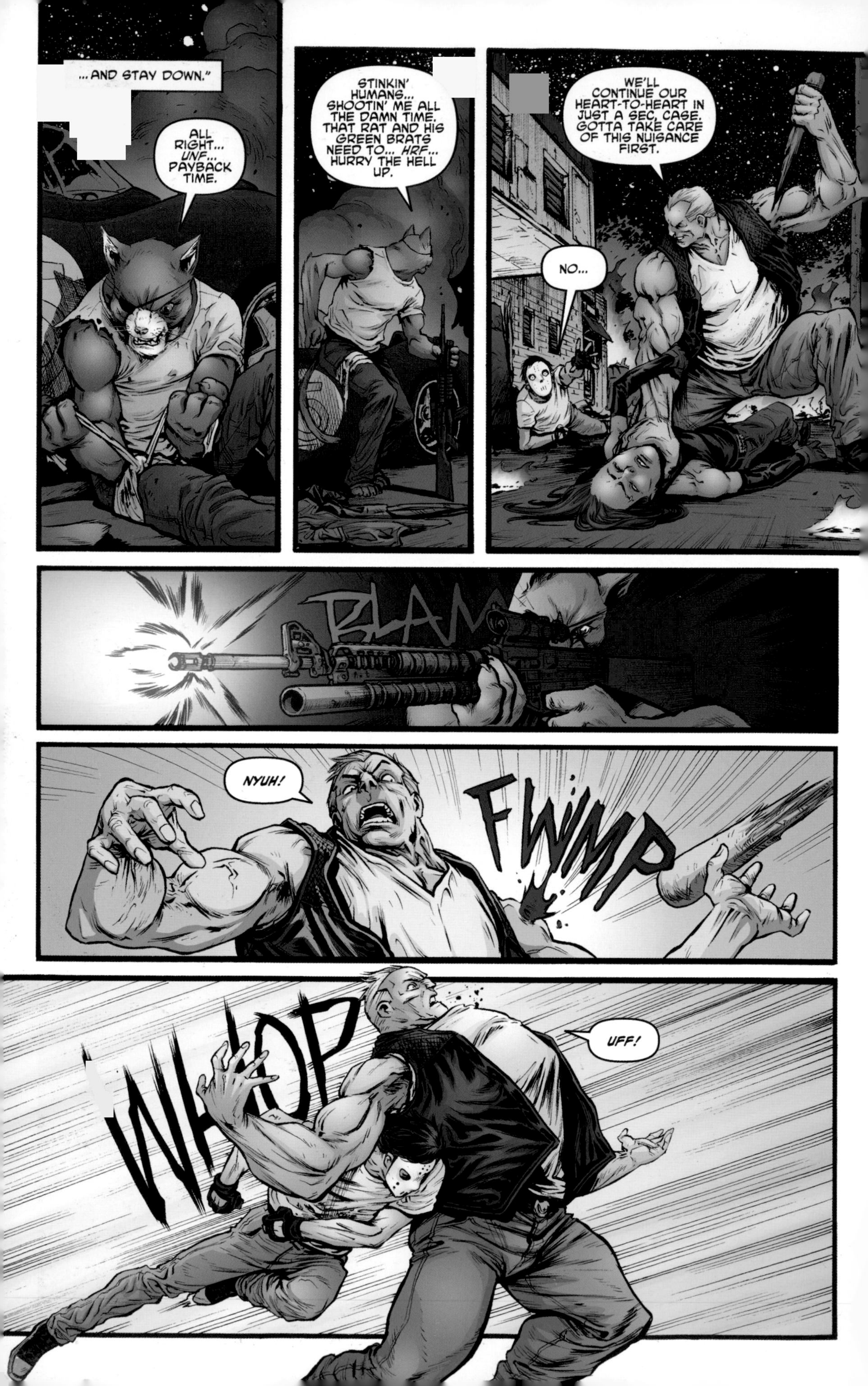
...AND STAY DOWN."
ALL RIGHT... UNF... PAYBACK TIME.
STINKIN' HUMANS... SHOOTIN' ME ALL THE DAMN TIME. THAT RAT AND HIS GREEN BRATS NEED TO... HRF... HURRY THE HELL UP.
WE'LL CONTINUE OUR HEART-TO-HEART IN JUST A SEC, CASE. GOTTA TAKE CARE OF THIS NUISANCE FIRST.
NO...
BLAM
NYUH!
FWMP
WHOP
UFF!

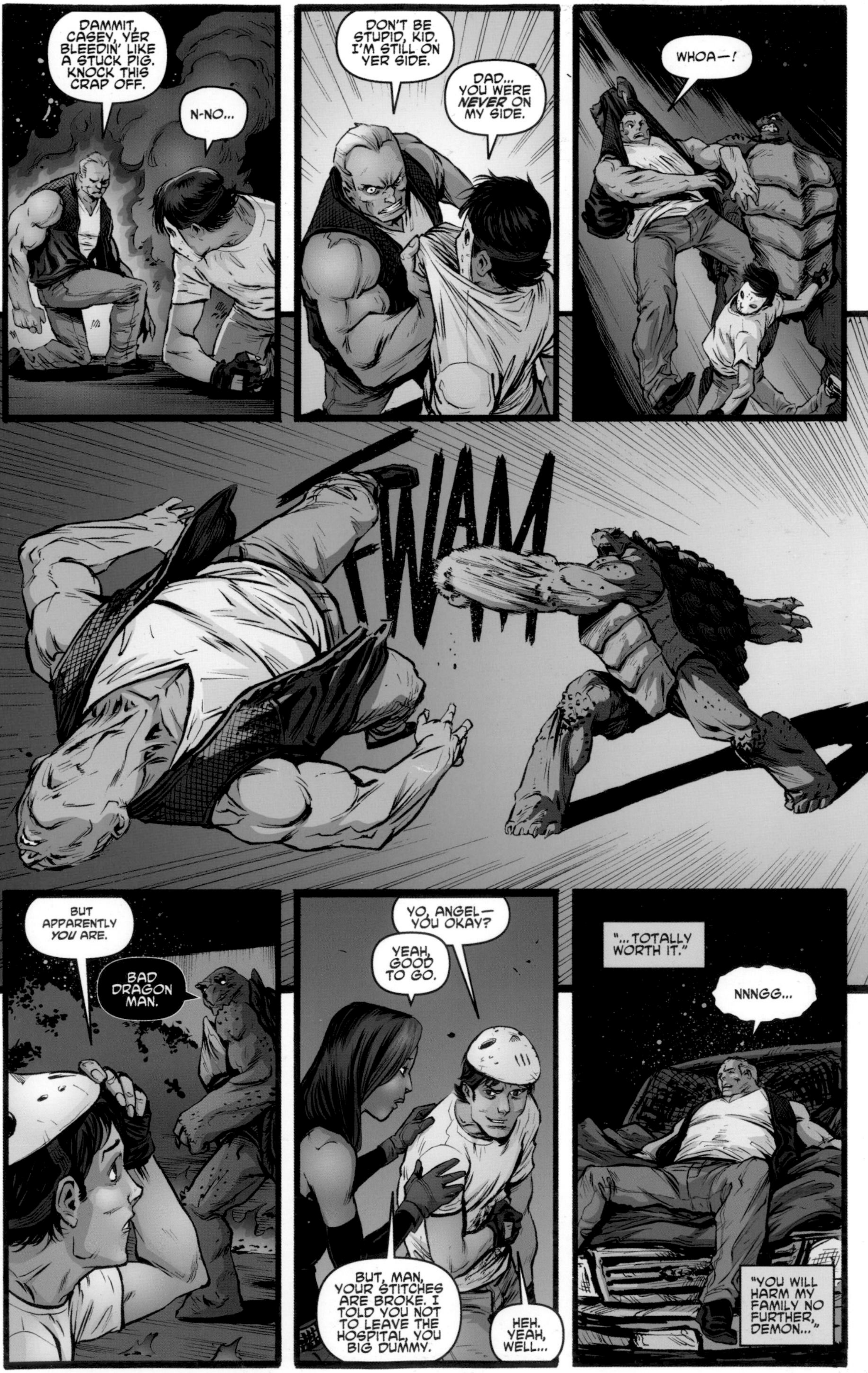
DAMMIT, CASEY, YER BLEEDIN' LIKE A STUCK PIG. KNOCK THIS CRAP OFF.
N-NO...
DON'T BE STUPID, KID. I'M STILL ON YER SIDE.
DAD... YOU WERE NEVER ON MY SIDE.
WHOA—!
TWAM
BUT APPARENTLY YOU ARE.
BAD DRAGON MAN.
YO, ANGEL— YOU OKAY?
YEAH, GOOD TO GO.
BUT, MAN, YOUR STITCHES ARE BROKE. I TOLD YOU NOT TO LEAVE THE HOSPITAL, YOU BIG DUMMY.
HEH. YEAH, WELL...
"...TOTALLY WORTH IT."
NNNGG...
"YOU WILL HARM MY FAMILY NO FURTHER, DEMON..."

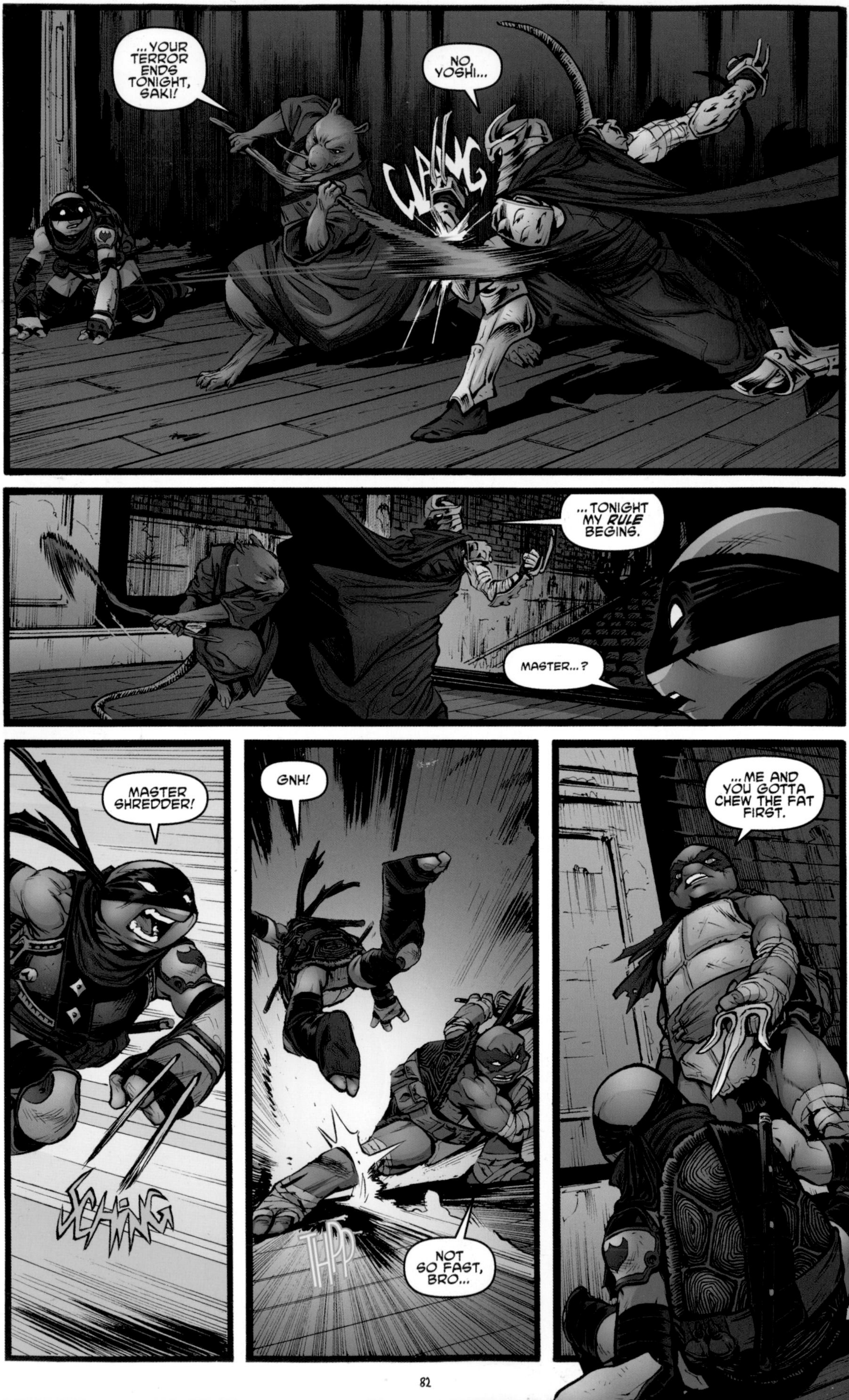
...YOUR TERROR ENDS TONIGHT, SAKI!
NO YOSHI...
CLANG
...TONIGHT MY *RULE* BEGINS.
MASTER...?
MASTER SHREDDER!
SCHING
GNH!
THPP
NOT SO FAST, BRO...
...ME AND YOU GOTTA CHEW THE FAT FIRST.

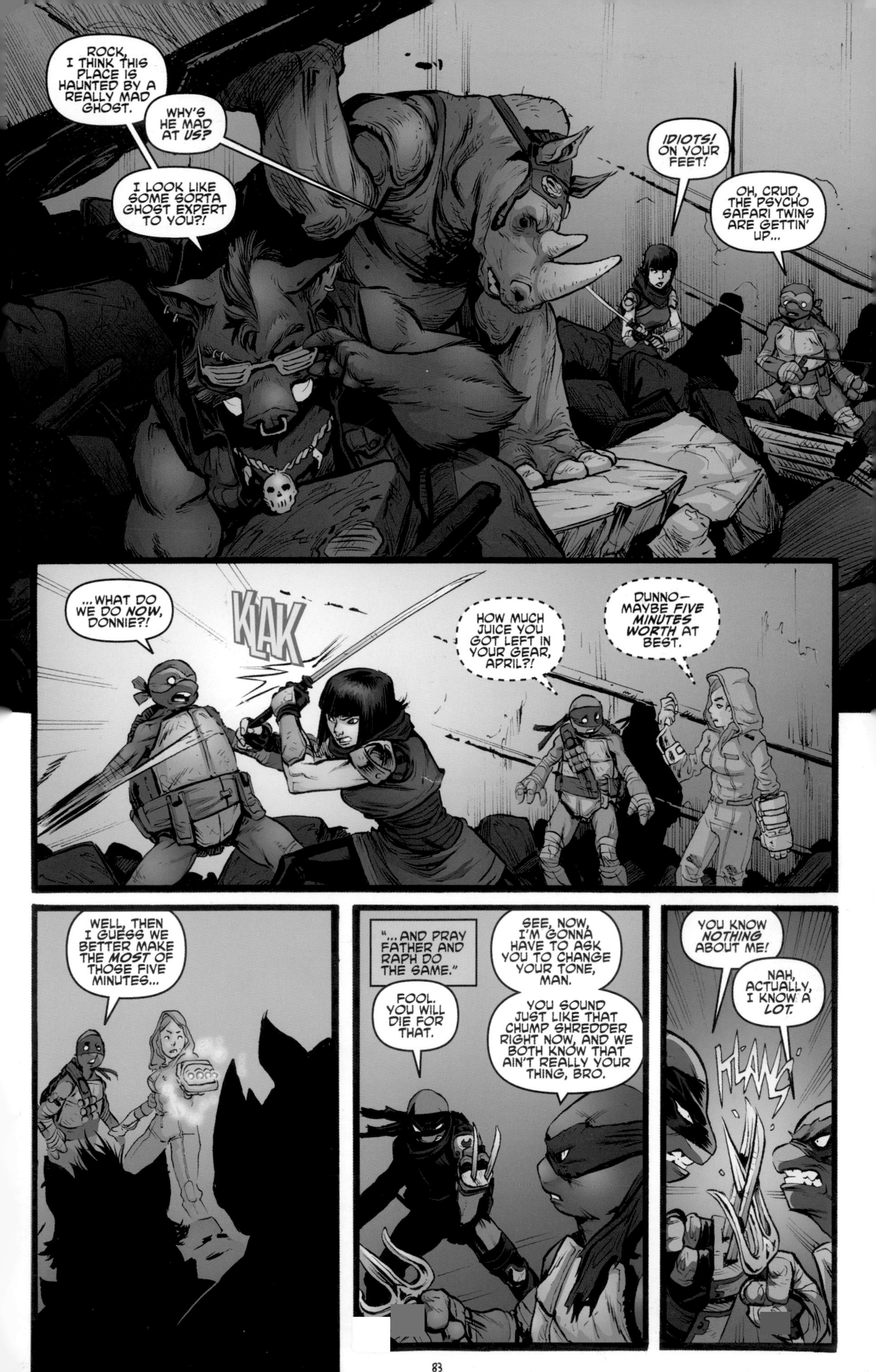
ROCK, I THINK THIS PLACE IS HAUNTED BY A REALLY MAD GHOST.
WHY'S HE MAD AT US?
I LOOK LIKE SOME SORTA GHOST EXPERT TO YOU?!
IDIOTS! ON YOUR FEET!
OH, CRUD, THE PSYCHO SAFARI TWINS ARE GETTIN' UP...
...WHAT DO WE DO NOW, DONNIE?!
KLAK
HOW MUCH JUICE YOU GOT LEFT IN YOUR GEAR, APRIL?!
DUNNO— MAYBE FIVE MINUTES WORTH AT BEST.
WELL, THEN I GUESS WE BETTER MAKE THE MOST OF THOSE FIVE MINUTES...
"...AND PRAY FATHER AND RAPH DO THE SAME."
FOOL. YOU WILL DIE FOR THAT.
SEE, NOW, I'M GONNA HAVE TO ASK YOU TO CHANGE YOUR TONE, MAN.
YOU SOUND JUST LIKE THAT CHUMP SHREDDER RIGHT NOW, AND WE BOTH KNOW THAT AIN'T REALLY YOUR THING, BRO.
YOU KNOW NOTHING ABOUT ME!
NAH, ACTUALLY, I KNOW A LOT.
KLANG

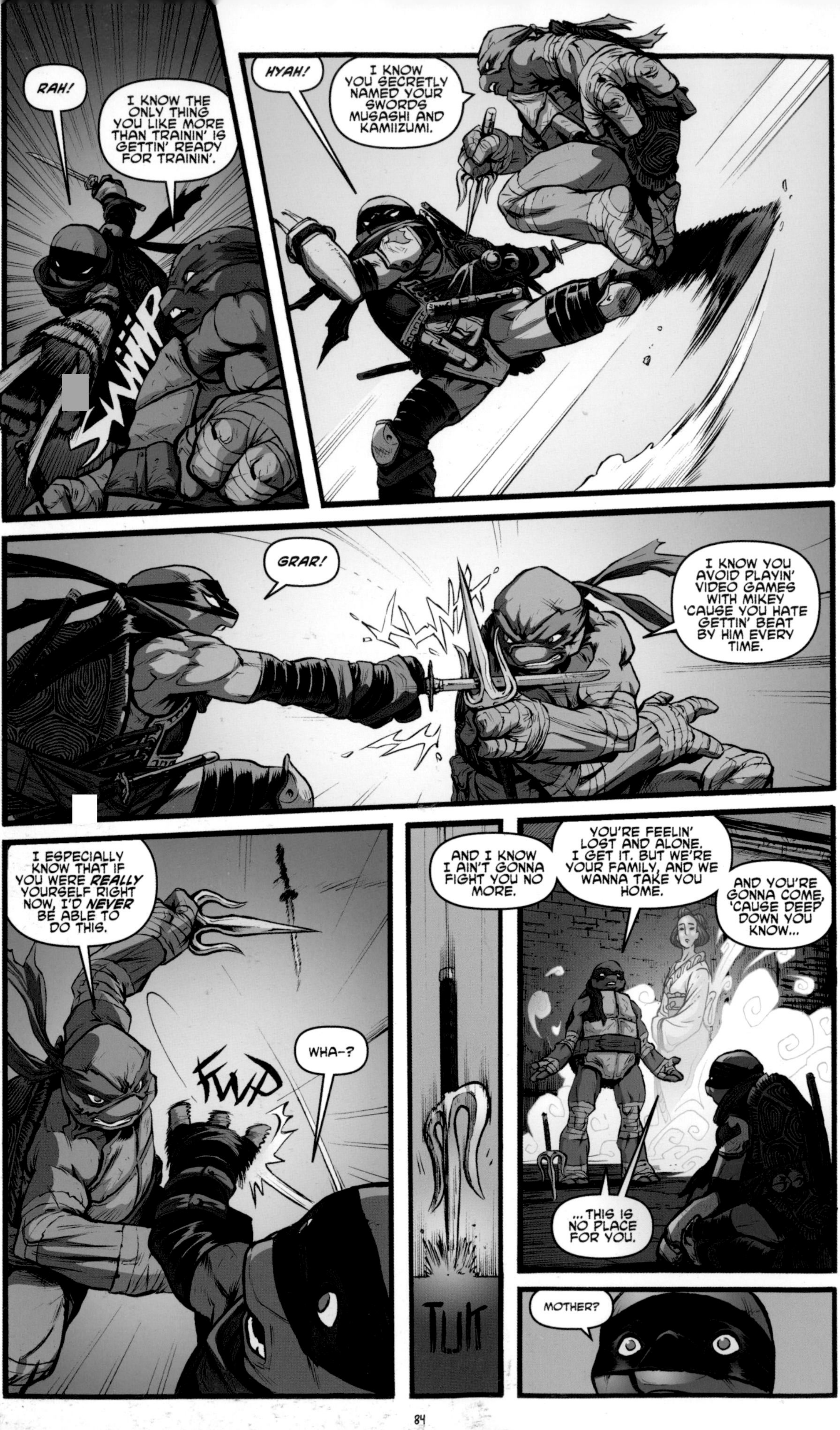
RAH!
I KNOW THE ONLY THING YOU LIKE MORE THAN TRAININ' IS GETTIN' READY FOR TRAININ'.
WHIP
HYAH!
I KNOW YOU SECRETLY NAMED YOUR SWORDS MUSASHI AND KAMIIZUMI.
GRAR!
I KNOW YOU AVOID PLAYIN' VIDEO GAMES WITH MIKEY 'CAUSE YOU HATE GETTIN' BEAT BY HIM EVERY TIME.
I ESPECIALLY KNOW THAT IF YOU WERE REALLY YOURSELF RIGHT NOW, I'D NEVER BE ABLE TO DO THIS.
FWP
WHA-?
TUK
AND I KNOW I AIN'T GONNA FIGHT YOU NO MORE.
YOU'RE FEELIN' LOST AND ALONE. I GET IT. BUT WE'RE YOUR FAMILY, AND WE WANNA TAKE YOU HOME.
AND YOU'RE GONNA COME, 'CAUSE DEEP DOWN YOU KNOW...
...THIS IS NO PLACE FOR YOU.
MOTHER?

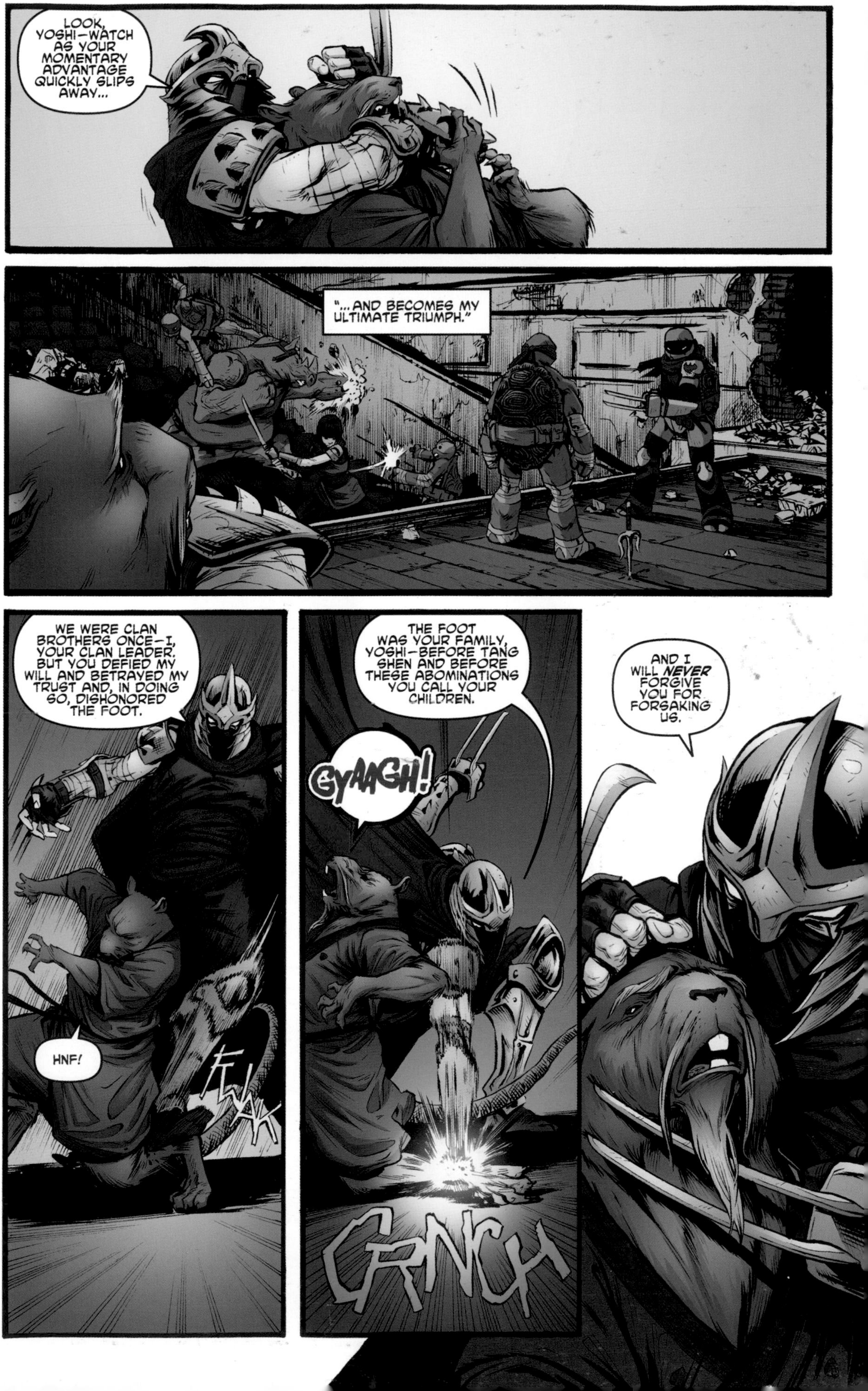
LOOK, YOSHI—WATCH AS YOUR MOMENTARY ADVANTAGE QUICKLY SLIPS AWAY...
"...AND BECOMES MY ULTIMATE TRIUMPH."
WE WERE CLAN BROTHERS ONCE—I, YOUR CLAN LEADER. BUT YOU DEFIED MY WILL AND BETRAYED MY TRUST AND, IN DOING SO, DISHONORED THE FOOT.
HNF!
FWAK
THE FOOT WAS YOUR FAMILY, YOSHI—BEFORE TANG SHEN AND BEFORE THESE ABOMINATIONS YOU CALL YOUR CHILDREN.
GYAAGH!
CRNCH
AND I WILL *NEVER* FORGIVE YOU FOR FORSAKING US.

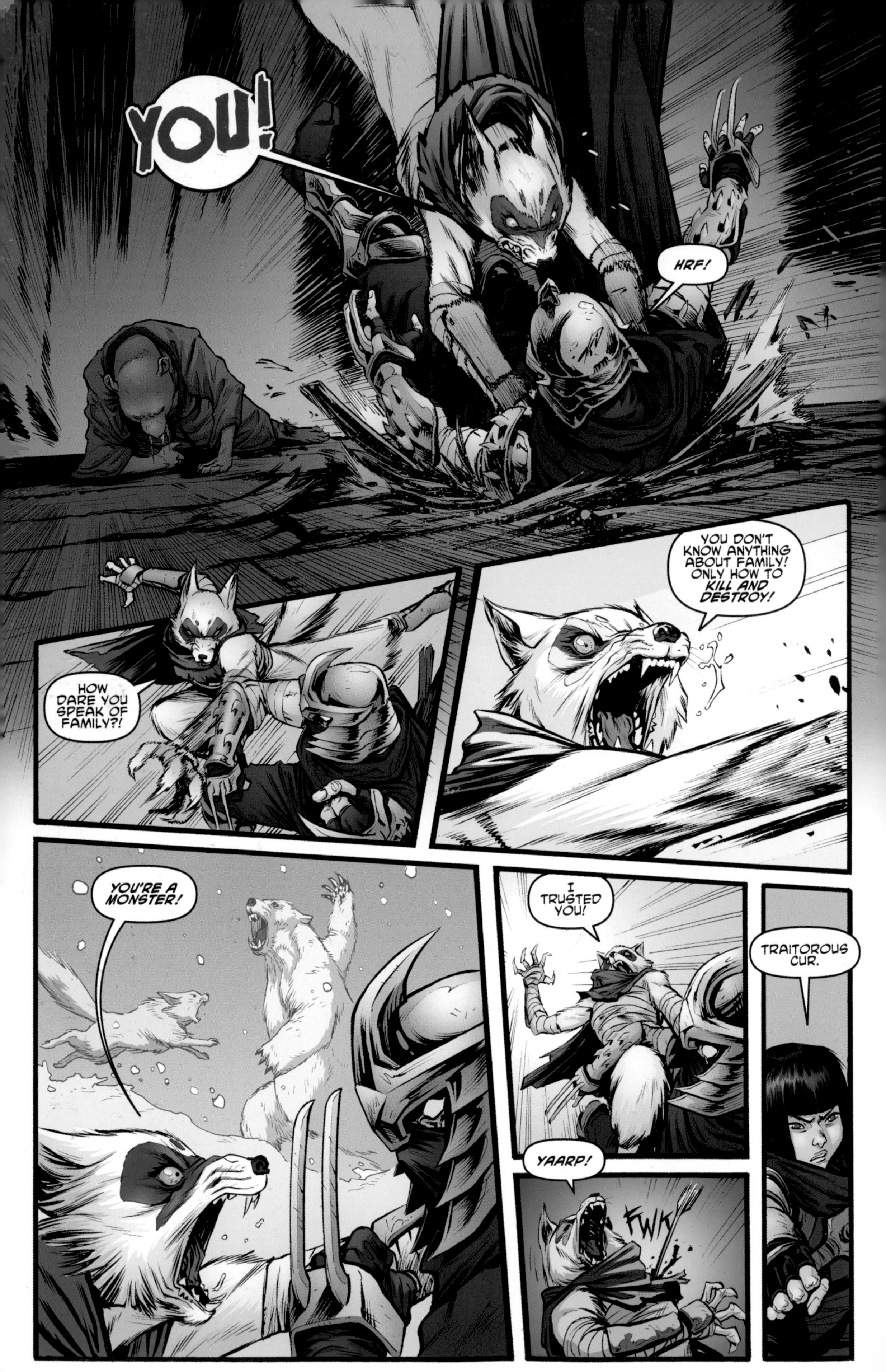
YOU!
HRF!
HOW DARE YOU SPEAK OF FAMILY?!
YOU DON'T KNOW ANYTHING ABOUT FAMILY! ONLY HOW TO *KILL AND DESTROY!*
YOU'RE A MONSTER!
I TRUSTED YOU!
YAARP!
FWK
TRAITOROUS CUR.

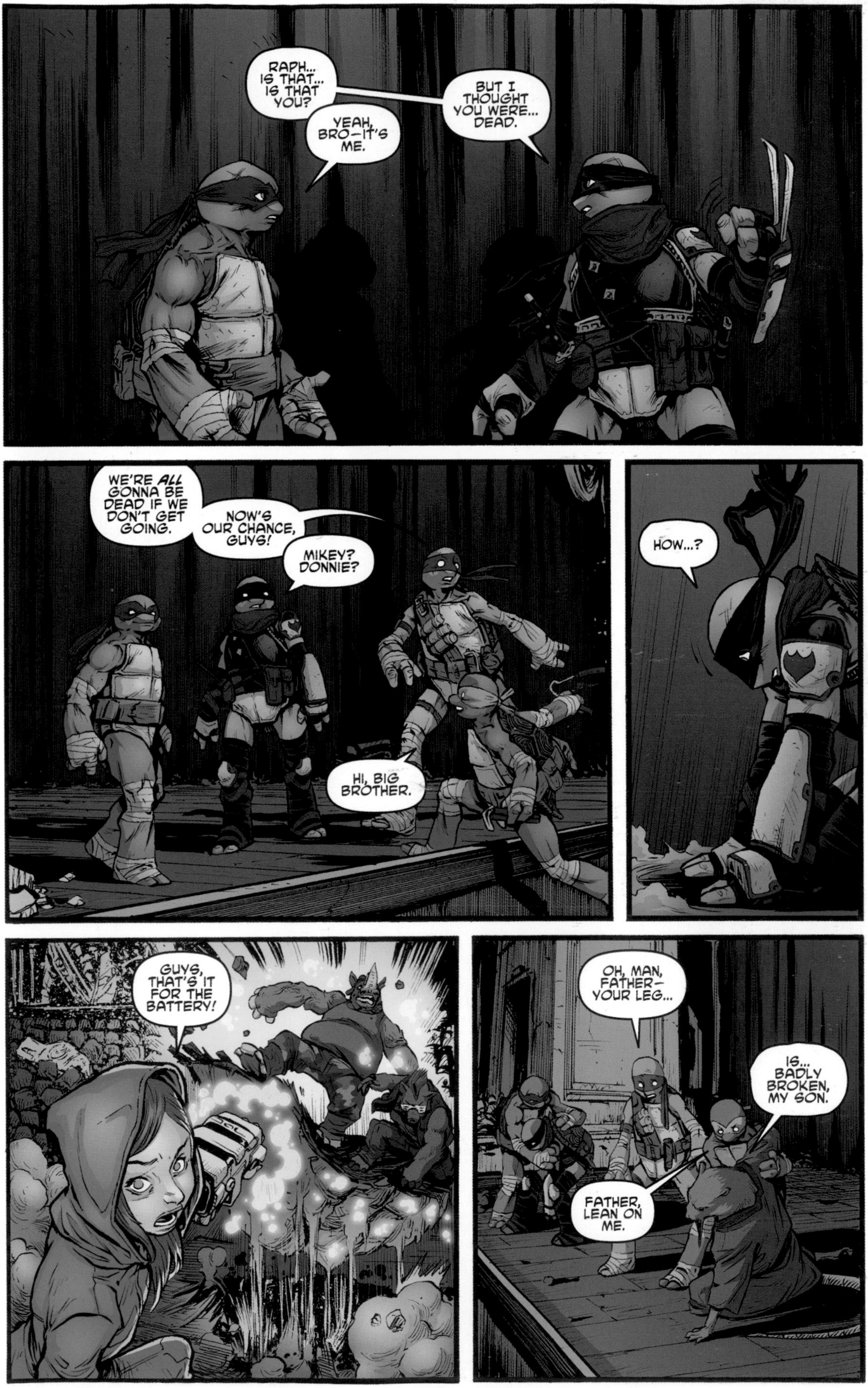
RAPH... IS THAT... IS THAT YOU?
YEAH, BRO—IT'S ME.
BUT I THOUGHT YOU WERE... DEAD.
WE'RE ALL GONNA BE DEAD IF WE DON'T GET GOING.
NOW'S OUR CHANCE, GUYS!
MIKEY? DONNIE?
HI, BIG BROTHER.
HOW...?
GUYS, THAT'S IT FOR THE BATTERY!
OH, MAN, FATHER—YOUR LEG...
IS... BADLY BROKEN, MY SON.
FATHER, LEAN ON ME.

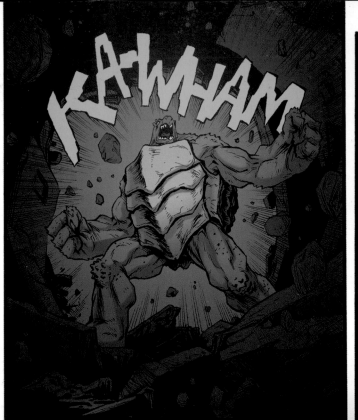

KA-WHAM

GUYS, TIME TO GO!

HURRY!

SLASH! LOVE THAT MOVE, BIG GUY! JUST IN TIME TO HELP ME WITH FATHER!

I GOT LEO!

COME ON, APRIL!

'BOUT STINKIN' TIME! ME AND SLASH HAD THINGS CLEANED UP OUT HERE WAY BEFORE NOW.

JUST... ERF... REMOVE US FROM THIS PLACE, OLD HOB. QUICKLY.

YEAH, YEAH, KEEP YOUR UNDIES ON.

NOT SO FAST, DWEEBS!

WE AIN'T DONE YET!

CRASSSHed

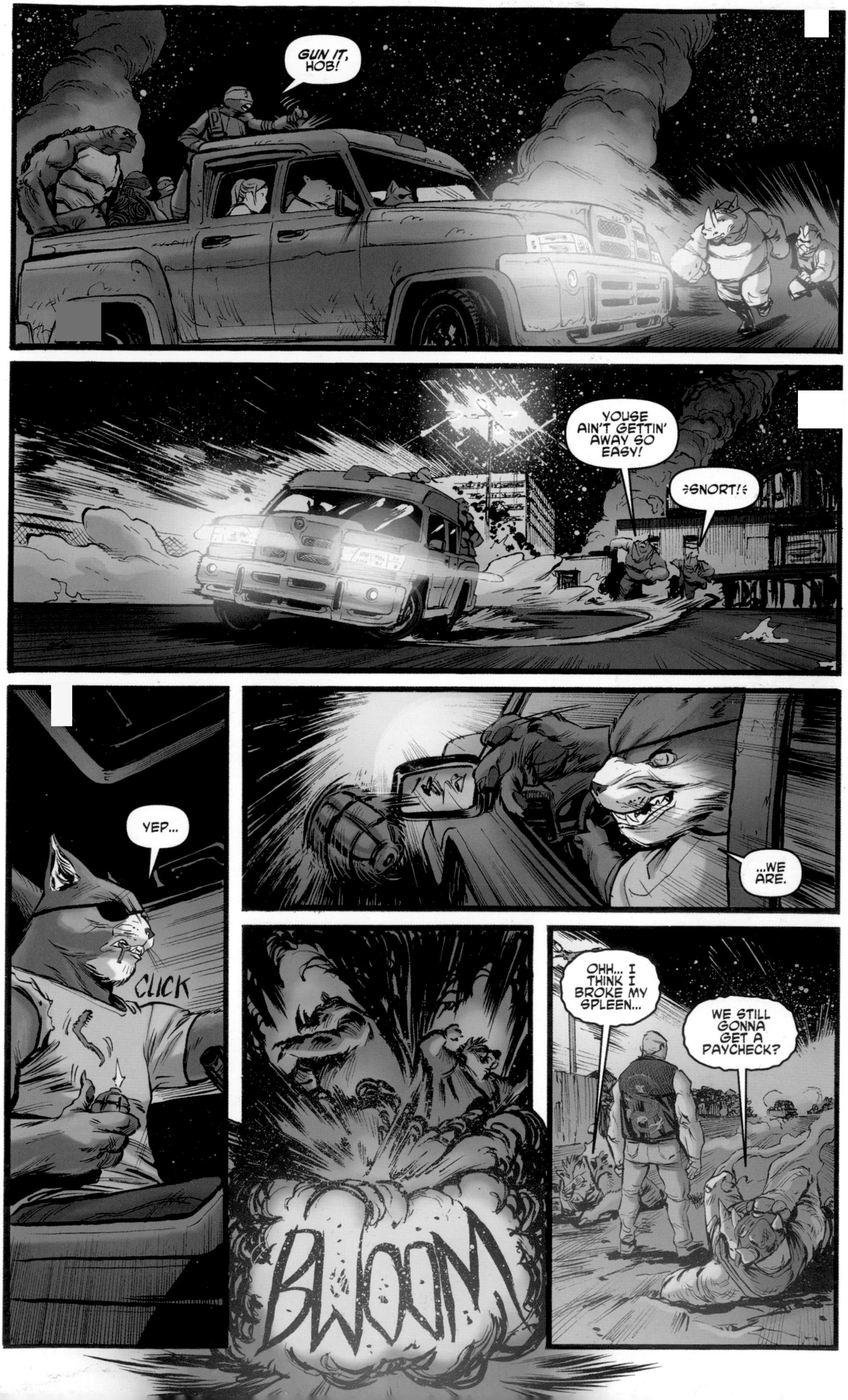
GUN IT, HOB!
YOUSE AIN'T GETTIN' AWAY SO EASY!
SNORT!
YEP...
CLICK
...WE ARE.
BWOOM
OHH... I THINK I BROKE MY SPLEEN...
WE STILL GONNA GET A PAYCHECK?

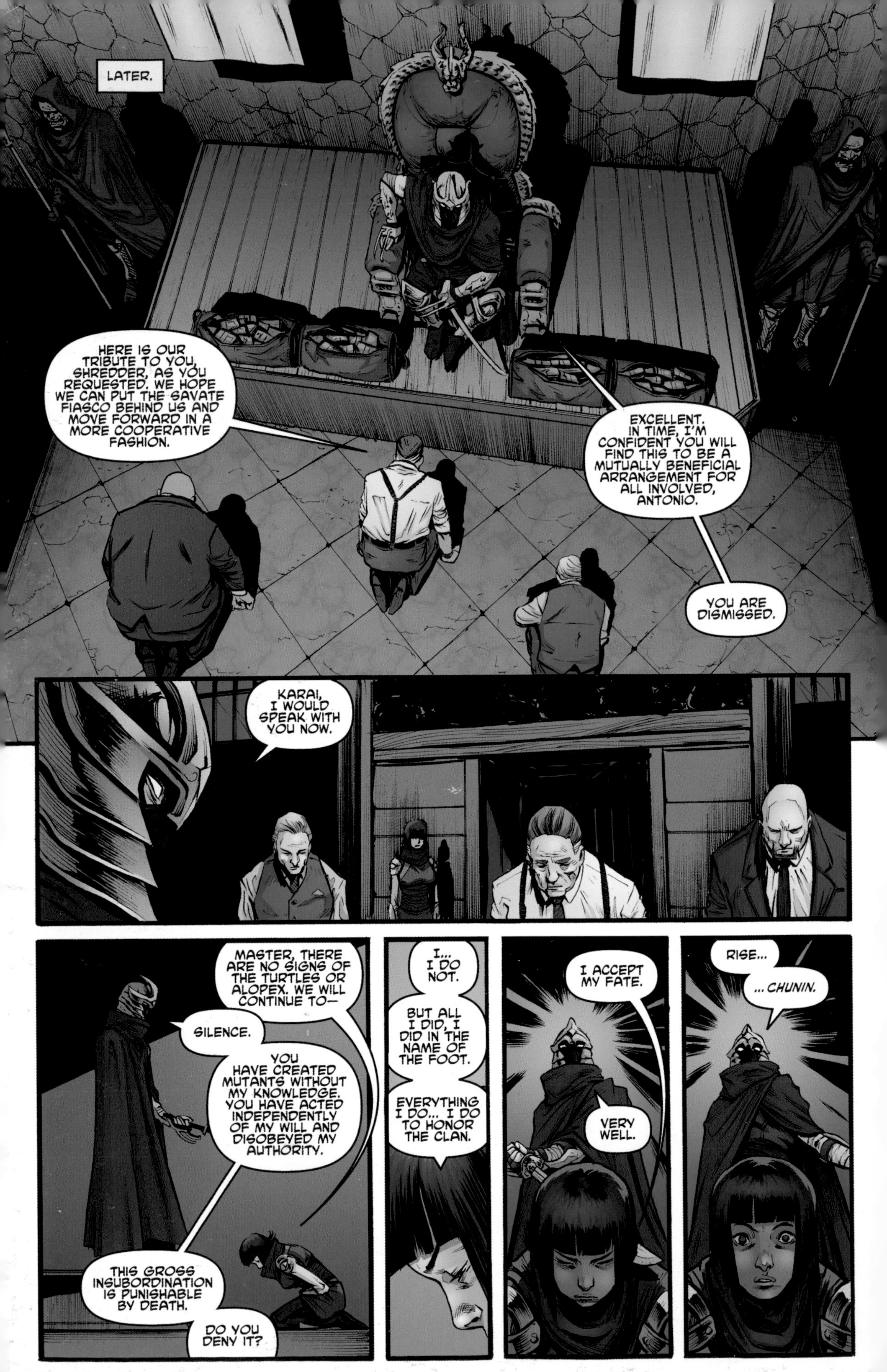
LATER.
HERE IS OUR TRIBUTE TO YOU, SHREDDER, AS YOU REQUESTED. WE HOPE WE CAN PUT THE SAVATE FIASCO BEHIND US AND MOVE FORWARD IN A MORE COOPERATIVE FASHION.
EXCELLENT. IN TIME, I'M CONFIDENT YOU WILL FIND THIS TO BE A MUTUALLY BENEFICIAL ARRANGEMENT FOR ALL INVOLVED, ANTONIO.
YOU ARE DISMISSED.
KARAI, I WOULD SPEAK WITH YOU NOW.
MASTER, THERE ARE NO SIGNS OF THE TURTLES OR ALOPEX. WE WILL CONTINUE TO—
SILENCE.
YOU HAVE CREATED MUTANTS WITHOUT MY KNOWLEDGE. YOU HAVE ACTED INDEPENDENTLY OF MY WILL AND DISOBEYED MY AUTHORITY.
THIS GROSS INSUBORDINATION IS PUNISHABLE BY DEATH.
DO YOU DENY IT?
I... I DO NOT.
BUT ALL I DID, I DID IN THE NAME OF THE FOOT.
EVERYTHING I DO... I DO TO HONOR THE CLAN.
I ACCEPT MY FATE.
VERY WELL.
RISE...
...CHUNIN.

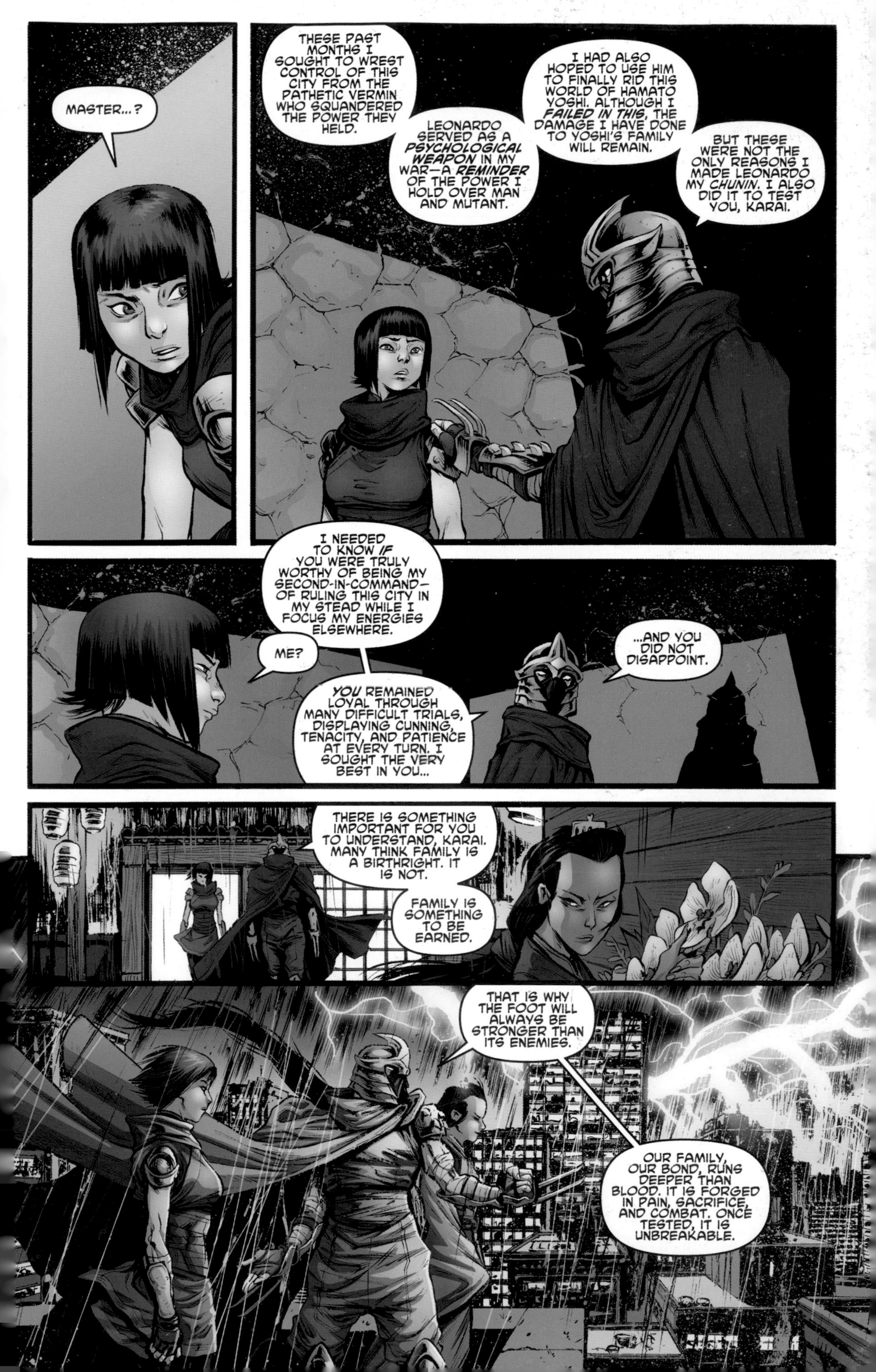

MASTER...?
THESE PAST MONTHS I SOUGHT TO WREST CONTROL OF THIS CITY FROM THE PATHETIC VERMIN WHO SQUANDERED THE POWER THEY HELD.
LEONARDO SERVED AS A *PSYCHOLOGICAL WEAPON* IN MY WAR—A *REMINDER* OF THE POWER I HOLD OVER MAN AND MUTANT.
I HAD ALSO HOPED TO USE HIM TO FINALLY RID THIS WORLD OF HAMATO YOSHI. ALTHOUGH I *FAILED IN THIS*, THE DAMAGE I HAVE DONE TO YOSHI'S FAMILY WILL REMAIN.
BUT THESE WERE NOT THE ONLY REASONS I MADE LEONARDO MY *CHUNIN*. I ALSO DID IT TO TEST YOU, KARAI.
I NEEDED TO KNOW *IF* YOU WERE TRULY WORTHY OF BEING MY SECOND-IN-COMMAND—OF RULING THIS CITY IN MY STEAD WHILE I FOCUS MY ENERGIES ELSEWHERE.
ME?
YOU REMAINED LOYAL THROUGH MANY DIFFICULT TRIALS, DISPLAYING CUNNING, TENACITY, AND PATIENCE AT EVERY TURN. I SOUGHT THE VERY BEST IN YOU...
...AND YOU DID NOT DISAPPOINT.
THERE IS SOMETHING IMPORTANT FOR YOU TO UNDERSTAND, KARAI. MANY THINK FAMILY IS A BIRTHRIGHT. IT IS NOT.
FAMILY IS SOMETHING TO BE EARNED.
THAT IS WHY THE FOOT WILL ALWAYS BE STRONGER THAN ITS ENEMIES.
OUR FAMILY, OUR BOND, RUNS DEEPER THAN BLOOD. IT IS FORGED IN PAIN, SACRIFICE, AND COMBAT. ONCE TESTED, IT IS UNBREAKABLE.

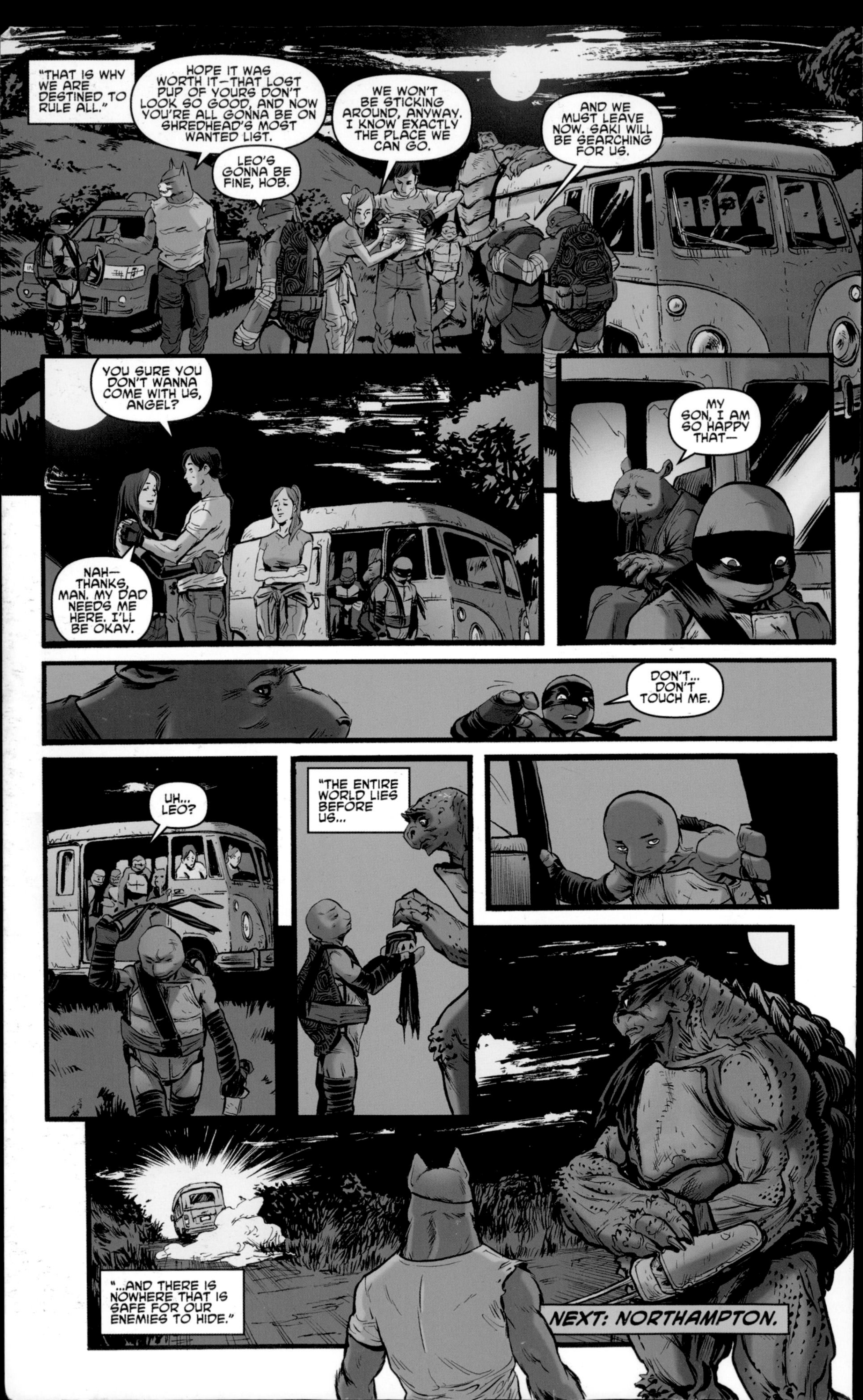
"THAT IS WHY WE ARE DESTINED TO RULE ALL."
HOPE IT WAS WORTH IT—THAT LOST PUP OF YOURS DON'T LOOK SO GOOD, AND NOW YOU'RE ALL GONNA BE ON SHREDHEAD'S MOST WANTED LIST.
LEO'S GONNA BE FINE, HOB.
WE WON'T BE STICKING AROUND, ANYWAY. I KNOW EXACTLY THE PLACE WE CAN GO.
AND WE MUST LEAVE NOW. SAKI WILL BE SEARCHING FOR US.
YOU SURE YOU DON'T WANNA COME WITH US, ANGEL?
NAH— THANKS, MAN. MY DAD NEEDS ME HERE. I'LL BE OKAY.
MY SON, I AM SO HAPPY THAT—
DON'T... DON'T TOUCH ME.
UH... LEO?
"THE ENTIRE WORLD LIES BEFORE US...
"...AND THERE IS NOWHERE THAT IS SAFE FOR OUR ENEMIES TO HIDE."
NEXT: NORTHAMPTON.

ART GALLERY

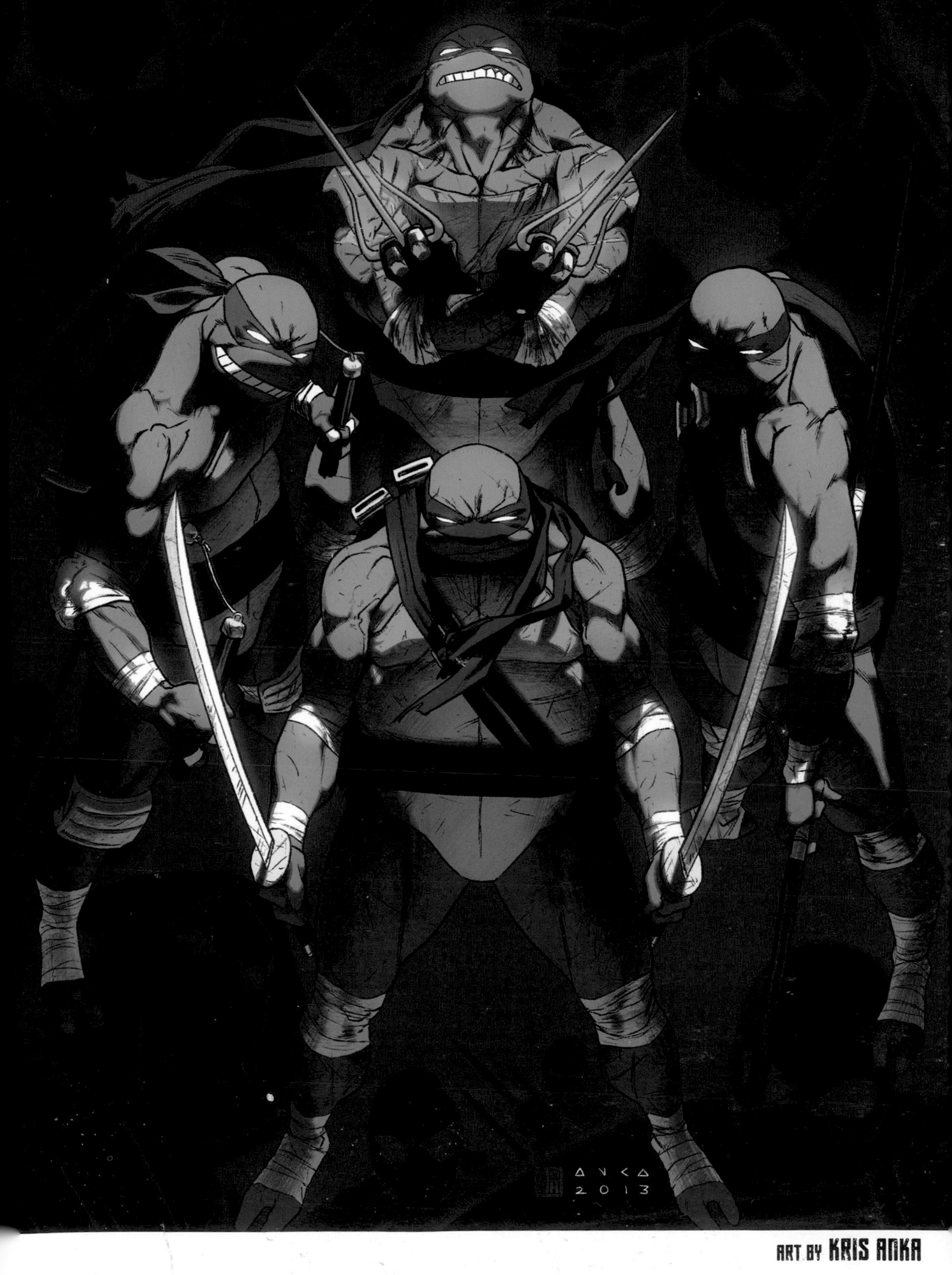

ART BY KRIS ANKA

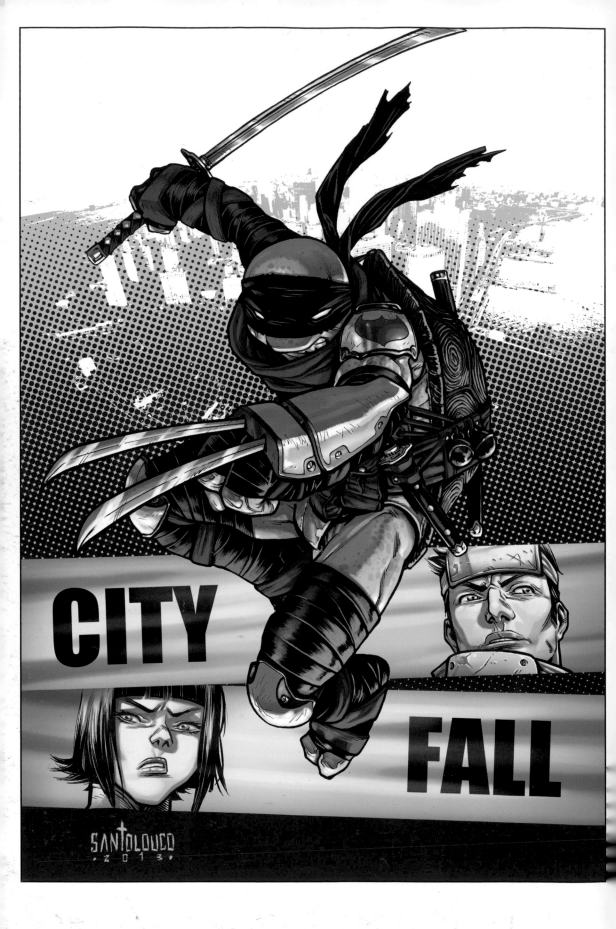

CITY

FALL

SANTOLOUCO
·2013·

THIS PAGE AND OPPOSITE PAGE: ART BY MATEUS SANTOLOUCO

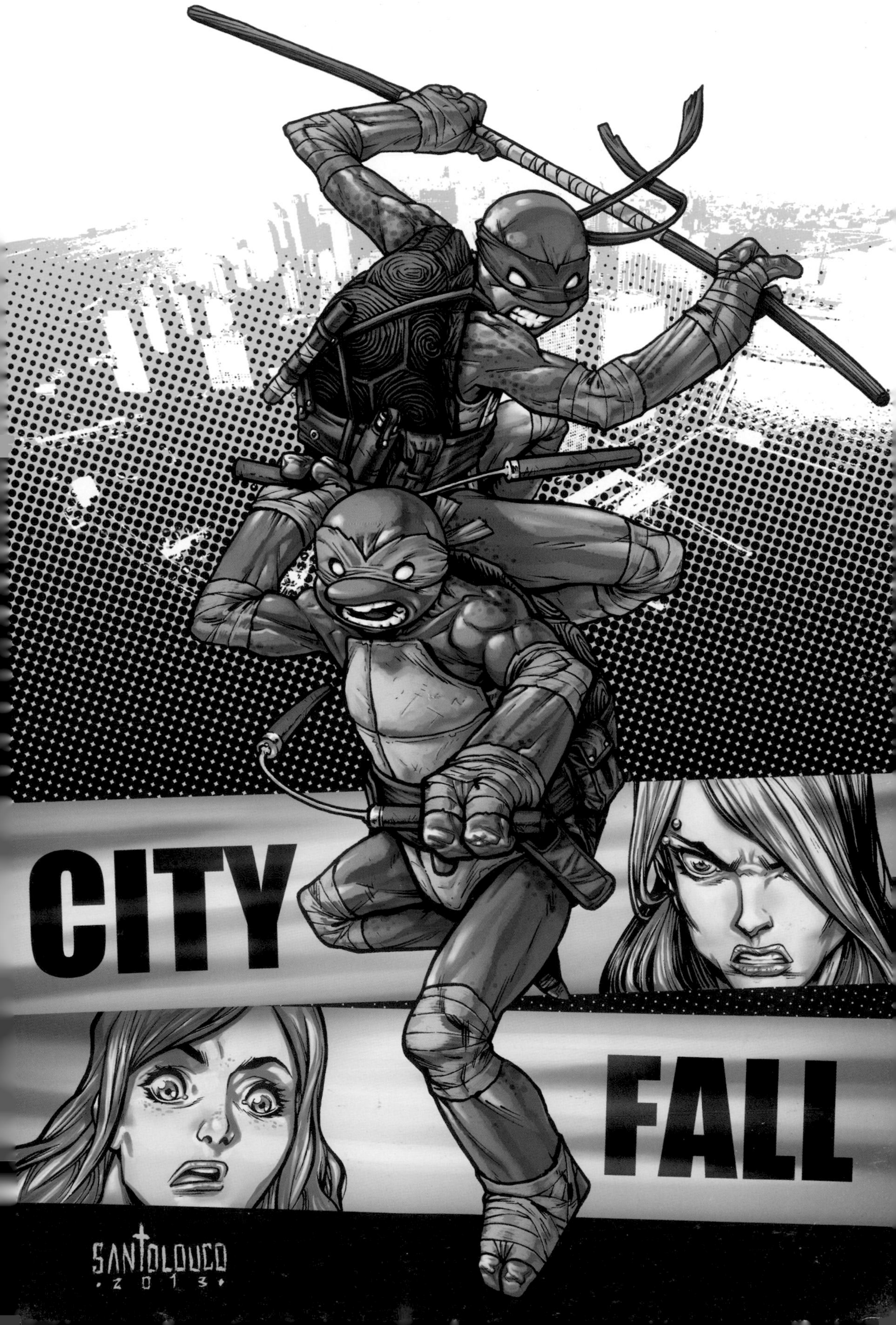
CITY
FALL
SANTOLOUCO
2013

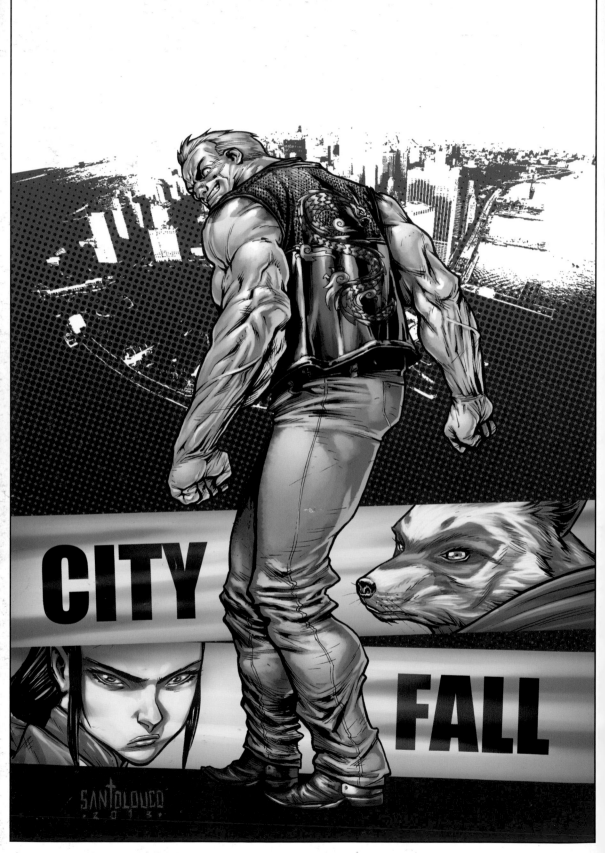

CITY FALL

ART BY MATEUS SANTOLOUCO

OPPOSITE PAGE: ART BY KEVIN EASTMAN · COLORS BY RONDA PATTISON

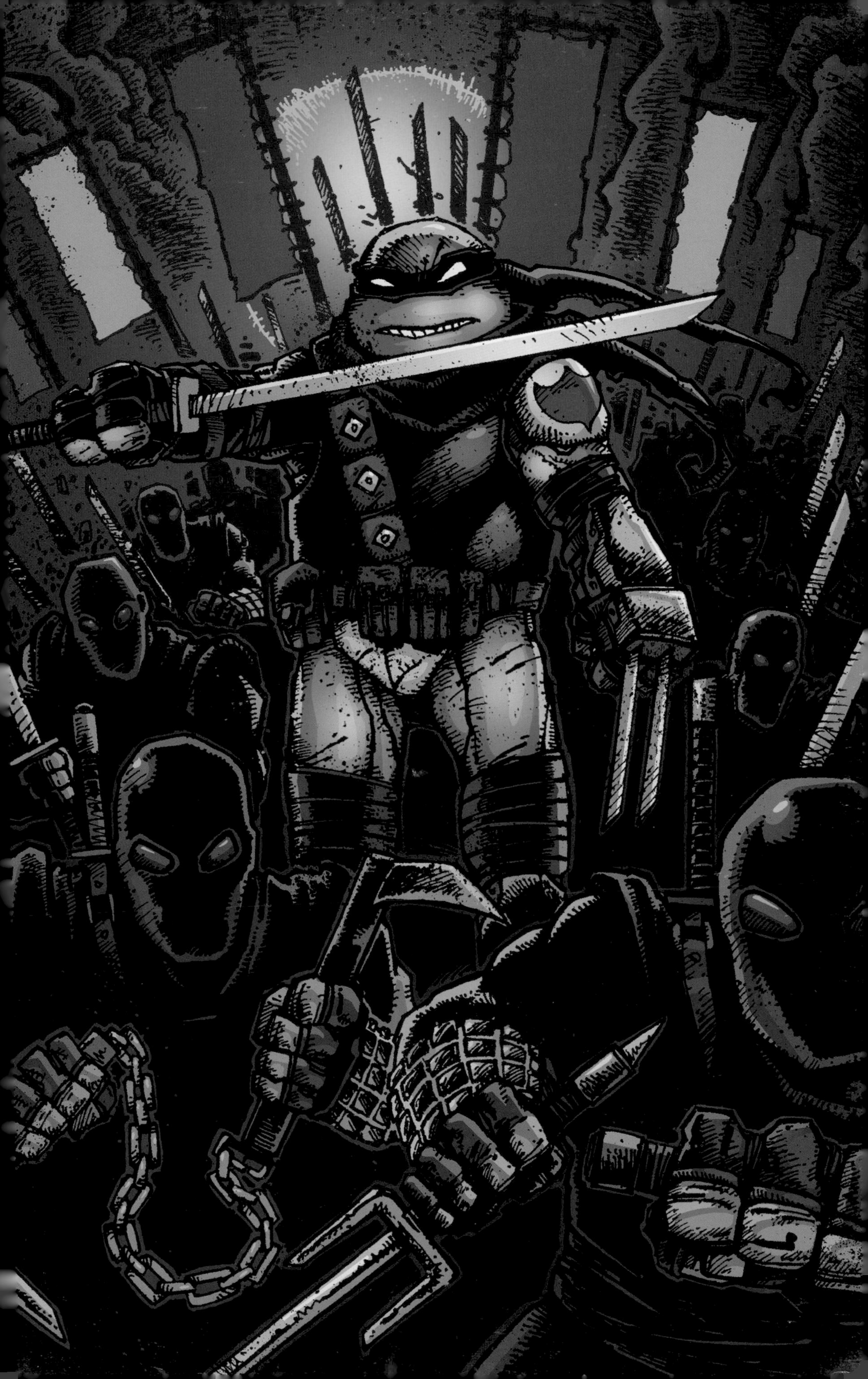

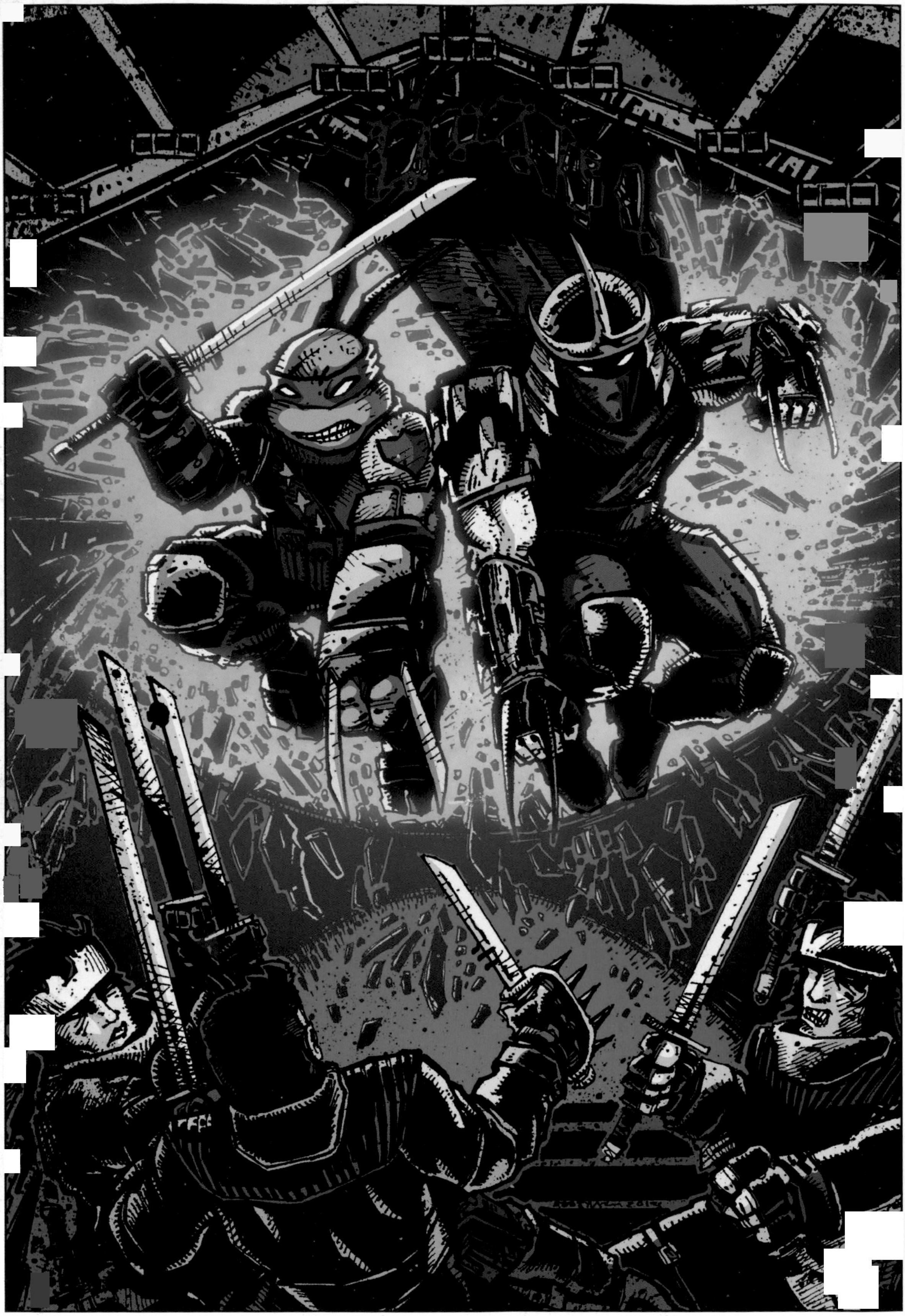

THIS PAGE AND OPPOSITE PAGE: ART BY KEVIN EASTMAN • COLORS BY RONDA PATTISON
FOLLOWING PAGE: ART BY KEVIN EASTMAN • COLORS BY IAN HERRING

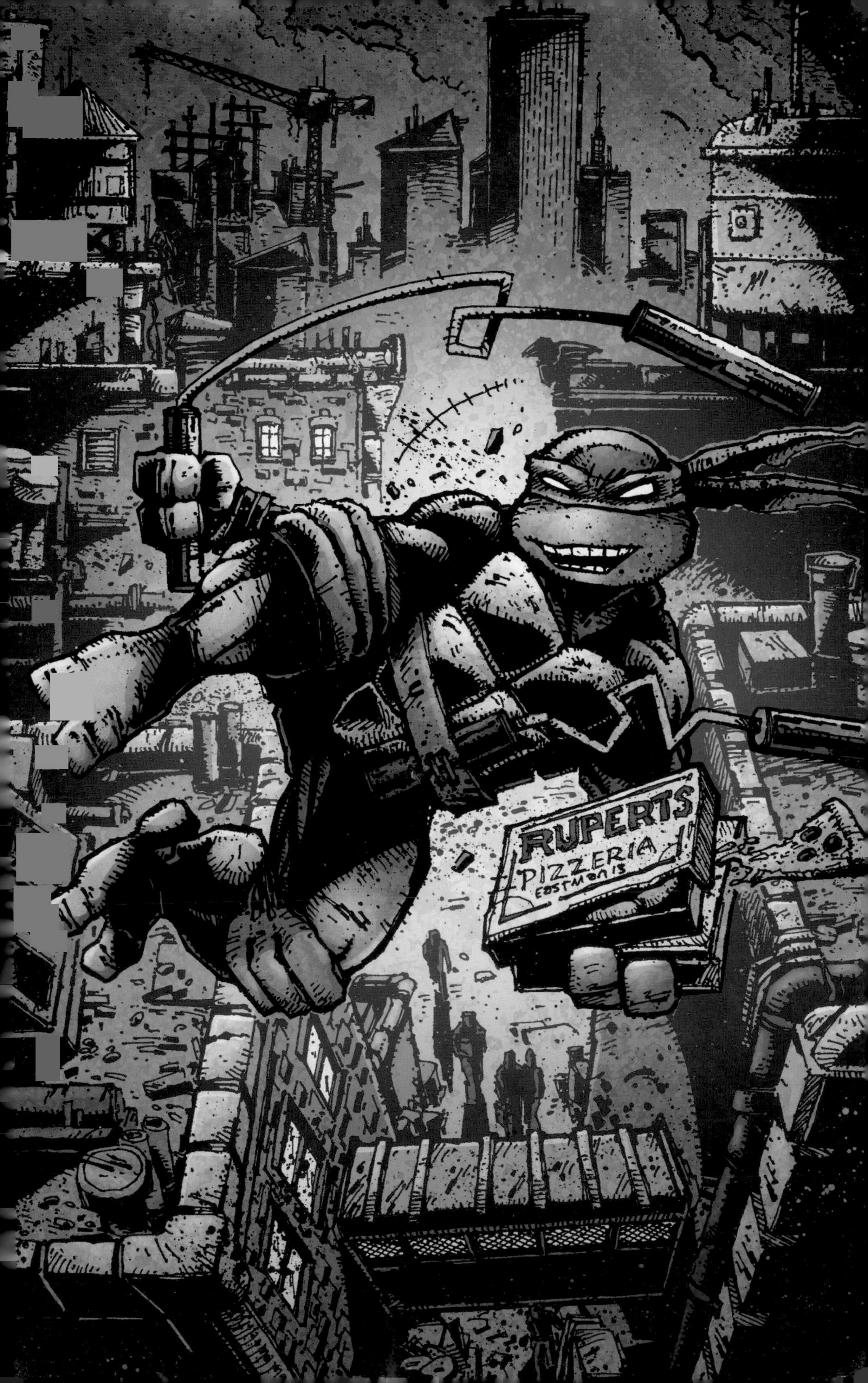
RUPERTS
PIZZERIA

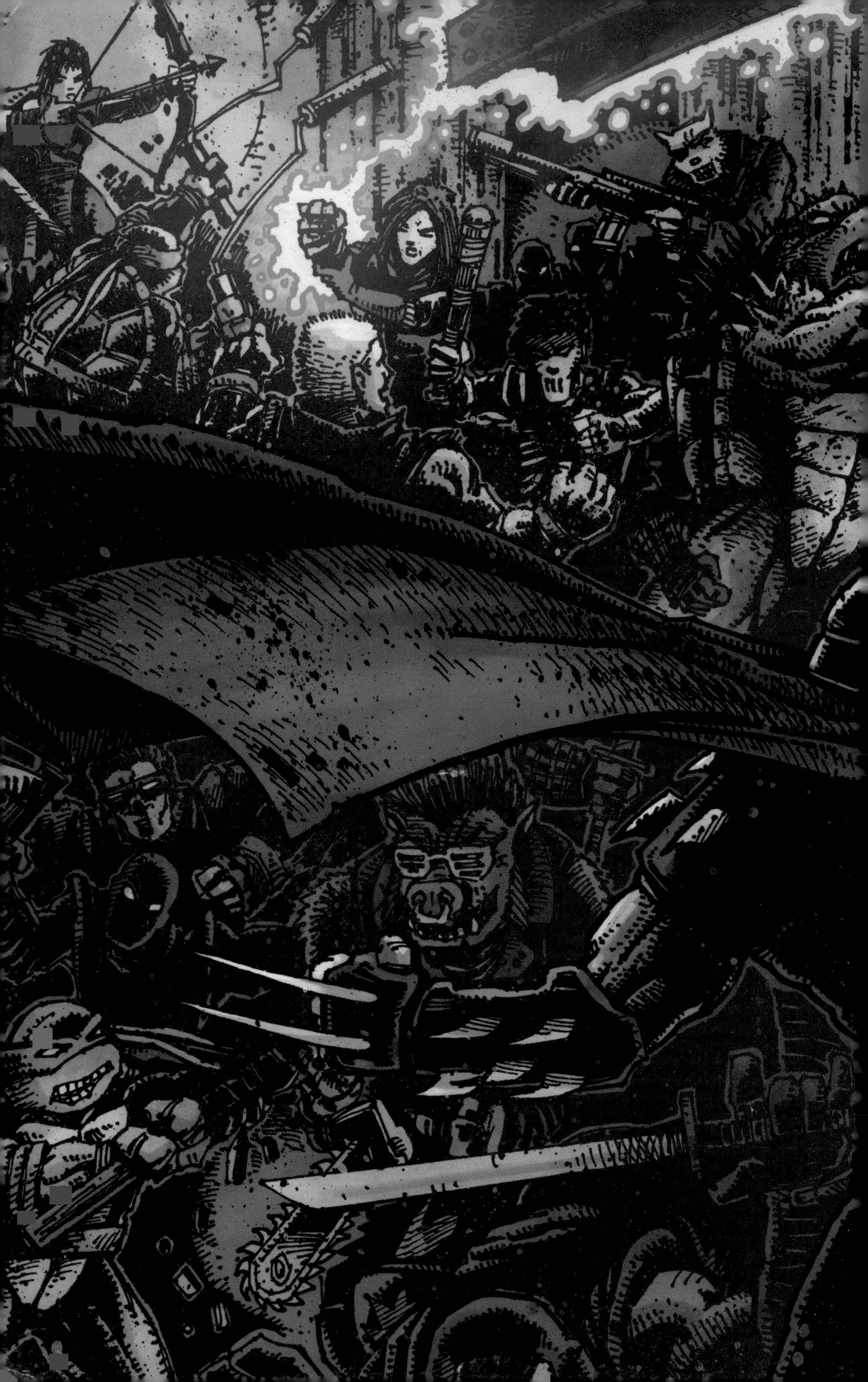

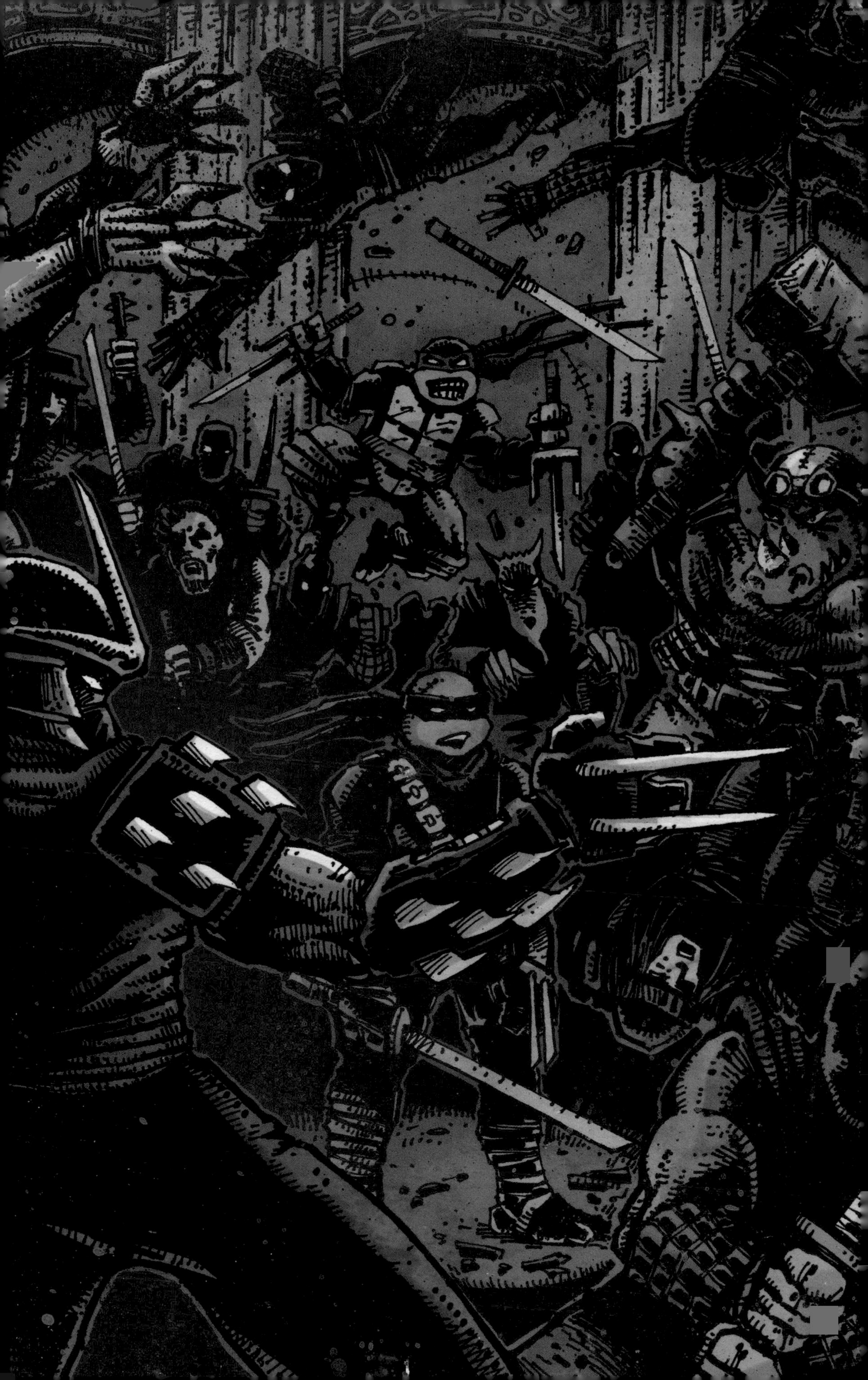

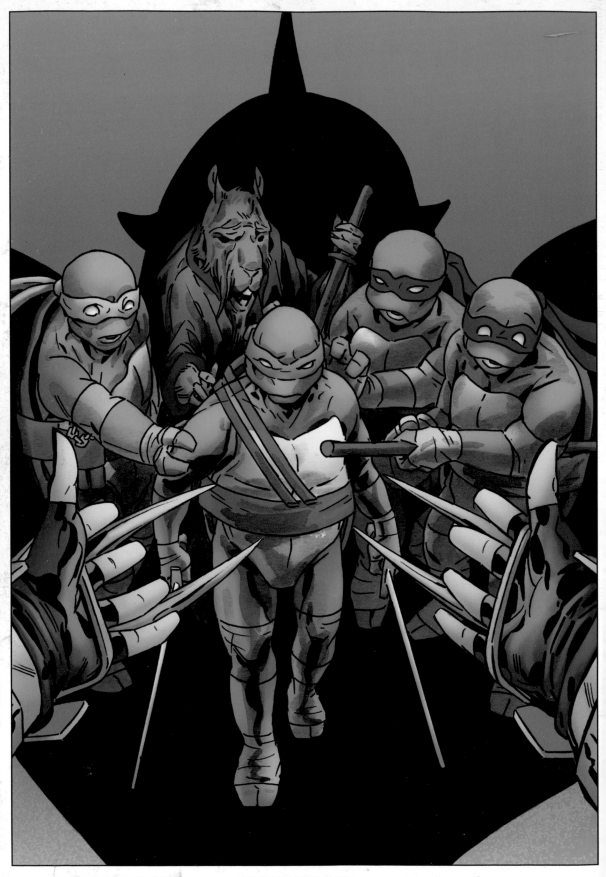

ART BY **MARK BUCKINGHAM** · COLORS BY **CHARLIE KIRCHOFF**

OPPOSITE PAGE: ART BY **KENNETH LOH** · COLORS BY **IAN HERRING**

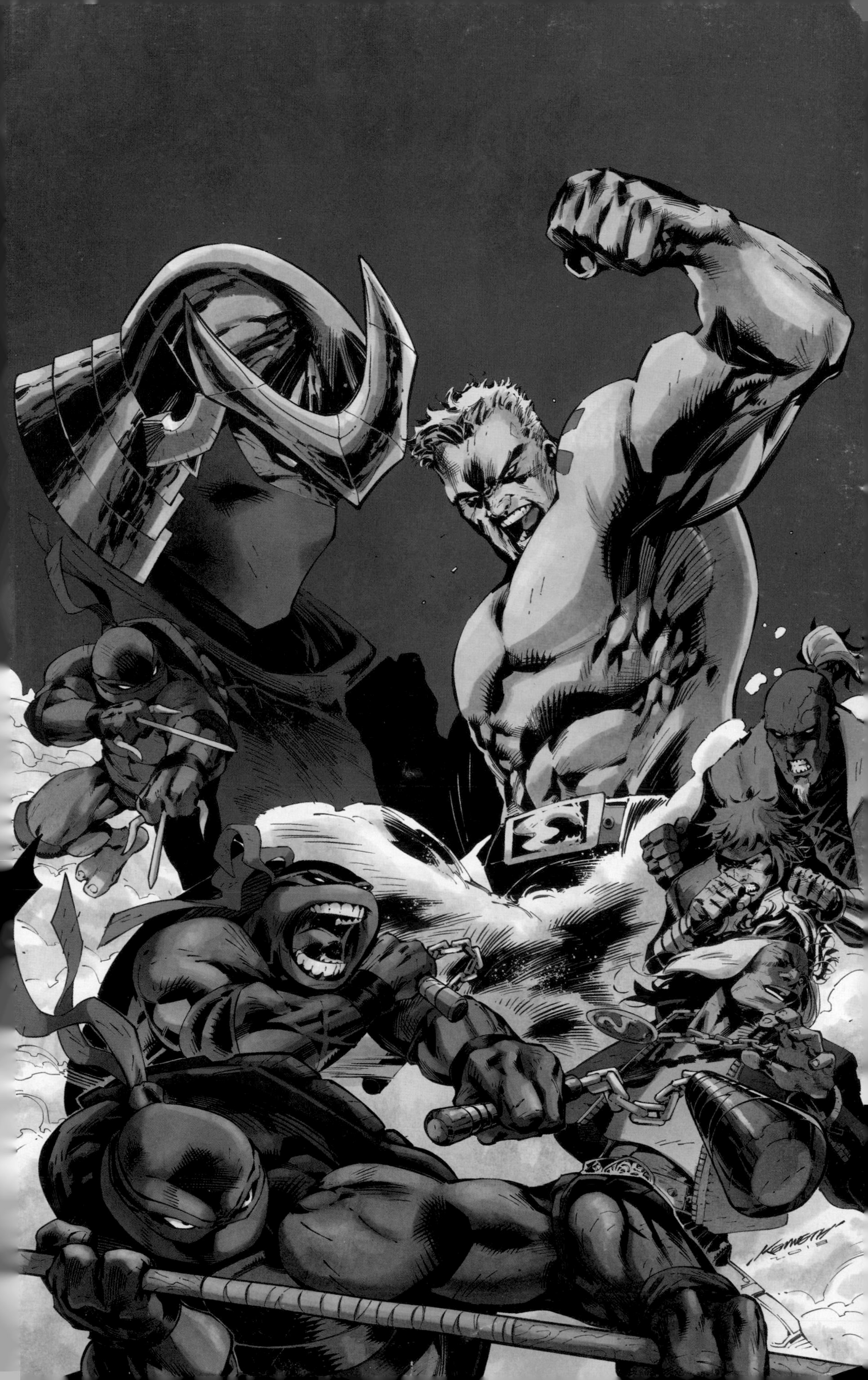

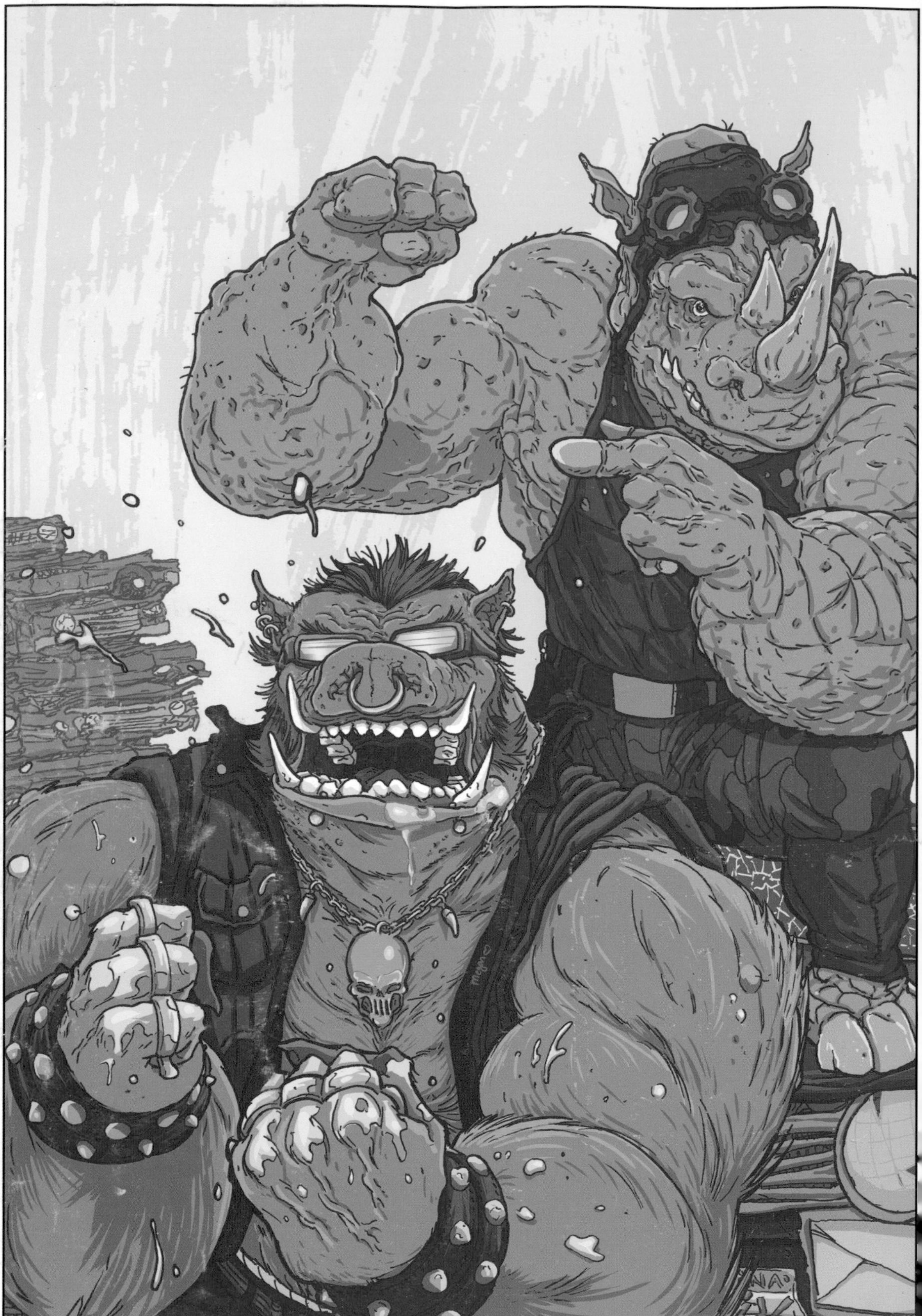

ART BY NICK PITARRA · COLORS BY MEGAN WILSON